Rick Salutin

WHAT WAS I

THINKING?

the autobiography of an idea
and other essays

* ecw press

If you can think — and not make thoughts your aim.
— Rudyard Kipling

*

To the memory of John R. "Jack" Seeley
(1913–2007)

*

CONTENTS

PREFACE

If this book had a motto, as books once did, it would be "Trust the thinking, not the thought." It arose from curiosity about why I write as I do, which is usually highly personal — even on large, abstract topics.

That wasn't congenital. Here's something from my first published piece, written in my last year of high school, an expository composition called "Fragments from the Fifties," assigned by my English teacher, Margaret Ford. She was a legend in the staff rooms. For decades, other teachers urged her to reveal her secrets in a book. Finally, she did. It was called *Techniques of Good Writing*. She asked to include my essay and ended it "by Rick S." It was my first byline.

Somewhere during those ten years, they
tossed a monster called rock 'n' roll
at us. . . . What did the president of
the United States stand for? Nothing.
. . . Yet there remained a basic fear of
the ultimate questions. . . . Out of a
deformed existentialism, came the beat
generation. . . . The sick joke has been the
most recent addition to Western culture.
. . . The '50s have been sick. The '50s have
been fearful. The '50s have been futile.

It has an assertive, confident quality that lots of
journalism and nonfiction had then. You could call it
the objective declarative style, though it's more of a
tone. I may have absorbed it from popular books like
H.G. Wells's *Outline of History* or John Gunther's
thick bestsellers about whole continents like Africa
or from newsmagazines like *Time*. It was the default
mode for journalism and nonfiction. It implied that
any bright person examining the subject would reach
the same conclusions, perhaps in the same words.
Subjectivity didn't enter in.

But by the time I wrote the first piece for
which I was paid, there were already big chunks of
me — my biography, my personal upheavals and
opinions — surrounding the assertions. It appeared
in *Harper's* in 1971, when Canada was in turmoil
and I'd just returned from ten student years in the

U.S. to try life as a writer. It was commissioned by a morose southerner named Bob Sherrill. "Ignorance in the South is like snow in Canada," he drawled. He idealized Canada, as Michael Moore and other Americans have. But as I left his Manhattan office with my first paying gig, he muttered, "Oh — and put your experience in." I asked why. "People seem to like it," he grunted. He wasn't ecstatic about the so-called new journalism, found in the *Village Voice* or *Rolling Stone*. But he acknowledged its dominion. I did so, with enthusiasm, and have ever since. Looking back, I think it wasn't just because he suggested it but because it struck a chord.

Here's an example. I covered the 2006 leadership convention of the Liberal Party of Canada for the *Globe and Mail*. The athlete-author-politician Ken Dryden, whom I'd known for 30 years, was a candidate. We'd met when he helped me write a play about his team, the Montreal Canadiens, in the 1970s. As I listened to his convention speech, I recalled how, shortly after we met, someone I was close to died and I spoke at the funeral. That got me thinking too much about my own death and I decided, whenever that time came, I wanted Ken to deliver my eulogy: not because he knew me best but because he's so damn conscientious that he'd have kept at it till he got it right, the way he played goal for the Canadiens, positioning himself to cover every angle, beating himself up each time he let one past him. He told me he sometimes wanted to apologize to fans for not making more of the "scintillating saves" that Habs broadcaster Danny Gallivan shrieked about — but, sorry, it was his way to anticipate everything in advance so he didn't have to lunge for pucks.

It never occurred to me not to include that reflection about him and I put it into my account of the convention. What shocks me, in retrospect, is that no editor or reader said, "Why the hell do I want to know about your morbid angst 30 years ago?" I could have said, "Dryden is diligent and assiduous to an almost bizarre degree; therefore, he would make as successful a national leader as he was a goalie." But that would have concealed what I *actually* knew: I wanted him to speak at my funeral because I knew how he was from knowing him. Instead of drawing a moral "lesson" or political generalization, I passed it on straight. Readers were free to make of it what they would. It was, in other words, about what we know and how we know it. It was epistemological.

What any of us have is direct experience. From it we abstract and generalize — as if you get to know more by knowing less — by going vague and concealing the origins of an idea, lesson, or concept that emerged from a particular moment you have lived. The generalizations obscure and dilute that specific moment. The abstraction stays tethered to the event that birthed it since we can't really separate them, but it's as if a veil has been thrown over it. It seems to me that if, as a writer, you reveal the experiential source, you'll enlighten your readers and revitalize the message. You transfuse it with the lifeblood of its source. Maybe they'll relive it with you, or revert to their own lives for insight and understanding.

It's true that you lose something by reducing a grand generalization to its experiential source: you lose grandness and generality. The direct experience is always limited and partial; it's bound to a moment in time. If you stick with those moments, then a larger picture — or a complete one, to the extent it's available to us — can only be built by assembling or collaging all the separate, partial views that each of us has. (This is sometimes known in philosophy as perspectivism. If I got to name it, it would be called experiencism.) In this light, the sum of all insights isn't the biggest, puffiest abstraction or generalization possible, like a float in the Macy's Thanksgiving parade. Instead, it's a larger composite picture, created by laying all those specific moments side by side — a puzzle that fits together, more or less, but awaits more pieces. Whether that would be a case in which the whole is more than the sum of its parts, I'm not sure. But I find it appealingly democratic.

I think that's also why I gravitated to journalism and especially to weekly columns, which I've done for almost 25 years, first in the *Globe and Mail* and then in the *Toronto Star*. I used to think that was also accidental, like my ardent, lifelong embrace of a depressive editor's chance suggestion. I'd started by concentrating on theatre, then added fiction. But they seemed to peter out while the journalism kept expanding, and as a freelance, you tend to do the projects on your wish list that you can get paid for.

But it also suited me. Columns are brief, fragmentary, and can easily drag in personal experience. We don't live our lives as well-wrought biographies, in ordered chapters. Something happens, something disconnected happens after that, maybe eventually patterns emerge, or not. If columns were literature, they'd be like short stories, one-act plays, or, most of all, lyric poems. Snatched, disconnected epiphanies. At least some columnists, ones I admire, write that way: Greg Clark, in his day; Pierre Berton, during the three brief years when he wrote five long columns a week; the incomparable Joey Slinger. Lyric poetry takes experience as it is; it tries to convey it but leave it whole. Then on to another poem/moment/column. Not all columns succeed that way; actually, few do. But most poems are also unsuccessful, yet poets keep trying.

The drift into journalism, by the way, wasn't happenstance either. When my mother died and I went through the boxes she'd hoarded in the tiny apartment where my dad kept her prisoner for 39 years (romantically, like Rapunzel), I found copies of the *Salutin Family Reporter*, made when I was seven or eight. It was printed, literally, in pencil, five or six copies per issue on carbon paper. The masthead listed Rickie Salutin as editor; my mother as publisher; and my brother, Lorne, as reporter. It had family news, sports, and classified ads from relatives ("Used blender: call Aunt Betty"). There was also a book on journalism from something called the College Outline Series and clippings of Pierre Berton columns that had enthralled me when I was in high school. I even had my own column in the high school paper. It was called The School Spirit, as if I hovered in the halls near the lockers, watching and passing judgements. That's scary, considering what I do now. You never know, as the old guys say in the sauna. Stuff is going on that we're not aware of, from which emerge our well-hewn thoughts along with our fateful decisions.

I should add that I care about *what* we think, not just *how*. But I've come to enjoy the process far more than its products, which always involve some letdown. You know that no matter how proud you are of an idea you've reached and preached, it will surely morph into an embarrassment before long. Getting an idea is way more fun than owning it. This may explain an odd feeling I often have: that people with ideas drastically conflicting with mine could as easily have been on the opposite side, including me. That too may be scary, but I don't think it makes me a relativist, as I'll try to explain.

I'll begin with a piece on a huge preoccupation of an era I lived through — the Holocaust — and how my experiences shaped my ideas about it. The Holocaust won't continue to grip future generations — like my son's, who was two in the year 2000, or Prince Harry of England's, who went to a costume party in 2005 dressed as a Nazi — in the same way. But for me, it's a good example of the connections between the thinking and the thought.

Then I will move on to a piece on psychotherapy as a lonely case where our society seems to prioritize the thinking over the thought. There's also a piece on Robin Hood and the way kids acquire their notions of good versus bad and one on the formation of Canadian culture through process in the absence of much product. I'm hoping they hang together, but, due to the nature of these things, who knows? There's a section traversing my anomalous 20 years at the *Globe and Mail*, including sample columns, a period that began precisely at the end of the Cold War and coincided with whatever the hell has replaced it. My responses to the world as it unfolded in those years were conditioned by my personal decompression from the left-right realities in which I'd grown up and then grown old(er). I've only realized that looking back. At the time, I simply thought I was observing the passing scene from a platform I never expected to occupy.

I've come to feel more ambivalent about writing itself. I now tend to think of it as a dumbed-down form of speech, despite the cachet it holds in our society.

That hasn't deterred me from writing, however —
and not just because it's all I really know how to
do. I'm hoping it's also made me a more interesting
writer. It's the process that's endlessly instructive.

Part I

WHAT SHAPES THE THINKING?

UNIQUENESS OF THE HOLOCAUST: THE AUTOBIOGRAPHY OF AN IDEA

*Our apparatus for acquiring
knowledge is not designed for knowledge.*
— Friedrich Nietzsche

I'M STANDING IN THE PHILOSOPHY SECTION OF THE bookstore at the University of Toronto one day in the early 2000s. I stepped in here bereft, after dropping off my poor laptop at the computer shop next door for service. They'll call when it's ready. I can't write or check email. I might as well read. I'm looking for something by Hannah Arendt, with whom I studied philosophy in New York in the 1960s. I'd gone into philosophy after dropping out of rabbinical seminary. It seemed a natural transition; I still hankered for meaning, but my faith was fading.

"Thanks a lot for that column this morning," says a man scanning the shelves beside me. "You're welcome," I say, blanking on the column, as I often do the day after I write one. "Based on what you said," he goes on, "you might be interested in the new book by Agamben, on the state of exception." Oh yes, the column was about torture and "the new normal" since 9/11. I don't know Agamben. I think of Agrabah, capital of a desert sultanate in the Disney film *Aladdin*. I'm up on kid culture these days.

He hands me the book from the shelf and moves on. It's slim and costs $15.95. I reshelve it, but as I'm crossing College, realize it's akin to a subject that has been preoccupying me, so I return and buy it. When I awake at three that night, I read it. Agamben, an Italian academic, says the state of exception — also known as a state of siege, martial law, or a state of emergency, depending on national proclivities — has been a normal political condition since the end of the First World War. In Canada it's known as the War Measures Act and was last invoked in October 1970, on the day I returned from my student decade in the U.S. Agamben traces the modern beginnings of states of exception to Germany but, surprisingly, not Nazi Germany. Rather, he connects it to the progressive Weimar Republic of pre-Hitler years. He quotes Walter Benjamin on the state of exception being the new normal, though not in that phrase. There's even a reference to "Taubes," who would be Jacob, with whom I did an M.A. in religion, before switching to philosophy. Nobody quotes Taubes. I didn't know he published a book in the '80s. On the night of the east coast blackout in 1965, I found him humming *nigunim* in the dark in his office — he came from a line of rabbis. We wandered up and down Broadway together, stepping into restaurants and bars that were operating by candlelight. But I digress. I'd recently been pondering the idea of uniqueness, or exception, associated for me with the Holocaust.

*

FOR TORONTO JEWS IN THE 1950S, THE HOLOCAUST was inescapable, the centre of everything serious — politics, morality, faith, identity. When I taught a grade three class at Holy Blossom Temple, we did a unit on it. We asked the kids to compose a letter from someone their age living in Nazi Germany. "Hello cousin Hymie," wrote Rickie Beck. "I hope things are good in Canada. Here in Nazi Germany there is a bad man named Hitler. He should be called Shitler." We herded our students into the second-floor auditorium one Sunday morning and listened to a *shaliach*, an emissary from Israel, say, "The world is finally learning, because of the state of Israel, that Jewish blood is as expensive to shed as anyone's." Sunlight streamed through the high windows. Across Bathurst, the stolid brick homes of Forest Hill Village stood calmly. We were comfortable scions of a people for whom, as Shylock said, "sufferance is the badge." How hard it all was to reconcile.

Over the next half a century, the Holocaust took on that kind of centrality more widely — in the West, at any rate. It became a focal point for historical and political discussion; nearly every contemporary crisis and confrontation evoked it. One needed to learn from Munich in order to prevent another Auschwitz, etc. After the Cold War ended, the Holocaust became a virtually mandatory element for justifying interventions in Bosnia, Kosovo, and Iraq. The first George Bush said Saddam Hussein was worse than Hitler. Bill Clinton bombed Bosnia and Serbia to forestall another genocide. The second George Bush compared Osama bin Laden to Hitler plus Stalin. Ethnic cleansing, a new term for the brutal territorial transfers and violence that had been routine in 20th-century conflicts, became identified almost exclusively with Nazism, as if they invented it. It was as though one could not talk or act internationally unless the subject matter had been correlated with the Holocaust

But I don't mean to cover the vast cultural space occupied by the Holocaust — its history as an idea. I want to focus on something smaller — its more compact autobiography in individual cases — in order to explore how the private itineraries of ideas can illuminate them. If that seems obvious — the fact that who I *am* affects what I *think* — I don't mean it as modestly as it sounds. Ideas have been treated deferentially in the Western tradition, from Plato, for whom they actually existed in another realm, to our age of experts with authority in their respective "fields": politics, sports, terrorism. There's also been a backlash, in some versions of postmodernism, as if ideas have no integrity *apart from* personal agendas. I want to examine these matters through the example of the idea of the Holocaust in my experience.

*

I BECAME A TEENAGE RELIGIOUS EXISTENTIALIST under the influence of Emil Fackenheim. I met him at Holy Blossom, where he taught us Jewish thought. I hung around there during adolescence, as some kids hang around the mall, because I was trying to avoid home and my difficult dad. (So I now think. Who really knows?) We were a precocious lot, and Heinz Warshauer, the principal, thought "challenging" us might keep us involved "post-confirmation." It did. We were enthralled by Emil's accent, gentle manner, impish look, cigars, and redoubtable mind. We had Emil contests to see who could mimic him. We'd phone each other and pretend to be Emil. But his ideas dazzled me. He believed in God, no apologies — yet he was clearly brilliant. He even gave some shrift to divine revelation and immortality. I'd thought those were reserved for the aged and credulous. It also had scandal value by insisting on spiritual meaning in our crass, acquisitive community. I went for it.

I used to ride my CCM bicycle down from Eglinton Avenue at the end of a high school day and wait for him outside the duplex he shared in the lower village with his wife, Rose, his former student. I don't think I ever said I was coming; I used to show up on people's doorsteps in search of, I think, parent or family substitutes. You don't call ahead to make an appointment with your (proto) dad. Many of the people I conscripted in this way had been teachers at the Holy B. Emil would unfailingly invite me upstairs, and we'd sit in his study. He'd talk to me about his latest book — it was on philosophy of religion from Fichte to Kierkegaard. I understood little, but his attention and respect were precious.

He'd been ordained in Nazi Germany by the sainted (as he was always called) rabbi, Leo Baeck. Emil then escaped to the U.K. When war broke out, he was interned as an enemy alien and sent to Canada, with other German nationals, including Nazis. They were all held together in what were widely called concentration camps. (Those were not a Nazi invention, though extermination camps were.) Eventually, with the war still on, the interned Jews were released. Emil rabbi'ed for a while but also acquired a Ph.D. in philosophy and began an academic career. In the camp he'd met Heinz, who gloomily presided over the Holy B. school and convinced Emil to write a textbook on Jewish theology. It explored the classic arguments for belief in God, Jewish survival, etc. Emil belonged to a mid-20th-century surge of religious existentialist thinkers whose starting point was concrete human crises versus abstract theories. They challenged smug modern verities like progress and rationality, in the wake of the Second World War and Holocaust. They took categories like sin and God seriously. Emil wrote in magazines like *Commentary*. To me it proved you could be brilliant, outrageous, *and* a successful writer.

In classes, he didn't focus on the Holocaust, but it would arise during a discussion about, perhaps, right and wrong. Then Emil would tell us it had been a unique historical event. "Because the Holocaust was evil for evil's sake," he'd almost whisper, hypnotically. His proof was that the mass murder of Jews in the final years of the war seriously undermined the German effort by diverting scarce resources needed for military purposes. In spite of that, the Nazis persisted. It was unreasonable; it was self-destructive. That's why he called it evil for its own sake. It served no other purpose.

This argument fascinated me. It stayed with me long after we lost touch — as if it held a meaning I'd finally discern if I turned it over and over, as the Talmud says one should do with each biblical phrase. Perhaps we all have intellectual touchstones — arguments, images, phrases that seize us and that we in turn seize. They suit us, so we make the most of them.

I puzzled, even then, about whether it made sense to say that Nazi leaders were irrational in their policy of exterminating Jews. Maybe there was a macabre but consistent logic playing out. If Jews were the ultimate cancer, the poisonous germ infecting the human species that had to be expunged in order to cure the organism and let it thrive, then destroying them might take precedence over shorter-term goals like winning the war. In that case, the Nazis were being both self-preservative and altruistic by pursuing genocide. In fact, if it looked likely that they were going to lose the war, as it did once the U.S. entered, there might be a ghastly selflessness in pursuing the long-term goal of eliminating the viral race for the sake of the species, even as one perished oneself. It all follows only if you accept the inane, insane premises: that race exists in some meaningful sense, that it is the overriding determinant in global history (and there is, therefore, such a thing as global history as a meaningful category), that humanity and individuals count little in making moral judgements compared to matters of race, and that Jews are a vile race. None of this shook my acceptance of the Holocaust as the epicentre of moral seriousness and a unique horror in history. But it made me think: it gave me a start point for asking other questions.

The confirmation textbook that Emil wrote at Heinz's urging (or needling) mentioned none of this concerning the Holocaust. It was called *Paths to Jewish Belief*. He wrote it with gusto since the competing textbook, by an American rabbi, took a naturalistic, humanistic approach. Its chapters were oh-so reasonable: they contained no embarrassing stuff about a personal God who might actually be present in a personal way to human beings. Such things would have smacked of superstition back then; they'd have sounded like Tevye in *Fiddler on the Roof* long before *Fiddler* became a beloved Broadway classic. My parents' generation were modern Jews of the 1950s; they wanted to be proudly Jewish, as well as contemporary and scientific. Emil, though, and other religious existentialists, like Protestant Paul Tillich and Catholic Jacques Maritain, wrestled with concepts like sin, prayer, and God.

So his book took up, in turn, questions of God, the afterlife, morality, the purpose of Jewish existence, the plausibility of prayer. It was no catechism; it was a demanding, reasoned discussion, using traditional sources but also informed by Emil's knowledge of modern philosophy. In his writing in journals at the time, he pursued similar topics for adult readers. I read them too — or tried. "Man will always pursue ultimate integration," one of those articles begins. I put it down and puzzled over it for weeks. (I still sometimes wonder about that line. I'm starting to think he may have been wrong.) He even wrote a piece for *Commentary*, before it became the catechism of the neo-cons, called "Apologia for a Confirmation Text," which did exactly what its title said.

In the mid-1960s, during my postgrad years, Emil began attending yearly gatherings, in the Laurentians outside Montreal, of like-minded Jewish thinkers from orthodox, conservative, and reform branches. The meetings were created and hosted by a Montreal orthodox rabbi, David Hartman, who eventually moved to Israel. Emil returned from his first attendance there and said he had met the high priest of Auschwitz. It was Elie Wiesel. What staggered him about Wiesel was his willingness to confront the Holocaust directly. I went one year as part of a small youth contingent. On a long walk, Emil told me he'd recently realized that, for 20 years, he'd been attempting to clear a place for faith after Auschwitz, yet he'd failed to tackle faith's main stumbling block: the Holocaust itself. He had been preoccupied with showing that faith was not precluded after Auschwitz, that it was not unreasonable even if it wasn't quite reasonable. But the subject he never wrote about in all those years was the Holocaust. He'd come to feel, without disowning those thoughts and essays, that they'd been a way for him to avoid the event that had deformed his own life and his generation.

That realization was a turning point. He wound down his philosophical concerns with a book on Hegel's philosophy of religion and turned increasingly toward the subject of faith — not so much *after* Auschwitz as in its shadow. He became, in a sense, the theological counterpart to Wiesel the novelist. He coined a phrase for which he became renowned: The 11th commandment for Jews after Auschwitz: thou shalt not allow Hitler posthumous victories. He said he realized this was what he'd been trying to do in all his writings on the non-impossibility of faith in the modern era: deny Hitler a posthumous victory. He also called it the 614th commandment, referring to the 613 rules of observance enumerated for traditional Jews in a medieval Hebrew treatise. His writing and thought dwelt on these themes for the rest of his life. Some of it was collected in a book, *To Mend the World*, based on a kabbalistic phrase referring to religious observance as a means to heal not only the individual soul but also the damaged structure of the cosmos. His life and thought took a deeply existential turn in the sense that each was recast by the actual circumstances of his experience and from then on proceeded differently. That may happen in the lives of many intellectuals, but you don't normally hear about it. The existential fulcrum gets papered over, literally, by books and articles. Only the theoretical conclusions stay in view: the biographical elements get hived off or ignored, as if they are incidental to the abstractions and generalizations they produce. But Emil was clear and honest. From then on, he based everything he wrote on who he was and what he'd lived through. In retrospect, 20 years of intellectual detour was not a long time for so profound a transformation to incubate in a context as fraught and dramatic as that of a Jew who came of age in Nazi Germany.

In June 1967, he followed the buildup to the Six-Day War between Israel and the Arab states in a mood of alarm and despair. It looked as if Hitler was about to win another victory. Then came Israel's sudden and total triumph. Emil declared it the equivalent of a miracle and announced that God had intervened in history. The presence of God in history, not just in the lives of individuals, had been a centrepiece in his theology of revelation. He was no fundamentalist: he never espoused the literal revelation of scripture on Mount Sinai to Moses. But like Martin Buber, he believed in an encounter between the "Eternal Thou" and the Jewish people, similar to the mystical or spiritual experience of individuals. In the abstract, this was a daring stance for a modern intellectual: it was a way to introduce a transcendent element into daily experience. It gave traditional scriptural religion a place in modern secular reality.

But applied specifically to the politics of the Middle East in 1967, it was a risky move and began to set Emil apart from many former colleagues and soulmates. In order to assert that Israel owed its victory to divine intervention, one had to accept the version of events presented by officials of Israel and the Western media. Yet there were grounds for being skeptical of this account. Perhaps Israel had not been so imperilled; perhaps their resources were more than equal to their enemies' and they knew it, but for strategic military and political reasons — to garner support and mislead the enemy — they presented the situation as more dire than it was. Perhaps Emil's anxiety and that of other Jews, including mine, had been due, in other words, to propaganda. It wouldn't be the first time in history. And if the real story of the buildup and the war itself were different, then there would be no need to invoke divine intervention as a "factor" in its outcome. He had begun moving down a dangerous path, potentially placing his theology and faith at the mercy of particular political and journalistic gambits.

We had stayed close. When I left home for university, first to the U.S., then Israel, he handed me on, more or less, to others: Judaica scholar Nahum Glatzer and medieval philosophy expert Alexander Altmann at Brandeis, both refugees from Hitler; Ernst Simon and Martin Buber in Jerusalem, where I spent an intoxicated junior year imbibing the language, ancient texts, and landscape; and Abraham Joshua Heschel in New York, at the conservative rabbinical seminary where I studied following my degree in Jewish studies from Brandeis.

In the summer of 1964, as I was turning 22, Emil came out of rabbinic retirement to officiate at my marriage in the little chapel of the Holy Blossom. He gave a Midrash, a rabbinic sermon, on the meaning of marriage, which was exquisite and stood as one of the reasons I remained in the marriage as long as I did though it was ill-starred from the outset. I hated the thought of Emil's homily having been preached in vain. In the spring of 1965, while I was studying at both the seminary and the Columbia grad program in religion (and Union protestant seminary too — I couldn't get enough), I walked to Columbia one rainy afternoon.

It was a grey drizzly day, and I was in a gloomy state about my marriage, my discomfort at the seminary, and, I suppose, the state of the world. The Vietnam War had poisoned discourse in the U.S. I was no kind of leftist — I still saw the world in religious terms. Politics seemed superficial to me compared to the existential cruxes of life, death, faith, etc. If anything, I leaned to the right. I'd seen Columbia prof Zbigniew Brzezinski demolish (I felt) some anti-war leftists on a panel at Union Theological Seminary, and I admired his sang-froid. I finished a cup of grey coffee at Chock full o'Nuts on Broadway and watched through the window as a column of New York City police marched briskly onto campus. I followed in the rain. By the time I got to the centre of the path that cuts across Columbia between Broadway and Amsterdam, a melee was in full flow. Bodies were being flung down the wide steps of Low Library — not a real library but the main admin building. I headed up to see what was going on.

At the top of the steps, among the columns that crossed the front of the stately domed building, the police had interrupted a protest against a Reserve Officers' Training Corps, or campus military recruitment, graduation ceremony. What I saw wasn't merely police pulling protesters off a picket line and flinging them down stairs in the rain. What hit me was an excitement in the faces of the cops and the thrill and animation of their body language. Many protesters were women with long hair in the fashion of the time. There was something sexual and provocative about them, and the police violence felt like a response, a politicized pas de deux. That's what struck me: the thrill and titillation in the armed agents of the state. They weren't just doing a job by maintaining order and allowing university business to proceed — or whatever they'd been called in to do. They were enjoying it — they were into it — as people said then. And I thought, *This is what it was like in Nazi Germany.* It went through my mind like the headlines that ran around the Times building in Times Square. The whole structure I'd imbibed — that Nazism and the Holocaust were *sui generis* — crumpled. *People are capable of this,* I thought, *because they're human.* Put these cops in Nazi Germany or Buchenwald and at least some of them would do what the SS, Wehrmacht, and guards did there, then. The uniqueness of the Holocaust and any elements of understanding and worldview built on it melted away. *So this is what the force of the state is essentially about — and human nature too,* I thought. That experience led on to my involvement in the leftist politics and attitudes of the time. The shift, looking back, seems almost effortless.

If someone, for instance, had to risk his or her academic career by speaking out at a university demonstration, I'd volunteer cheerily, as if I'd already written off the future of my past. I took my comps for a Ph.D. but never began a thesis. I spent a summer on an island in Temagami reading through a small mountain of texts on Marxist economics. My relationship with Emil did not weather these changes well.

When I returned to Toronto in 1970, I went to see him at the university. He said, "I've been hearing things I don't like about you and Israel." He didn't ask what I thought. I found it presumptuous, but it was true: I had changed. I'd lived awhile in Quebec City, where I'd gone to rent a garret and become a writer. I used to drive out to Laval to be around students and attend political meetings. One of the active campus groups was Palestinian. I began to apply my newborn leftism, anti-imperialism, and so forth to the case of Israel. It was easier to think through up there. It had been hard to examine Israel in New York (and hardest of all to rethink Canada, but that's another story). So Emil was right. It's odd that we never discussed my fall away from faith; it didn't seem to interest him or me. We had both been, in some way, absorbed by politics.

Our contact waned. In 1981, when Israel invaded Lebanon, I wrote a piece for *Maclean's* called "Hitler's Last Laugh," in which I quoted Emil's 11th commandment against him. I said that supporting the invasion amounted to ceding Hitler a belated victory. When the article appeared, Emil wrote to *Maclean's*, angrily disassociating himself from my use of his aphorism. We had sporadic, indirect, always bitter contact. He retired and moved to Jerusalem with his family. Years passed before we spoke again.

Then, it was at the behest of Dov Marmur, a sophisticated European who'd become rabbi at the Holy Blossom. He told me that when he arrived in Toronto, he was told to avoid two people, and I was one. So he got in touch. He and I became friends, and in 1988, he told me Emil would be in Toronto, launching a book. Dov asked me to come. When I winced, he said, "I'll stand between you." After speaking, Emil signed books. I got in line. He looked up and I said, "It's Rick." He pushed his glasses onto his brow (another loveable trait), rose, and embraced me. We met next day, and I brought up our disputes. He said generously, "We can do two things. We can talk about it. Or we can say, that's all in the past." I suggested we talk about it a little. We got nowhere, but it didn't matter.

We were back in touch. We'd see each other when he was in Toronto and talk about an autobiography he was writing. In 1996, on his 80th birthday, the Holy Blossom held a dinner in his honour, which I attended. It all came apart again after 9/11.

"Emil Fackenheim mourns for you," someone told

me. "I'm not dead!" I whined to Dov Marmur. "For Emil, you are dead," said Dov. I got a tart email from Jerusalem. Emil said he'd followed my recent debates in print with backers of the war on terror and "of course" I'd lost every round. Then he veered off. He said that when I was 16, and he judged a sermonette contest for Jewish youth, he awarded me first prize; yet looking back, he realized that I had quoted one verse from Exodus but failed to mention the next, which invalidated my point — as if he'd like to take back the Goldman Oratorical Cup, more than 40 years later, if he could. I pondered how to reply for months; a copy of his email still sat on my desk a year later when I heard he'd died. Then I realized I could have said something about his famous phrase, my use of which incensed him. It was open ended, that 11th commandment (or 614th) for Jews after Auschwitz; it told you how to approach your obligations as a Jew but not what to actually do. It left that to each of us, in our existential situation, much as the categorical imperative of Kant (whom Emil revered) said only in broad terms what you must do: behave as if your act could serve as a rule for all people, or: treat human beings as ends, never as means. Both Kant and Emil left the application, the living of life itself, to each person's free choice. He had respectfully cleared that space, despite how vehemently he disagreed with the decision in my case.

*

After 9/11, pure evil was in the air again. George Bush said it was the source of the attacks. Others, like my colleague Marcus Gee at the *Globe and Mail*, with whom I had some of those debates in print, found Osama bin Laden an "embodiment of pure evil." There was even a sense of him as being uniquely evil, like the Holocaust. It changed the world forever, people said; nothing would be the same again. They sometimes mentioned, by way of contrast to their view, Hannah Arendt's phrase — the banality of evil — which she coined at the Eichmann trial 40 years before. It was a conundrum for me. 9/11 certainly didn't seem banal. It was spectacular: huge towers collapsing as if swallowed by the earth. The drama and symbolism were extraordinary and unique, but it all had a grimly ordinary result: some three thousand innocent lives extinguished in the name of cause and grievance, hardly a rarity in the 20th century.

I studied with Arendt at the New School, after drifting out of the seminary/religion stream. I hadn't even known she was Jewish or that she'd spent a decade after fleeing Nazi Germany working for Youth Aliyah in Paris, helping Jewish kids reach Palestine — as Israel then was.

She was a great teacher. She had a directness. "Look," she said, when two of us Marxists explained to her, after she lectured on violence, that capitalism is inherently violent. "Look, violence is when *he* hits *you*." She didn't support the student left or the anti-war movement, so we young leftists considered her one of *them*, though she had her own trenchant critique of U.S. shortfalls. But in years to come, I found myself turning to her books. I didn't become a disciple — she isn't that kind of thinker — but I take a regular dose of her thought. After 9/11, a book of her essays jumped off the shelf into my hands one day as I stood in Book City. Then a few of its pages, from a 1950 piece called "Social Science Techniques and the Study of Concentration Camps," leapt out again. Near war's end, she wrote, the gas chambers were counterproductive. Himmler knew it. Yet he ordered that "no economic or military considerations were to interfere with the extermination program." This, "for all immediate practical purposes," was "self-defeating." It was the same argument I'd heard from Emil, which had never stopped resonating.

Humans are obsessive, repetitive beings. It's how we grow and learn. We return to scenes of significance, intellectually and geographically, because we haven't yet solved the puzzles of our lives, ones that often first confronted us when we were small. I came back to Toronto after ten years away, I now think, mainly because I wanted to unravel some dilemmas I hadn't solved when I left (and that were more or less the reasons I went). It's the reason artists rework the same themes throughout their lives. So, years after I heard Emil argue for the unique evil of the Holocaust, I found a chance, post-9/11, to re-engage with that notion.

"NORMAL MEN DO NOT KNOW THAT EVERYTHING IS possible," Arendt wrote, quoting a Buchenwald survivor. They have not been through the inferno. Yet it has always seemed to me that many "normal" people *do* know everything is possible. They may shake their heads sadly but are not surprised. Arendt feared her social science colleagues of the 1950s would be stymied by Nazi conduct since they could not comprehend how "objective necessities . . . , adjustment to which seems a mere question of elementary sanity, could be neglected." She meant necessities like using trains to get troops to the front instead of filling them with Jews on their way to the gas. But I don't find that hard to grasp, and I don't think I'm abnormal. It seems to me that people routinely fail to adjust their behaviour to "objective" reality. They regularly live and make decisions on bizarre, irrational grounds. She wrote that the insides of the camps look to an observer like an insane asylum, and that's true. But the inside of a hockey arena during the playoffs looks pretty insane too, and you could say the same of many family dinners. Hockey games and family dinners don't carry the weight of a death camp, but they are irrational and perhaps clinically insane in a normal, everyday way. Practical calculation and "common sense" may not be as normal as she implied.

And, when I got to the top of the stairs at Low Library, during the Vietnam years, to see police flinging around protesters, I thought, *Ah, so this is what politics is about: authority, brutality, sadism, and violence.* That's when the social context in which I lived started making more sense, not less. That probably says as much about me and how I "normally" tend to view the world as her view says about her, which is the point I want to linger on.

Arendt described the camps as a world in which "punishment persecutes the innocent more than the criminal, where labour does not result and is not intended to result in products, where crimes do not benefit and are not even calculated to benefit their authors." Yes, it's all true, but that too, I'd say, happens all the time. Reread her list. She called it a realm of "complete senselessness," which it may be. But it can also be seen as at least one part of the normal fare of human life. I find none of it bizarre or rare. Humans act irrationally, in the sense Arendt employs, because what matters to them in their own eyes often has little to do with the rational calculation of benefits. There are surely benefits — emotional, psychological, and short term perhaps — but who decided that short term is irrational and long term is rational? If people behave emotionally and quixotically, who gets to say that is an aberration from, rather than the essence of, being human? You see it in religious martyrdom and daily life. My only point is that irrationality — in the narrow sense of being impractical, short term, or counterproductive — is chokingly common.

Whatever happened in the camps was not a new beginning to human affairs: it was on the continuum.

During the rebellion of 1837 in Ontario, for instance, the rebels against British imperial rule retreated to Navy Island on the Niagara River, in U.S. territory just above the Falls, where they exchanged cannon fire with loyalist troops on the Canadian side. A local man who had enlisted with government forces was hit by a cannonball that ripped off his leg. His name was Miller — that's all the brief account says on his identity. And he was an "old Navy man." Perhaps he served during the Napoleonic Wars under Nelson at Trafalgar; lots of impoverished English kids shipped out and then migrated to the colonies in North America. "After the mangled member was cut off, he desired to see it, gave three cheers for the Queen" — Victoria, the slip of a princess who ascended the throne in faraway London that year — "and in a few hours was dead." He made some kind of sense of his life by giving it away gladly, even giddily, for the sake of the gratitude of a queen who would never hear his name or deed. I have been thinking about Miller for 30 years, since I read about his death in a passing phrase in the historical record, while working on a play called *1837. If I could understand him*, I thought, *I'd understand a lot of what there is to know about human behaviour.*

So when Arendt speaks of "our common sense, trained in utilitarian thinking for which the good as well as the evil makes sense," and calls it a possession of those "normal men" who do not know that everything is possible, my question is, who are these normal people, with their common sense, that she calls "us"? What if the varieties of common sense are more mysterious, multifarious, and subterranean than she supposes and the "calculations" of benefit made by Miller and others (like my dad, who I'll come to) are far from utilitarian? Nor is this situation new or unprecedented since the Holocaust. It constitutes the human condition, which Arendt wrote about brilliantly. In fact, what seems to me neither normal nor common would be a world in which people live basically utilitarian — in her straightforward, no-nonsense definition — lives, ones in which they do not die (or live) for the sake of a distant monarch, or God, or ideal, or revenge, or vindication, or simply for a sense of respect and significance bestowed on them by neighbours or progeny — that is, a world in which they behave reasonably, moderately, and predictably according to "common sense" calculations of risks and benefits. Doesn't *that* sound more utopian and exotic than the lives we see everywhere on the historical stage or in the houses on our street?

Then why did Arendt assume that it — her kind of common sense — was the normal state? Well, utopian or not, it is a view of human behaviour that may have suited the world in which she grew up: the worldview of the European bourgeoisie: calculating and self-serving yet proudly modest and realistic in its own way. An attitude of putting and taking, which Dickens satirized in *Hard Times* and Eliot scourged in "The Love Song of J. Alfred Prufrock." It was easy to ridicule because it was so entrenched and taken for granted. We attack the fortresses that confront us. For me in Toronto in the 1950s, it was the smug bastion of middle-class North American contentment and materialism, perhaps the last gasp and remnant of European bourgeois self-satisfaction. The desperate way I found to undermine that smugness was to become scandalously, traditionally pious: to pray three times a day facing Jerusalem, lay tefillin — the straps and boxes Jews wrap around their arms and forehead during morning prayers — and unashamedly call out the name of God in the shopping plaza at Bathurst and Lawrence. We easily forget the power of a moment, like the moment of the European bourgeoisie, because once past, it exists only in a diminished state, as an object of ridicule or romanticization. The fortresses become windmills to be charmingly tilted at. We and all we hold seriously — our own graven images — will be diminished too, in time.

Arendt was a child of that bourgeoisie, still in an age of ascendancy then, though at the start of its twilight. She was, wrote Arendt scholar Jerome Kohn, "born into a well-established nonreligious German Jewish family" in 1906. "Prodigiously intelligent, bountifully educated, and heir to an old and rich culture." The rest of her life, you could say, consisted of being torn from that setting or having it dismantled and pulverized to dust around her. The First World War, the gas(!), the trenches, Weimar, the Great Depression, the rise of Nazism, the Second World War, the aftermath of refugees, Cold War, Stalinist enormities, the ugly McCarthyite campaigns. And yet she writes, it seems to me, as if the demise of her own childhood milieu was not just the close of a brief, geographically limited, historical episode but the end of a geological era. For her, perhaps it was.

Emil was a child of the same bourgeoisie. His father was a wealthy department store owner in Halle, in what became East Germany. His family had roots in German and Prussian culture that went back centuries. Late in life, at the end of the Cold War, when he had, in a surprising turn, become more revered in Germany than he ever was in Israel, his new (or old/new, in Herzl's phrase) homeland, he received compensation for the expropriated property and died, his friends say, a wealthy man. He had been born a decade after Arendt but may have shared her sense of bourgeois culture as the ethical or anthropological baseline for human nature. He told me once that he aspired to a bourgeois life in the sense that Hegel meant it: one that afforded him time to philosophize.

I don't mean either he or Arendt had a view of human nature that was bourgeois. Or even that they had an explicit view of human nature. Arendt said the essence of existentialism (an odd notion) was the way it replaced the old philosophical focus on *what* human beings are with amazement that they simply *are*. But stuff slips back in, especially if you've decided that essences are out of bounds or nonoperative. And in their ideas about normal human behaviour, or the constraints on action, both she and Emil may have been — to some degree and perhaps without being fully aware — harking back to that early *bürgerlich* ideal. Did they do so in revulsion at what was happening around them? It sounds crudely Freudian — and condescending toward such fine, unflinching minds.

But then Freud himself explicitly repudiated that same bourgeois view: that human nature is pragmatic, realistic, commonsensical, and calculating. He did so long before the Holocaust, from the very heart of the European bourgeois model — *fin de siècle* Vienna. He died in 1939, on the eve of the Holocaust, having chillingly anticipated it long before. Who knows? Perhaps it was easier to foresee an alternate jagged, disorienting model of human nature in theory, as Freud did, than to encounter it in history, as Emil, Arendt, and their generation did. Freud wasn't alone. In his time, there was a cottage industry in rejecting the bourgeois ethos, like Artaud's theatre of cruelty in the arts and other manifestations in academia and politics. Nazism itself was built on antibourgeois revulsion. Arendt and Emil were certainly aware of all that. So I find it surprising that German Jews like them could maintain that they were *surprised* by the descent into barbarity. Horrified and enraged, certainly. Disappointed and devastated, even in theory. But not surprised. Unless you grant, as I say, that it is one thing to anticipate the theoretical possibilities of a holocaust or gulag or breakdown of civilization, but another to find it shatteringly forced before your gaze while you pass through the fire yourself. That could send you scurrying back to embrace an earlier worldview, even if it had once seemed banal. I can sort of hear Arendt say, "Look, Artaud was theatre. Freud was theory. But this *happened*. No one *really* expected it."

Emil, by the way, went through a full-blown Freudian analysis after coming to Toronto. But he remained a partial skeptic. He used to say, "It's like treating a sick horse with a pill through a blowpipe: everything depends on who blows first." He said it in what he called his deadpan. Still, he didn't deny Freudian interpretations — he just said something witty about them. As for Arendt, she rejected interpretations based on unconscious motives. She felt they deprived people of their dignity, even their freedom, and down that road lay perdition. She is not someone you can picture in therapy, especially Freudian. "Look," I can hear her again, "he says that's his reason. If I don't take him seriously, why should I take you, me, or anyone seriously?" She believed in will and choice and would not see them disparaged. Despite that, her writings include brilliant construals of the "real" meaning of events. As if she couldn't refrain from it.

*

AS FOR ME, IF I TURN NOW TO ASK WHAT MADE ME make these judgements about the judgements made by Emil or Arendt, it is not because I want to get into an infinite regression, a whirlpool of endless subjectivity. Or that I equate the depth and value of my thoughts based on my experience to theirs, based on their experience. It is because none of us has any choice about viewing the experience of our times, except through the prisms of our lives. It's a given. I'm not trying to glorify my experience; I'm trying to emphasize everyone's, which is unique and a potential source of insight for others. This is what living a life in awareness of one's times is about: your two cents also count — at the very least for you and possibly for others.

My own version of common sense, as I've said, tends not to be perplexed when confronted by destructive, vile, self-negating behaviour of the sort that, writ large, infused the Nazi system and the death camps. I tend to be surprised by the opposite — when people behave practically and constructively, as individuals or together. As it happens, I also grew up in a smug, bourgeois community — though it was not secure or confident. But I am not suggesting there is any single underlying "factor" behind one way of viewing the world or another. Many elements enter in; everything is modified by everything else. In my case, I'm guessing it had to do with my dad.

He would explode, for no apparent reason. I used to think it was about his gambling and debts, the threats from "the guys" — the loan sharks on the Danforth — to break his legs. But mum told me after he died that he was energized by the danger and narrow escapes. So maybe fear wasn't the source of his cruelty and explosions; maybe it was his loaded relations with his older brother Al, who founded the little firm of A. Salutin and Bros. but forgot to include *brothers* on the sign in the window at Adelaide and Spadina. (The other sign read "No Retail.") Or it could have been lifelong resentment of his own dad, Hyman, who had done nothing in life, he told me, except neglect his family and run around with women. Maybe he just had a rough ride through the birth canal and never got over it or was simply a mean guy, born that way, and remained true to himself.

Whatever the source, it was brutal. Screaming, abusive, deriding. Mostly at my mum for being stupid, ignorant, incompetent — when he couldn't find a tie in the morning or we were leaving on a trip or, rarely, going to a family social event, which seemed to fill him with dread and he always wanted to leave early, muttering "Fre" (for Freda) through his teeth, making everyone tense. I should add that they had a stupendous, historic sex life, whether in spite of or due to all the rest. Everybody noticed it (except me, but that's another story). The tiny apartments in which we lived were drenched in sex. She told me that when I was in high school, he still came home for "lunch." She said it continued until a year before his death at 85, at least three times a week. I asked if she ever had an orgasm, and she said every time. I thought about that (we were driving), then asked what she meant by an orgasm. She guffawed (not her usual mode), "An *orgasm!*"

He'd come home from gambling in the middle of the night and flick on the overhead light in the cramped bedroom my brother and I shared, bellowing that we'd be on the street tomorrow and it was my fault. When I got into trouble with high school authorities over what I saw as questions of principle, I told him, expecting sympathy and hoping for pride. He said they were right. I said, "But they're wrong!" "Even when they're wrong," he howled, "they're right!" When my brother connected headphones to the TV so he could do his homework without the din from the set, Dad ripped them off and threw them at Lorne. When I mused to an analyst that it was almost as if he wanted me to fail, the shrink delicately inquired, like an anthropologist trying not to upset the primitive worldview of the natives, if there might be a reason for that. It stunned me. I'd never considered that he actually bore me ill will, which he clearly did. Seeing others fail was his only way to not feel left behind, since his own failure was a given. It may also account for the gambling. Sheer luck was the sole potential route to success. He bullied his own family because he could.

I'd say he knew it was bad, wrong, however you want to phrase that. When he was dying and still bullying my mother, who was frail and ill herself, I told him she'd go the day after he did if he kept on. He said she had to die sometime. That's when it occurred to me that he knew what he was doing and knew it was wrong. Perhaps it started with what seemed like uncontrollable outbursts against his wife and young kids. Back then, he may have regretted it or felt guilty. But he came to realize there were no consequences, and from then on, he embraced it, without regret. I could go on about this, and I have.

It wasn't Auschwitz. I know, I know. Yet the possibilities of awesomely cruel behaviour got established in our minds and remain. There is a chasm of quantity and quality between Auschwitz and the familiar family cruelties. Yet when a kid sees his dad behave that way, he knows — or I think I did, like the Buchenwald survivor quoted by Arendt — that everything is possible. If my dad can let go like this at any moment with me, he can go to the end, whatever it might be; nothing can surprise me. Like that sight of the cops on the Columbia campus.

They weren't the SS, but under other circumstances, some might and would have been. The first glimpse unveils the potential, and surprise will never again be an option. The possibility of the Holocaust was contained in those dynamics inside our apartment, whether it seems ludicrous to compare or not. Maybe this is a "category mistake"— I don't much care. How could I fail to understand, in some rudimentary way, the Holocaust and other potential atrocities, after growing up there? My dad surely had his good points; he wasn't a Hollywood monster, but he had monster potential. Nor do I mean he'd have been a Nazi if he'd been in Nazi Germany (and not been Jewish, etc.). In fact, I'm sure he wouldn't have; his form of brutalization — the domestic fascist, as it were — was different from the politicized mass version. In his explicit politics, he was an FDR Democrat. But I can't be surprised when people behave wretchedly.

I should add, in deference to Arendt and Emil, that they both knew well that brutality and sadism were hardy perennials and didn't occur for the first time in Auschwitz. But each insisted on the uniqueness of the Nazi case: Emil, because it was self-destructive; Arendt, for a different reason. She argued that the distinction under Hitler wasn't barbarism; it was the cold intellectuality of it — it was founded not on emotional satisfaction and release, like my dad's and so many other bullies', but on logically carrying out an ideology. You can call this a crucial difference, or you can say it's just a variation. Everybody gets something from the exercise of cruelty. It's true that the motives of the Nazi leaders were articulated in relatively cool ideological terms: they were serving the cause, history, or however else they put it. Does that mean there was no vicarious charge, like the sense of release my dad once acknowledged to me? I guess that depends on how seriously you take the Nazis' own professions. Not as the last word, in my view. There's always something new and something ancient, a unique version of timeless propensities. Everything was always possible.

*

For me, claims about the transformative, unique nature of 9/11 — that everything has changed, that the world will never be the same — evoked Emil's assertions about the Holocaust as uniquely evil. It wasn't a big leap. The Holocaust was widely invoked post-9/11. It looks problematic, since if the Holocaust was unique, how can you compare it to 9/11 or anything else? But *unique* has become a comparative term like *famous*, and logic isn't essential in these matters. So Americans in particular tended to elide the two, as if only the Holocaust was "unique enough" to compare to their trauma. This also fit the U.S.'s sense of exceptionalism: both Jews and Americans are "chosen" peoples, while the ascent of fundamentalist Christianity in the U.S., with its apocalyptic and catastrophic expectations, easily attached itself to the 9/11 imagery. The Holocaust and 9/11 seemed fated to meet. And when I saw the essays in Arendt's book, it was naturally the pages on the uniqueness of the Holocaust that jumped out. Around Remembrance Day that same year, I found myself reading poetry arising from the slaughter of the First World War, another apocalyptic event thought to have changed the world forever so that nothing would ever be the same. That was probably as true as it was for the Holocaust or 9/11. We live in an age of ongoing uniqueness. States of exception (which are all unique) have also become normal since at least that war, as Walter Benjamin wrote and as I discovered in the book recommended by the man in the university bookstore.

So the autobiographies of Emil and Hannah Arendt influenced the way they responded to the decisive event of their time — the Holocaust — and helped shape their interpretations of it as a uniquely evil moment. And my own autobiography — perhaps my dad's screaming fits — shaped my response to their response. Then another event — 9/11 — and the reactions to it evoked those earlier responses, theirs and mine, along with an endless unfolding set of exchanges — with them, with myself, with the man in the bookstore.

*

IT IS THIS HOMEY PERSONAL CONTEXT OF THOUGHT that I want to insist on — even the heaviest thoughts of the weightiest thinkers on the thorniest topics. Every idea I have is an idea of mine! It arose in my head, in a specific context, and so did every idea anyone has ever had, including the big ones, as a moment in the chain of associations and digressions that comprise each conscious life. You can strip an idea from its context and lend it a certain autonomy, like an orphan — though with an austere and intellectual dignity (a dignified orphan) — disconnected from the mundane details of a particular life. But that won't change the fact that it has a background, an address it came from, which affects its content and authority. Most intellectual histories take account of the autobiographical setting of thought but as lip service, the way biographies often deal with childhood: a quick chapter left behind and rarely treated as the decisive period in every life ever lived, its effects reverberating till the end. (Rosebud, Rosebud — always Rosebud.) We remain the kids we were, and our ideas stay rooted in our autobiographies. Those bios are not mere backdrops for thoughts, a sort of outer garment that the ideas themselves can put on or off. The thoughts don't exist at all, apart from the lives in which they are embedded. They are warp and woof. You can't always know the background, the return address, but you can at least assume it's there and that something important is probably missing from your comprehension. So proceed with caution, and don't be too intimidated by great thinkers and their thoughts. A recognizable life like your own lurks there somewhere.

I hope it doesn't seem tawdry to use the Holocaust and 9/11 to make this simple point. Perhaps I've leaned to overkill since the approach I'm embracing — replacing the majestic history of ideas with more modest autobiographies of ideas, or private little diaries — runs against the Western intellectual tradition (which I tend to feel deferential toward, for my own autobiographical reasons), a tradition in which ideas seem to have an independent life — whether literally, like Plato's forms, or embodied historically, à la Hegel. When I studied philosophy or the history of ideas, a notion like free will seemed to migrate from thinker to thinker and era to era, as if on a journey all its own, like a worm wriggling across a Persian rug. When an idea inhabited actual thinkers, it did so like a parasite in an optional or interchangeable host. There have been postmodernist rejections of this approach in recent decades, but I'm speaking of the main tradition, over millennia.

I don't believe a homier approach diminishes the role of thought. But it does emphasize thinking itself more than its end products, such as ideas, truth, and knowledge. Knowledge seems to captivate us, and yet as Arendt said, echoing Nietzsche, what we are actually good at is thinking rather than knowing. Our instruments for knowing — our minds — are only capable of partial approaches to truth, because we exist in specific, limited contexts: our lives and times. One sign of that is the way all knowledge, no matter how confidently posited, is embarrassingly outstripped before very long. I include impersonal scientific views in areas such as physics, medicine, and nutrition (Wasn't breakfast once the most important meal of the day? Before that, it didn't exist!) as well as sudden personal flashes about why I always partner up with the wrong people. Eventually death intervenes to prevent further embarrassment. There's nothing wrong with this state; it's not even genuinely embarrassing; it's simply the best we're capable of when it comes to knowledge. Less partial and perspectival beings, like gods or angels, would do better. Nor does it mean we're hopelessly confined within our views. We can access the perspectives of others and, by a collective and democratic process, build toward a larger view — an aggregation of perspectives. But there won't ever be a grand synthesis, putting it all together, because, well, who would do that? No one can get outside their perspective. It's only the process itself that can do the synthesizing.

You can call this relativism — but not in the sense that nothing is true or everything is equally true. It's a relativism in which there is no complete truth and humans, as "finite modes," in Spinoza's mind-bending coinage, catch only partial views of the whole. So, in the absence of a perspective taking in everything, we must constantly turn the kaleidoscope to get another view, while never seeing it all at any moment. We must count on each other to complement and supplement; there's no alternative. The point is not that the Holocaust was unique (Emil) or a new historical moment (Arendt). Or that it was instead a variation on an old theme, as I've suggested. It could, in some senses, be any, none, or all. They all contain a piece of the full truth, which only God could comprehend, if He existed, which She doesn't. Since this provisionality is the way to truth for us, it seems to me useful to shed light on the origins of ideas, since their meaning will be illuminated and inflected by their provenance. It is an argument for the role of origins in ideas, not for the invalidation of ideas by virtue of them having origins.

Nor does it mean everyone is right, in a postmodernist way. You can be more or less right or wrong, depending on how well you reason with the materials you have at hand. There is a broad playing field on which all thought takes place — or we wouldn't be able to communicate at all. But the "rules" involved hardly suffice to bring us to identical conclusions on most matters, given our particular startpoints. Uncovering the constraints that act on your thinking — what Harold Innis called your bias, whether it's individual bias or the bias of the "civilization" in which your thought developed — can stretch those limits to something broader and truer — but only up to a point. The boundaries remain.

I don't find this discouraging. I'd say it makes thought *more* interesting: an endless, evolving detection process, in which you investigate and complexify your previous ideas. There's always something to learn, somewhere deeper to go. It explains why philosophical activity (in a broad, nonspecialist sense available to all) never ends yet seems to make no progress; it's because serious thought is always specific and part of someone's biography. It changes as your life changes, and will end when you do. There is no way to transfer others' thoughts to you, since one size always fits one. Words and concepts are not the same from person to person or situation to situation. All conclusions must be reformulated, rethought, and brought home, as it were. No one can discover truth for others. And no one makes thinking about anything obsolete for anyone else. This makes philosophy a universal human activity not in the old sense (because everyone has access to it through their inherent rationality) but because we all must redo it for ourselves. After that we can compare notes with others and see what a more comprehensive view *might* look like.

2

THE SINGER NOT THE SONG: ON THERAPY

We have added a dimension,
and there is no more radical act.
— John R. Seeley

ACT I

I WENT TO MY FIRST SHRINK IN MY EARLY 20S. I WAS married, a seminarian, and a grad student bound for an academic life. I was terrified by what might happen if I put my precarious sense of self under scrutiny. I talked to a rabbi and theologian I knew named Gene Borowitz. He confirmed the risk. "You will question all the pillars of your life," he said. Then he listed them, showing how well he knew me: "Melanie. Judaism. Academics. But the marvellous thing you'll discover," he went on, in his sonorous sermon voice, "is that after you've gone through the process, they will all still be there." It was like a warranty. I suppose it's how his own therapy had gone. I exhaled with relief and signed on. Four years later, I came out the other end divorced, an atheist, and a dropout. Yet I still *was*.

My pillars had crumbled; I remained. It turns out that what you think, including who you think you are, is adjustable.

Psychotherapy is a process of thinking about what is thought (or felt or done). There are other ways to do that. In philosophy, both linguistic analysis and phenomenology focus on the thinking more than the thoughts. But nothing is pervasive in the way therapy is. I'm using the term nonspecifically and untechnically — for a way of examining and explaining what we mean or do — which assumes that what we say we mean isn't exhaustive and might well be misleading. Therapy began as a medical specialty for treating mental pain and suffering; now it's in the air everywhere: a sense of unconscious motives, underlying meanings, slips of the tongue, fixations, obsessions, complexes. It has spawned a vast vocabulary (like *unconscious*). You can't even attack it without resorting to its language. In medicine, it falls in and out of favour, like its procreator, Freud. That hardly matters; it has long since been generalized and "added a dimension."

*

MY SHRINK'S NAME WAS HARRIS PECK, SO FILM STAR Gregory Peck appeared often in my dreams of those years — sometimes as *Mirage*'s distraught amnesiac who watched in horror as *his* mentor hurtled through a plate glass window at the top of a skyscraper. He spent most of that film repressing the trauma. The skyscraper in the film was in Manhattan, probably on the East Side, where, with *my* Peck, I was trying to remember what I was trying to suppress. *Casablanca* (the site of Rick's Café) also figured in my dreams.

Peck — a *Pilgrim's Progress* kind of name for an analyst — happened also to be the patron saint of a psychiatric social work agency where my wife worked. He was legendary there. That mattered to me since, like most people who go into therapy and lots who don't, I lacked confidence in my intrinsic worth and sought proof of my value in the approval of others — in my case, via a series of intellectually imposing father figures. I urgently wanted to land Peck as we "explored" the idea of "working together" in an early session.

I told him Heschel didn't want me to do it. Peck suddenly leaned in over the coffee table between his armchair and the couch I was on (an ordinary couch; the "couch" couch was on his other side). "Abraham Joshua Heschel?" he breathed — and I knew he was hooked.

Not every shrink would have known that name. Descendant of a dynasty of charismatic Hasidic rebbes, there's an Abraham Joshua Heschel chapter in Buber's *Tales of the Hasidim*. Heschel wrote books with fabulous names like *God in Search of Man*. I had added him to my collection of father figures when I went to the seminary. Before enrolling, I'd told him I couldn't choose between the wide world of universal knowledge at Columbia grad school and what seemed like the parochial seminary. He said, "My son, in the end, Moses was probably a very parochial man." It struck me to the spot with sudden, shattering self-awareness, the way Fritz Perls, founder of gestalt therapy, used to cut to the core in an instant: an Aha! moment. In fact, Heschel was a therapy kind of guy himself, despite his aversion to it.

Peck knew the name, he may even have known Borowitz's. Many shrinks have (speaking technically) a fixation on religion, especially Jewish shrinks like Peck or Freud. Freud had a little statue of Michelangelo's *Moses* in his office. He wrote about Judaism and picked it to pieces but always treated it — not just Judaism but religion — seriously. (As did Marx, who called religion the opiate of the masses but also "a sigh from the heart of the distressed, the heart of a heartless world." Opiate in a good way, you could say.) Many shrinks are Jews who left their Jewishness along with any religiosity yet return to the scene of primal desertion with fascination, respect, and guilt; it's a way of having it in spite of leaving it behind, much as even a happy child must grow up and leave home. When I said Heschel's name and Peck leaned in, I felt I'd snared him. Maybe he did too, because the topic never arose again till I was almost done, four years later.

*

PECK WAS A CLASSICAL FREUDIAN OF THAT ERA,
which meant neoclassical and post-Freudian;
alternately, it meant eclectic and pragmatic. I'd
known people who were treated by *echt* classical
Freudians, men (mainly) with a foot in earlier eras;
they'd leave their patients to sit — that is, lie in
silences lasting weeks or months — because the iron
law of free association decreed that the analyst *may
never intervene* in the eruption of the unconscious.
(By these standards, I think the record shows Freud
himself was a neo-Freudian.) At those impasse
moments, if I moaned, "But *nothing* is in my mind,"
Peck would snap testily, "Oh, there's always *something*
in your mind" — as if he couldn't bear the boredom
of analytic silence. His outburst would release some
thought in me, though there's no way to know
if it was already there or I had manufactured it to
keep him from yelling at me. Peck even fell asleep
sometimes and occasionally took calls, saying it must
be important since someone was clearly desperate to
reach him. I'd picture a rival patient at the other end
about to step out a window, like (the other) Peck's
mentor in the movie. Peck (the shrink) liked to say as
a witticism that it would be wrong for an analyst to
simply nod neutrally as a patient announced, "Now I
am going to jump out this window." He repeated that
one so often it made him seem a bit dotty, not that
it was my place to notice such things. Maybe he was
the desperate one, desperate for some contact outside

the damn room where he spent so much time cooped up with other people's streams of consciousness. Maybe *he* had the jump-out-the-window impulse. Sometimes it was hard to keep the movie Peck and the shrink Peck distinct.

Near the end of year one, at his suggestion, I brought my wife in for a few sessions, a sort of gift to her in our effort to save our catastrophic marriage; she'd been jealous that I had the famous Dr. Peck as my personal saviour, since she'd heard about him first. And perhaps it was a gift to him too, since he had an annoying way of flirting with her. He once told me that even gorgeous fashion models deeply doubt their own attractiveness, adding that having them as patients was one perk of a therapist's life. I can see that: something to look forward to all day or week, while folks like me troop in and out kvetching. It's a fascinating profession, of course, in principle, when you're not nodding off or reaching for the phone during a session. I spent long evenings at the bar of The West End, on upper Broadway, sipping Guinnesses in doughty brown bottles and working through dreams I'd managed to salvage, since he insisted that what happens between sessions is more important than the sessions. It was like a therapeutic version of the Protestant ethic, the faith that effort and hard work will be rewarded in this world. Decades later, when I signed on with Harvey Freedman for a different kind of therapy, he told me not to bother thinking about things between sessions. He was like one of those teachers who don't believe in giving kids homework.

Peck was classic enough, in his neoclassical way. We seemed to be travelling on a grid he knew, a program that was relatively rigid, like dots we had to spend time connecting but that were in fact already out there, at the back of the puzzle book, with the other answers. Eventually we would pass through the phases (rhymes with *mazes*), dissolve the transference, terminate my treatment, and . . . Bob's your uncle. It had to be anticlimactic for him; maybe that's why he sometimes dozed off. "What we just did is telescope the whole process," he said near the end of year one, after he'd talked more than usual, perhaps not having meant to, drifting further than he planned into regions we hadn't yet touched on. But he knew what we were headed for, like a tour guide who's done the trip too often. It sounded odd, even with me tending to assume he had total control. "Of course," he added, making it hard to tell if he was trying to convince me or himself, "we have to go back and proceed through the entire thing in the right order at the proper length." Besides sounding boring, it seemed an old-fashioned notion of knowledge. The truth is out there for all to see; you just have to acquire it yourself. One size fits all, or at least fits some, and the process is just a particular way to get where you already know you're going. Freud had something of that about him too, at least some of the time.

At those moments, Freud seems a lot like Lenin, his European contemporary of the *fin de siècle*. Leninism, which dominated 20th-century left-wing thought, appeared to be based on the proposition that for every political problem, there is one and only one solution, or "correct analysis" — Lenin's term. If you get the analysis right, the rest follows, like diagnosis and cure (Bob's your uncle). Correctly comprehend the social contradictions at work in your nation or society and out will pop the revolution — bada-bing bada-boom. That kind of model, or fantasy, also suffused Freud's thought and some of his practice — but only some: he wavered between stern scientific determinism of the 19th-century kind (so did Marx and all the Marxists, like Lenin) and a kind of giddy, panicky, exhilarated anarchism of the mind. In photos, we only see Freud as the former: starched shirt, upright posture in his office chair, the *Moses* statuette just out of frame, a cigar balanced in his fingers. What was behind his reluctance to abandon devout scientism, that one-and-only-one-correct-analysis model? Fear of chaos? Sexual pandemonium?

I read Freud's *Introductory Lectures on Psychoanalysis* in my teens. His confidence, or pseudo-confidence, was breathtaking. "I don't have time to tell you how we know this," he told students at Clark University, where he gave the course. (I'm paraphrasing.) "But we have learned what certain symbols in dreams always mean. For instance, walking upstairs always means having sex." Yet at other times, in high theoretical flight, he could be far less dogmatic. When he wrote about the death impulse, he speculated wildly, like someone behind the wheel of a car who'd never driven before. But those untamed thoughts arose in a nonacademic context, the maelstrom of treatment, where an individual's life was, one way or another, at stake. False immodesty there could have serious effects. He fretted, late in his career, about the apparently inevitable failure of all psychoanalysis and how to know the moment to terminate, which was difficult since no treatment ever seemed to conclude, er, conclusively. He laid this result at the feet of a force he called the death drive. It was hardly science in the stiff-collar sense; it might as well have been an episode of *Star Trek*. The death drive was "the urge of the living to return to a lifeless state," a tendency in all "matter imbued with life" to revert to the torpid, inanimate condition from which it sprang. He knew it sounded peculiar and spooky, but sometimes, he said (with true intellectual courage), you had to "call in the witch" — the metaphysical one, not the gal from Oz. He didn't sound embarrassed about the gambit; he was more concerned with the practical dilemma of how the hell you know when a treatment has gone as far as it can and will advance no further and whether to end it there. That essay is called "Analysis Terminable and Interminable." I knew people in New York who'd been in therapy so long they said they couldn't leave because their analyst needed *them*. They'd take him or her along for holidays, on a cruise or at the cottage. Peck told me he once attended a seminar with Erich Fromm, a revered Freudian at the time (he wrote *Escape from Freedom*, which you saw people reading on the subway). One shrink appeared unhurried as he presented the case of an analysis that had bogged down. "I thought I smelled something, you son of a bitch," snapped Fromm, who seemed like a kindly man in his books. "This poor guy is in pain. You ought to be going into each session hoping it will be the last so he can get out, finished, fixed, cured!"

Freud sounds splendidly undogmatic in that essay — published only a couple of years before his death — spinning theories into the stratosphere, not defensive about the proven inadequacy of his life's great work, psychoanalysis itself. *What the hell — this is the real crunch for doctors and patients*, he seems to feel. *So it's no time to get pompous about my theoretical legacy; I'll toss this death thing out there and see if it helps.* "We must submit to the superiority of the powers that defeat our efforts," he wrote, after hypothesizing inventively on the chthonic grip of inanimate primal stuff over the life force. He does a kind of exuberant embrace of the inevitability of failure, not exactly what you expect from the cocky know-it-all who gave those lectures at Clark 20 years ago. He doesn't seem demoralized. In fact he appears energized, going by the language he uses at the moment of definitive breakdown: "It is only the cooperation and conflict of the two basic drives, eros and the death drive, and never one of them by itself, that accounts for the colourful variety of the phenomena of life." That isn't a voice exhausted at the end of the road, though it's clearly where he's arrived. He doesn't fasten on all the grimness and hopelessness in the phenomena of life, which have defeated him. He rhapsodizes over their lush variety! As if it's a pleasure to be vanquished by such a multifarious, prolific antagonist: that twosome in one, eros/Thanatos.

I once saw Bob White, the magnetic leader of the Canadian Auto Workers union in the 1980s, get totally invigorated by defeat in the struggle for social justice. It was the night in 1988 when we lost the epic battle over free trade in Canada. "I knew we were gonna lose this election," he burbled, "but I had no idea we'd lose this badly!" He brimmed with energy. I got the same sense from my friend and union mentor Kent Rowley in similar catastrophes: Right, let's get on with it; we've a lot to do now, more than ever. It's exciting — as if life acquired renewed meaning when you failed and had to start over, as though they almost feared success more than failure, since the *joie de combat* might depart then. Or perhaps they always knew it would be defeat in the short run and medium run too, and as for the long run, chances are that's a loser as well.

Optimism is facile because no one knows what's coming down the line, and it's a relief to face the likelihood of defeat still feeling the effort was made, that some good might yet occur. "But surely infantilism was meant to be overcome," Freud wrote in *Future of an Illusion*. He was talking about religion, but maybe he was thinking, consciously or un, about psychoanalysis. I find that the most touching line — I was going to say that he ever wrote, but I may mean that I've ever read. It has the quality of a prayer. Infantilism, that mighty, demonic force, may have been meant to be overcome, but there's no assurance it can or will be. It's the "surely" that gives away his doubt. At best we can hope, so let us pray. Freud never claims it *will* be overcome. The process — as Marxists used to say about the struggle — continues.

Analysts too, Freud wrote, closer to the end than the beginning of his life's work, "have not achieved in their own personalities the degree of psychological normality towards which they would like to educate their patients." (For him, normality was a good thing, not the dubious compliment it would be today.) He wondered if the movement he created had already become the third "impossible profession," marked by certainty that "you will fall short of complete success." The other two were teaching and politics. Even an analyst's own analysis will have to terminate too soon, since failure is inevitable — total, redeeming knowledge, a definitive analysis, is apparently unachievable.

There's a brisk, sensible, not-at-all-morose note in his conclusion. It is "a practical matter," a case of trying to "create the optimum conditions for the functioning of the I." That's it — no muss, no fuss, two cheers for us (or me). You've done the best you can; you're no longer striving to reach an impossible dream, like normality or mental health. You've met the limitations of your vision, and it seems accompanied by some delight at reaching the truth, along with frustration. At least you're not under illusions. Cheer up, there's no hope — a line Peck offered me at some point, which I used in a play about the false Messiah of the 17th century, Shabtai Zvi. The hope was false anyway, pleasant as it was to entertain. What you can do is still worthwhile.

By this point in his trajectory, Freud takes a noncategorical, nonmessianic approach to helping people in their sickness. In fact he sounds kind of, um, normal, well adjusted, realistic, and, er, healthy? Health and illness have come down to a quantitative matter, as Freud sometimes put it, because "a normal I, like normality in general, is an idealized fiction . . . every normal person is simply averagely normal; his I approaches that of the psychotic in one respect or another, to a greater or lesser extent, and the extent of his distance from one end . . . to the other end of the range serves us provisionally for what is so vaguely called the transformation of the I." That sounds awfully nonjudgemental and kind of anarchic. It's a matter of degree; we all lurch along on the scale between somewhat crazy and somewhat healthy (or normal, though, as I mentioned, people today, a century later, tend to prefer crazy to normal — anything but normal, please, it makes us feel so unspecial). It's chiefly a question of how far along that scale between psychotic and normal you can get; but overall, the human enterprise sounds, at its heart, as nutty as a fruitcake — little animated piles of matter tugged between surging vitality and debilitating inertness — as inept a metaphor as any for the ridiculousness of human life. Who ever thought this thing up? If there really is a God of creation, he's got a lot of 'splaining to do, and it's impressive the way that Freud, both a scientist and rationalist, doesn't try to hide the underlying absurdity. What would be the point? After all those years of reasoning and treatment, he too seems relieved; he didn't do a bad job, he's not a failure, and he doesn't feel like one, but still the task itself is ultimately futile — so let's get on with it. Cheer up, there's no hope.

Real hopelessness would probably be arriving at the end with a complete analysis. How dreary. How deathly. Maybe that's why he seemed exhilarated by the inevitability of failure. You get some small, often shitty, victories against pain and anxiety, but overall, no completion. The process proceeds, endlessly, till the end. It was the best and only real part: the thinking, not the thought.

PECK HAD A WILD-MAN SIDE TOO — *WILD ANALYSIS* was Freud's term — that cohabited with the guy in the buttoned-down lab coat plodding methodically through treatment and filling in the anticipated blanks. In fact, it was the unexpected moments when there was nothing much for him to do but improvise that proved truly therapeutic, whereas I barely recall the details of my history with its "complexes" that we excavated and reconstructed like a dino dig.

Early on, he vetoed my plan to separate from Melanie, my wife. He said shrinks got a veto on major life changes like that; it was part of our deal. Like the way he way he agreed to waive some of his hourly fee till the treatment was finished (which, come to think of it, was like a promise that he wouldn't keep me hanging around in pain forever). The theory was that, just as patients were getting close to some liberating insight, they might try to avoid it by "acting out" via a dramatic, life-changing gesture. The shrink had the right to forbid this in order to let the insight force its way into awareness rather than get dissipated in . . . acting it out.

There are lots of psychohydraulics like that in Freudian theory: thoughts and feelings get sidetracked into various "channels" by being suppressed or repressed and then burst out elsewhere, like explosions in a water main. I found it a little obscure as well as irritating, and I protested loudly that here I was finally trying to take control of my life and he of all people was standing in the way. Then one day he stopped me dead by "removing" the prohibition. I think he said it was either that or, from the sound of it, she and I might end up killing each other. He had called my bluff. I moved out.

Some time later, Melanie returned from a trip to England to announce she'd replaced me with my polar opposite: a white supremacist London bank teller. We'd been separated about six months. I'd moved into International House on Riverside Drive, where Leonard Cohen set his first novel, across from Grant's Tomb. But, of course, at the instant she told me, I was consumed with remorse and — presto — my love and devotion to her burst forth again.

I staggered up to Tom's Restaurant on Broadway — the model for the hangout in *Seinfeld*. It was 10:30 at night. I went to a phone booth inside and made my first emergency call to my shrink. I knew you were allowed a few, and I hadn't cashed any. A maternal operator ("Stay right there, honey") told me she'd get him to call me back. When he did, I burst into sobs. "She's got someone else, just when I realized I love her, now it's hopeless . . ." No response from him. I didn't know if we'd lost the connection. "Are you there?" I said. He said yes. "Don't you want to ask me anything?" "Like what?" he said, not sounding stressed. "Um, do you want to know if I'm all right?" "Are you all right?" he said. "Yeah," I said. "I'm okay." "That's good," he grunted. "I'll see you tomorrow," I said. "Oh?" he said. "Yeah," I said, "I have an appointment with you." We hung up. It was like emergency curbside mental first aid. The parashrink arrives by phone and gives you enough to staunch the blood loss; the rest can wait till you get to the hospital. I'd say now he was working on dissolving the transference.

*

BY THEN I WAS TRANSITING FROM THE SEMINARY to the oddly similar world of the left. One afternoon, Peck rushed in late to his Madison Avenue digs, saying some of my "friends" had blocked his car (a Lincoln, I assumed) outside a conference downtown. They were called Radicals for Psychology. I'd begun a Ph.D. in philosophy at the New School for Social Research in the Village. There was a radicals-for group corresponding to every faculty. The psych radicals were campaigning against the oppression of the poor by means of psychiatric programs that tried to adjust them to a vile social structure, rather than "empower" them — a word not yet invented, but it's what they meant. They had targeted a huge community mental health project at Lincoln Hospital in the South Bronx, which Peck, my Peck, headed. (Maybe that's why I assumed he drove a Lincoln: free association. A shrink like Lincoln: authoritative, moral, top of the line, utterly devoted to my welfare as Lincoln was to the Union's. He was going to solidify my fractured identity and was willing to sacrifice his time —

perhaps even his *life*, like Gregory Peck's mentor in the flick — for me.)

The program at Lincoln got massive federal funding; it was the pilot for community mental health projects nationwide and sounded extremely worthy; it was one of the credentials that had made me feel I'd scored a top-notch shrink in Peck. He must have been shocked when people on the side of the people, like my friends, labelled him the villain. (Though by then I'd learned that the left, like any orthodoxy, can always make some members feel apostate. If you laid tefillin at the seminary you'd soon notice someone else who laid two sets of tefillin.) But it made me wonder for the first time if we really would be great lifelong friends if I weren't in therapy with him, a fantasy lots of people in treatment nurture. Did he drop the detail about why he was late to plant that little doubt — as part of the process of dissolving the transference and weaning me away from my father figure addiction? Maybe he'd have said it anyway, out of pique or as chit-chat, and simply didn't interfere with it coming out of his mouth, for whatever use it might serve.

*

Shortly after that, our sessions shifted from his private address on the Upper East Side to Lincoln Hospital in the Bronx, where the big, contentious community health program run by him was based. I had to take the subway. Since Yankee Stadium was on that line, I sometimes made time to catch a few innings of an afternoon game. One afternoon, I sat in the waiting room outside his office in the hospital as the harsh sound of harangues and denunciations seeped through the wall. Then his door burst open, and a line of black and brown people in dashikis paraded by. They didn't spare me a glance. When I went in, he didn't seem to want to talk about it, as if he was repressing. A week later, I phoned his secretary about my schedule for the week — it was always changing, to my annoyance, which gave us something else to analyze. "It's Rick Salutin. I'm phoning about this week's appointments." (Peck also put stock in my reactions to his secretary, who was a crucial part of my life in those years.) "This is the community, dear," said an unfamiliar voice. "We've taken over the hospital." For the rest of the occupation — they were common; I was involved in some myself — I scrambled to meet him in various locations at Albert Einstein, the hospital and med school in the Bronx where he taught. He seemed rattled, and who wouldn't be? But did he, again, *decide* to let it show — or, rather, not *prevent* it from showing — as part of the therapeutic plan? How devious: you treat the patient by, in effect, *not* treating him.

*

THEN CAME A DAY THAT HE AGREED RELUCTANTLY, as if signing up to pass a kidney stone, to discuss with me what I should do about my marriage. Melanie's white supremacist lover had been eclipsed shortly after her return by a surprising blizzard I managed to generate of flowers, poems, remorse, ardour, rented cars for weekend trips to the tip of Long Island. Rejection had set me free. Then, at the very moment she announced the other guy was over and I could move back in, it was if I'd got a telegram saying "NOTHING HAS CHANGED. STOP."

After all the emotion and commotion, little really had. A year later, she and I were deep in discussion about whether to quit, again. It was better than the first time, since we were talking about what to do, instead of generating so much conflict and pain that we ostensibly had no choice but to get out: the shot-from-a-gun method of ending a relationship. Peck said he'd discuss it with me, but solely as a window into my garbled psychic structures, not, God forbid, for the practical purpose of making the right choice so that I could get on with my wretched life. That wasn't the kind of therapy he did. I paid scant attention to his pro forma declaration of purpose; what mattered for me was the chance to uncover his carefully concealed opinion on whether I should get out of the marriage. I tuned my radar for clues on what he truly, underneath, thought I ought to do. The more I looked and listened, the less I found.

No tips. Not a hint. "I'm starting to think you don't *have* an opinion on whether I should split from her," I said in frustration. "That's true," he said, smiling proudly, as if I'd finally grasped the nettle. "And furthermore," I rolled along, like a prosecutor daring him to deny it, "I don't think you even *think* about it." I'd assumed till this moment that he regularly did, while shaving in the morning or listening to some other poor loser's dilemmas. That's what sank me. He spent no time at all pondering what I ought to do!

"Right again," he said, as if delighted to have been caught out. "And I'll tell you why. First, because *you* are positioned to have far better information about this decision than I will ever have. Second, even if I had an opinion, it would be irrelevant, since it's your life and you have to decide."

I can still hear the smugness — smugger than any interpretation he offered as we went through the analysis proper. On those he was confident, sometimes glib, but never smug. This, however, was his own little number, like a stage actor with a tiny part but who relishes his moment each night during the show. It was *him* as therapist, not just him being the therapist he was trained to be. What he said had the extra virtue of sounding true. He wasn't offloading responsibility for my decision on what I should do about my marriage because it said on page xxx in the shrink manual that you must indicate to the patient he has responsibility for himself and needs to accept his autonomy. Or because now was the time to dissolve the transference, right on schedule — though what he did had precisely those effects at exactly the perfect moment. Sometimes the right things happen at the right time because that's when they happen to happen, not because anyone scheduled them. Anyway, motives don't always matter, even in therapy. Whatever pleasure he got from it or from my pain at being tossed back out into the world on my own, he genuinely did *not* have the information on this subject that I possessed; it *was* my life and not his, so the choice would, sorry, have to light on me. "Nobody here but us chickens," he liked to say. It went as a pair with the joke about the guy stepping out the window. It was the best advice — treatment? — he gave me in the whole four years and seemed largely unrelated to my, by then, well-documented Oedipus complex and other standard components of Freudian theory. The beguiling question is, did we need to assemble that whole analytic suitcase in order to get to Peck's self-satisfied little outburst that proved so beneficial and therapeutic? Did the latter depend even remotely on the former? Oceans of theorizing to allow one unpremeditated moment of real interaction and insight. It was all, in the end, a matter of the process, not the content.

*

MELANIE AND I SEPARATED, FOR THE SECOND AND final time. She decided to move to Vancouver. We bought a car and drove out together, camping along the way. I helped get her settled, then rode back alone across the U.S., arriving at my newly bachelorized pad on Riverside Drive early one morning. Sometime that year, my first unmarried year, we decided — Peck and I, as if we were equal partners — to terminate when spring came, just as Mel and I had separated a year before. I was impressed. No one I knew had terminated; it was the legendary flaw in psychotherapy. The one that defeated Freud.

One day that winter, I went in to see Peck at Lincoln, where he'd been reinstalled. I was about to offer a dream, but I got an odd feeling from across the desk. (I was upright again, after years on the couch.) Now he seemed to be pondering some kind of proposal. "I think we should switch chairs for this session," he finally said. I started to rise. He motioned me back — he didn't mean literally — and began describing his grandson, who lived in New Jersey or maybe Long Island. A teenager, bright, of course, good grades, loved sports, played in a rock band. He sounded like a kid from St. Louis I met in my teens at a Jewish youth camp in an Indiana town called, I swear, Zionsville who talked like the Voice of America: "Rick, I live three things. I live football, I live youth group, and I live my girl." Like all adolescents, the Peck grandson was trying to find himself. It was a great era to go looking, since the economy was good and, if the self-search lagged, you could just head home, assuming decent jobs were available, or back to school. The kid had gone to Israel that summer to work on a kibbutz, a common form of quest for self, especially before the Israeli occupation of Palestinian land in 1967. For my stifled, pampered generation, Jew or Gentile, the best treatment available often seemed to be a stint on a kibbutz.

For this kid, though, it didn't take. So he boarded a train back to Tel Aviv, where he was to catch a plane for the U.S. But on the way, he was accosted by a Lubavitcher Hasid. The Lubavitchers were descended from the followers of Rebbe Shneur Zalman of Lubavitch, just as Heschel was a successor to the first Abraham Joshua Heschel. There were dynasties in those days, though the Lubavitchers had grown less ecstatic over time: their line had been routinized (the current rebbe, Menachem Schneersohn, married in); their practice, less spontaneous and more ritualized; and their organization, bureaucratic. From the start, they'd been one of the more orderly, theologically systematic Hasidic groups. I had spent time with them during my year in Israel. They had a community outside Tel Aviv called Kfar Habad, or Habad Village. The bus dropped you at a shelter on the highway, and you slogged across muddy fields till you entered a place that looked like an 18th-century Polish shtetl. When I was helping Roger Kahn write a book on Jews in America, I took him out to their world headquarters at 770 Eastern Parkway in Brooklyn, a fabled address among the faithful, to interview one of the rebbe's adjutants. After our interview, they gave us a peek at the massive records the rebbe kept of his far-flung flock and let us have one of the file cards they all filled out. When any of his Hasidim had a major life decision to make, they'd write the rebbe, who'd consult the file card before telling them what to do. I kept it as a memento.

The Hasid on the train had asked my shrink's grandchild to perform a mitzvah — that is, to fulfill a religious duty, though the term sometimes means just "good deed." Would this kid, en route from kibbutz to suburbia, please wrap his arm and forehead in tefillin and repeat after the Hasid the morning prayer? The boy agreed; a conversation followed. He ended up going to Kfar Habad — and he was still there. It made sense for him; he didn't know for how long (and I have no idea what finally happened), but it felt right at the time, and so, as we were often urged to do back then, he just did it. His granddad, who was no practising Jew though he married a rabbi's daughter, had recently visited and found him seemingly at peace. Just the previous weekend, Peck had been invited by the Lubavitchers to Eastern Parkway for a private audience with the rebbe, and came away impressed. "He's a remarkable man," said my formidable shrink. "Did you know he has a degree from the Sorbonne?" Since I was familiar with this world of Jewish religiosity — though we'd assiduously skirted it throughout my years of therapy after the original Heschel moment — he'd like to know what I thought. That's what he meant by switching chairs.

"I am *so* embarrassed," I blurted. The horror: embarrassed by my own shrink! "Look," I went on, "you are a psychotherapist, an analyst. You are dedicated to cultivating the autonomy of the individual. Surely infantilism was meant to be overcome, Freud said — and you have shown me you take that seriously. You helped me overcome infantilism and dependence. Don't you remember our breakthrough session in my first year when I realized how damned dependent I always felt, despite the many signs I scatter to the contrary? Do you know what the Lubavitcher rebbe's idea of the dignity of his followers, his Hasidim, amounts to — his idea of their independence and autonomy? He has a file card — not a file, a card — on each one. It's three by five. I can show it to you, and you know what it contains, in Hebrew? Astrological data. Full stop. Date of birth, time of day, constellation. In bulging cabinets out there in Brooklyn, where you just were. When one of these inherently autonomous human individuals somewhere like Israel or Australia has a momentous choice to make involving whether to take a job or have an operation or even end a marriage, they write the rebbe in Brooklyn, and he — or maybe an assistant — plucks out the card with the gibberish, and on that basis the rebbe writes back saying exactly what course to follow. Is this your idea of the dignity of a freely choosing human agent? He suckered you and you went for it." (Hooked you, I could have said, just the way I hooked you.) "They know what marks Jewish shrinks are for this mumbo-jumbo. Like Freud with his statuette of Moses. You all left it with a show of superiority and self-awareness, but underneath you're worried and guilt ridden and hoping to be forgiven and reintegrated. It's the Jewish shrink syndrome, and they are shrewd operators: they run a global recruiting operation and target people where they're vulnerable. The rebbe a great man? A degree from the Sorbonne? You know what his degree is in? Engineering! What did you think — he was drinking *rouge ordinaire* with Sartre at the café Les Deux Magots? I am mortified that my analyst, my East Side shrink who liberated me in this age of freedom for individuals and nations, was seduced by a huckster with earlocks. It is so humiliating."

Something like that.

He heaved a sigh, which served to shift the seating back to where it began and should have stayed, probably. "I may not know a lot about religion," he muttered, "but I am one of the best damn analysts in New York. So let's get back to work." Technically speaking, and I have no idea if this was in the back, or front, of his mind, but he had just finally, definitively dissolved the transference, at precisely the point in the process when that ought to have occurred. If he knew he was doing it, that's impressive, because he used the materials at hand — the odd experience about his grandson, the trip to Brooklyn, my crushing embarrassment at his behaviour, the accompanying outburst — and employed them creatively to accomplish the task at hand.

We terminated a few months later. On T-day, with all the pillars of my former life obliterated like Ozymandias's remnants in the desert sands, the I that nevertheless persisted despite all the psychosurgical amputations was nattily self-observing my state of mind. *Hmm*, I thought as I drove my new used car to Lincoln, the one I'd bought to transport my wife out west to her new life. *Hmm, no observable symptoms of anxiety, despite the impending finale.*

I parked and stepped out to transfer something into the safety of the trunk before I went inside to graduate. This was the South Bronx after all, which was well on its way to war zone status. As I raised the lid and leaned over to deposit whatever it was — maybe my skates — I threw up, right into the trunk.

INTERMISSION: HAROLD INNIS

Think of therapy as part of the oral tradition. We tend to think of the oral tradition quaintly, as in preliterate cultures or storytellers in Kensington Market on car-free Sundays. But for most of human history, it was the means of discovering and amplifying knowledge, then recording and transmitting it. After the relatively late creation of writing, the oral tradition coexisted with the written one in reasonable balance for two millennia. With the invention of the printing press less than six hundred years ago, it began its slide toward quaint status. Today it survives in only two serious institutional forms: therapy and teaching.

Could anyone seriously advocate a revival of the oral tradition as a serious way to pursue knowledge and not merely the self-knowledge of therapy? Well, standing almost alone is Canadian scholar Harold Innis (1894–1952). He's not much known now, though he's the only professor after whom a college at the University of Toronto is named. (I'm told the fight song of Innis College goes "Who the hell was Harold Innis?") During the last phase of his academic career, he wrote a great deal, ironically, in praise of the oral. Book after book, article following article, he declared his "bias" for the oral, over the written, tradition. For him there was nothing quaint about it. He saw it as one of two fundamental "technologies of communication" that marked the journey of the human species. They'd now be called media, but he rarely used that word. He saw the oral and written traditions not just as two different ways to transmit content but as different ways to approach, discover, and convey insights, wisdom, and truths. Each implied an entirely different way of thinking; they asked different questions and emphasized contrary values. Each had its own "bias." He ascribed the disasters of the first half of the 20th century — two world wars and a depression, for starters — to the triumph of the written over the oral. You could hardly take orality more seriously or consequentially.

Why his bias for oral over written? Speech is the human specific, and thought is inseparable from it: they appeared first in spoken form and then more recently in written versions. There is no method of thinking, wrote Hannah Arendt: thought is the method of thinking. And, in its origins, the oral is closer to the natural structure of thought. It reflects what thought is really about.

We all pass through the oral on the way to the written when we acquire speech as kids, but the oral wasn't always just a way station en route to adult modes. In the oral traditions of ancient Greece, ancient Israel, Aboriginal peoples everywhere, and even churchgoing rural societies of the 19th century, people heard the same epic stories year after year. It was how everyone was enriched: by hearing something new in repetitions of the old, peeling layers away, anticipating what was coming, and then being thrilled by it yet again — often in new, unexpected ways. All adults share with children this inherent propensity, but it can be trained out of you as you age, so that you bridle — you feel a kind of discomfort — if "forced" to sit through something you've already "seen," meaning once before. But really, how much have you taken in when you've watched a movie, read a book, or listened to a song for the first time? You get the plot, the twist, and the outcome, as if they are all that's there or all that matters. Like passing through a country or ocean once or chatting for a few minutes with a person. Less is gained by moving on than by going back. That's the oral tradition, in essence, that has dominated most of human history, though not the relatively brief recorded, written-down part.

Innis, though, had a bias not just for the oral as ritualized and repetitive but for the version of it found in ancient Greece. As an economic historian, he had studied the role of Canada's Native peoples in the fur trade, but he never mentions *their* oral traditions; it was the oral tradition of ancient Greece that impressed and obsessed him. Why? Because that was the glorious fountain from which Western "civilization" emerged, yet it had all come to such a grim impasse in his own lifetime. Where did it go wrong? He used to sit at "high table" during lunches in Hart House at the University of Toronto, alongside the classics scholars as they discussed the rise of Western thought in Plato's or Aristotle's academies. The great thing about the oral tradition in a context like ancient Athens or the Hart House high table is that everything gets asked. If you're pursuing thought on your own, as you are when you're writing a book, you can ask yourself questions inside your head (as it were), but it's easy to avoid some of the sharpest ones, to prefer to glory in the answers you've already reached rather than to treat them as tentative; this allows you to swiftly move on to the next phase of your subject, undelayed by nagging uncertainties, and to meet your publisher's deadlines.

Innis didn't disparage the written; he thought it was splendid for recording conclusions reached and disseminating them to wide audiences — far superior to the limited range of the human voice. But the written was hampered in the exploration of difficult and complex issues, scientific or ethical. Authors are supposed to be deep thinkers and write complex works, but pause long enough to discuss any page of a book worth discussing — with students in a class, for example — and you'll notice how slowly the discussion unfolds. You can barely cover a paragraph in an hour. You realize how frequently the author has not lingered to consider or explain — or even to properly think through — a great deal of what's laid out there on the page. The oral is hideously slow — often circular, cumbersome, and limited in its reach — but it's "overwhelmingly significant," wrote Innis, "where the subject matter is human action and feeling and it is important in the discovery of new truth" even if it is of "little value in disseminating it."

He wasn't an idiot. He didn't think you could go back to preliterate times. Besides, he liked reading — and writing. It's who he was. But he came to feel that what mattered was a balance between the two approaches to knowledge, as it had once existed.

That balance was exemplified in Plato's dialogues, which were written accounts of oral encounters. The "immortal inconclusiveness of Plato," he felt, dominated Western thought for two thousand years until Gutenberg and his press tipped the balance toward the written. From then on, information, knowledge, insight, and wisdom came to be entombed almost exclusively in the printed word and in books. So Innis pleaded for universities to recognize that students and teachers were still human, not just vessels between which printed notions could be poured back and forth. He wanted a restoration of that balance, for the sake of human survival and moral value. That's all.

I should add that, though he died early in the TV age, he was aware of electronic media like radio and TV, which seem to be oral in the sense that they contain voices and spoken words. But that didn't disturb his grand division into two basic technologies of communication. Because what mattered wasn't the simple fact of human voices; what counted was interaction, dialogue, and question and response in live human presence, with all the nuance that a live presence involves: facial expression, gesture, tone, hesitation, anxiety, shrugs, grunts, vague searching intimations. Writing flattens out and drains all that because there's no response and no response to the responses. So radio and TV, which are one-way because they brook no reactions and don't alter themselves in response to reactions, belong in the written tradition. (What Innis might have made of the internet is hard to say.)

So his focus on the oral drew him toward the process of thinking and not just the resulting thoughts. The written tradition, of course, involves a thinking process, but it is routinely obscured in favour of its results. What we get on the page tends to be the thoughts that emerged, along with a final, declarative version of the arguments that support those conclusions. In the oral tradition, the whole messy thought process is highlighted.

You hear that focus on process in the tracing of tradition, in the chain of seers, singers, and bards who are often recited. In the interactions of Plato's dialogues: "Why, Socrates, what a strange conclusion you reach." "Far from it, Thrasymachus. Listen to my reasoning." Or in the Talmud, a written record of a chain of oral disputes and adjudications: "Two men come upon a garment lying in the road. Each seizes an end. To whom does it belong? Rabbi Yossi says . . . Rabbi Zechariah disagrees. He says . . ." This contextualizes the judgements reached and exposes the whole dynamic. You gain a sense of the real-life settings from which conclusions emerged and often of the personalities who arrived at them. It becomes possible to backtrack and retrace the process of reasoning. And if the conclusions turn out flawed, it's relatively easy to say, "At what point did this get derailed?" Or, "What are the alternate routes that might have been pursued, and can any of those paths still be taken?"

I don't know of a better advocate than Innis for the oral tradition, of which therapy is a rare example today. But there's another reason he comes to mind here: he's a classic candidate for therapy himself. There's no sign he ever indulged in it. The very thought is hilarious. I picture him as someone who'd consider psychotherapy self-obsessed, self-indulgent, and narcissistic — terms derived from psychotherapy itself. Yet his whole intellectual career, including his tortuous, brilliant studies in communications and the oral tradition, cries out for interpretation. That's because there's a huge mystery in his trajectory as an intellectual. His writing on media and his bias for the oral appeared only at the end of his career, without preparation. From everything that brought him to his station as Canada's leading thinker in the 1930s, you'd never have expected a radical turn toward media. Biographically speaking, it's a gobsmacker.

He'd made his reputation entirely as an economic historian, the founder of the "staples school." His most renowned book was *The Fur Trade in Canada*. It was witty, erudite, original, detailed. He also studied the natures of the timber industry, the fisheries, and the railroad, all with an eye on interactions between metropolitan centres and colonial hinterlands. Then at the height of his acclaim and power, he dropped it all and began writing on what's now called media. He had no expertise in the subject and no original research. He relied on secondary sources and wrote elliptically and cryptically. Some of his disciples struggled to explain it as a continuation of his earlier work. But there was a hint of embarrassment, as if they thought he might have wigged out.

And perhaps he did — but in an understandable, admirable way. His original career goal was the ministry. He wanted to serve. The First World War intervened, where he experienced the horrors of the trenches. There's an eloquent photo of him coming off duty one night, drained and appalled. When it ended, he abandoned his plans for the clergy because of the church's collusion in making the travesty possible. He turned to scholarship instead as his way of contributing, through greater historical understanding, to the creation of a world where future catastrophes might be avoided. But in the 1930s, just as he reached the peak of his powers and reputation, the Depression was ravaging lives, fascism seemed triumphant, and he could see the signs of a coming war even more horrible than the one he'd survived.

In a state of despair but hanging on to hope, he sought a better explanation of how Western civilization had come to this. He reverted to a question his philosophy professor posed when he was an undergraduate before the war. It starts his book, *The Bias of Communication*: "Why do we attend to the things to which we attend?" He concluded that we, the Western world, had paid attention to the wrong thing: written knowledge. It wasn't that we'd failed to find answers; we'd been looking in the wrong place, in the wrong way. He dove into an exploration of how this wrong turn occurred and what its effects had been. Above all, the invention of the printing press by Gutenberg in 1452 had destroyed the balance between the oral and the written, which had characterized culture since the age of Plato. Print broke down bonds of community and replaced them with an individualism that left people disconnected and fearful, eventually turning them toward nationalism and demagoguery. It substituted cold, unresponsive pages for living dialogue between human beings. From it emerged the superficiality and hysteria mongering of journalism. Print was inattentive to its readers; it lacked the dialogic quality of oral interaction. Yet he was the most distinguished representative of the written tradition that Canada had ever known. He spent most of his adult life reading and then writing books. His success and prestige were based on them. It was as if he turned on himself.

Innis became aware during the same period, still in his 40s, that he was dying of cancer. Perhaps first by the kind of hints a person receives from his body and then by medical diagnosis. This surely increased his sense of urgency: he'd gone down a wrong road, in some sense. Now he'd try to take, or at least indicate, the way back. He was fond of quoting Hegel, who said the owl of Minerva — the wisdom bird — takes flight at dusk. Hegel meant that societies gain insight only when they're in decline. But it can also apply to individual lives.

There was one other factor: a woman. According to Innis's intellectual biographer, John Watson, he fell in love with a graduate student, Irene Spry. He would never have left his marriage, but he offered her a sort of intellectual partnership alongside him at the university. She turned him down — spurned him, really — to marry a man active in left-wing politics, a cofounder of — it's a bit much — the Canadian Radio League, which led to the creation of the CBC. Graham Spry was a kind of anti-Innis. He made all the other choices, ones Innis hadn't made when it was his time to choose early in life and couldn't remake afterward. Was this part of Innis's crisis? (There isn't always a lover or an unrequited love to help explain things, but it's striking how often there is.)

I know this amounts to doing posthumous psychotherapy on Innis more than half of a century later. Did he have a life crisis, an identity crisis, or an attack of insight and remorse — over what he'd done, or not done, and what the cost had been? Was his turn/pivot/flight to media theory a form of self-therapy, following a sort of self-analysis, though he'd never have called it that? Did he reject the overt components of his intellectual life and expose its underlying *unconscious* motives, its covert meaning, then try in those last years to adjust the life according to that new *insight*, but only so far as possible, only as much as the *reality principle* permitted? I know it sounds like straight, or revised, Freudianism. And Innis, as I've said, is an unlikely candidate.

Yet few questions could be as Freudian as the one he re-posed to himself, decades after his first-year philosophy prof assigned it: *Why do we attend to the things to which we attend?* Any question that stays lodged in your mind for 40 years is something you have paid attention to. And it seems to me his entire late career, when he did that huge 180 from economics into an effectively nonexistent field, is a kind of attempt to answer that question. He turned against the scholarly written word itself in order to embrace its opposite, the oral, in yet more *books* — writing against writing, publishing against publishing in books against books. Even the cryptic, aphoristic, fragmentary nature of his writings on communications — they're *in* books, but they really don't amount to books in the stately, unified way his earlier ones do — suggests he was trying to escape the shaping influences of the written tradition, or what he called the "grooves of motion of thought," even while remaining a writer. They read more like

Kafkaesque fables or Nietzschean aphorisms than scholarly works.

It's as if he'd taken a look back over his shoulder, with a sense that death was near for him and the civilization to which he adhered, in the light of that question. To what had he attended all his life since he first heard (not read) that question? To books, the printed record, the written tradition. First he read it; then he wrote it. Why did he attend to that all his life? Because he grew up in it, it shaped him, it seemed the way of nature, and it fashioned the grooves of motion of thought along which his mind, and that of his culture (or civilization), moved. Perhaps, as a boy on a farm in rural Ontario — with no electric light, few books, and little abstract conversation — it was reading that saved him, like many others. So, after a long and distinguished writing career, as dusk fell and the owl of Minerva rose, he pondered why he'd spent a fruitful lifetime absorbed in just *this* way of deciphering the world, the print way: fact- and information-based one-way communication between author and reader, inflexible and stripped down. First you read someone else's writing. Then you write and someone else reads you. No live, immediate, prickly back-and-forth between minds — or a minimal amount, mediated by print or through the mail.

At that late point, when he finally had an answer to his professor's question, it was too late for him to remake his life. One lives forwards only.

Innis's own students, now aged themselves, recall him as a poor, mumbly, unforthcoming teacher. But that's no argument against his belated endorsement of the oral tradition over the written. How better could you get to know a system or adversary than if it has pinioned and controlled you all your life — without you even being aware of its grip, till too late? Changing yourself — basically: how you are, who you are, the way you view the world, what you do in it — just because you abruptly understand the sources of your character late in life is unlikely. (It's like Andre Agassi, who says in his autobiography that he always hated tennis, from the first moments, but didn't stop. Why? Because by then, even early on, it's who he was. There was no one else to be.) By the time you've gathered enough evidence to know the choice you *should* have made, it's too late to make it. The owl has flown the coop. Who would you turn into, at that point — another person, the one you might have been? But Innis *could* write about the insight — in a bitter, contradictory, self-lacerating form of payback.

None of this speculation negates the value or originality of his insights on communication. Why would it? The question is whether it enhances those insights. I think it does. It adds to their power and cogency (adds value, an economist might say) by providing a better sense of how they arose and where they came from, fleshing them out and making them more specific. For instance, it increases a sense of the fateful, even tragic, *power* of communications technologies, as Innis strove to explicate that, the way they underlie and channel our energies and choices, usually unknown to us yet often in ways destructive to our own interests. This may be especially poignant to those who've "chosen" to live as scholars or writers. But we can all identify with the people we are not, the people we didn't become.

ACT II

HARVEY WAS MY LAST SHRINK. HE'S RETIRED NOW, but he still gives me tune-ups, as he says, when I need them, over coffee in the hood. He's the shrink who became a friend, the way I expected Peck would till the occupation of Lincoln Hospital or the debacle with the Lubavitcher rebbe. After our treatment relationship ended, Harvey said he'd like to get to know me as a person, which sounds odd but was typical. He had a way of flooring me. I went to our first session leaking blood from reviews of what I considered, of course, a fine book I'd written. I always found being reviewed a lacerating experience. He asked me to describe the reviews. I extracted some phrases from where they were gouged in my self-esteem. It happens, he said, that I have discussed this matter with Saul Bellow. That's what I mean by flooring me. His daughter had attended the University of Chicago, became Bellow's assistant, and married him. So Harvey, much younger than Bellow, was his father-in-law.

If I asked miserably, as we sat in his study, why I kept repeating some self-destructive behaviour, he'd look at the library of psychotherapy that lined every wall to the ceiling and say, "You mean, is it in any of those? Nah. That's all bullshit." He didn't say it arrogantly: he said it thoughtfully, as if this was the first time he'd looked hard at those volumes and wondered what they were worth. He was an in-the-moment kind of guy who didn't work on a grid.

He'd been through the mills of therapy. He trained in psychiatry, then psychoanalysis, and joined the medical faculty at the University of Toronto while still young, when he already had three kids. He felt pretty puffed up, he said. But he was attracted by less reputable forms. He joined Fritz Perls's gestalt movement in the 1960s, the therapy (or maelstrom) my ex-wife went into after moving to British Columbia. Perls named Harvey his successor, but his sudden death in 1970 preempted a transition. After that, Harvey started the Gestalt Institute in Toronto. He stuck with it for five years then left. "You can't teach that stuff," he said in an offhand way. It's the tone he used when he revealed conclusions that probably took a lot of hard mental labour. It wasn't a pose, as if he was wearing wisdom lightly, but more as if he'd already moved on to newer conundrums, so that any conclusions won, at whatever cost, were always provisional. It sounded as if he'd revamped his views often and had no deep investment in what he thought at any particular moment. Even his blanket dismissal of the accumulated psychotherapeutic wisdom on his sagging shelves had a tentative quality.

In our second session, after I sketched my earlier bouts of treatment, he asked in that careless way if I'd ever dealt with sadism and masochism. "Not that I recall," I said. "Why?" "No reason," he said. Years later, it poured out — the memories around pain I inflicted and pain I absorbed. "How did you know?" I asked. He shrugged, as if something had struck him that he didn't recall. In an abject manner, I said I felt I was meant to live alone. He looked surprised, as if someone had knocked on the door by mistake. He said he thought I was meant for the opposite. I told him he was kind to say that. He shrugged again and said it had nothing to do with kindness; he was responding on the basis of a lifetime of experience and a load of confidence in his instincts. It was neither benevolent nor therapeutic; it was more like describing the weather out the window: "It's starting to snow." He didn't seem to second-guess his reactions, which may be normal for many people but is unusual in a shrink. Perhaps it took him years to override the impulse to examine his intuitions or it just came naturally.

At the end, I was the one who suggested we draw to a close. Terminating wasn't a therapeutic preoccupation of his, though he didn't, as they say, resist it. He noted that my main reason seemed to be embarrassment at how long I'd been coming, albeit only weekly. For him the process seemed to have an indeterminate quality; it wasn't as if we were covering a course or pursuing a cure. Instead of encouraging me about my progress, as Peck had, he talked about a patient who'd been with him far longer and still came — he may have said "interminably," though I don't think he meant it technically. I asked about the patient's motive. Harvey said he thought that for this person, therapy was really a form of purchased intimacy. It sounded unsavoury, the kind of thing most of us would dislike being known for. But he said it in that sanguine, accepting way. He appeared intrigued by it, as if it might teach him something, because nothing human was alien to him and we can all imagine ourselves in that position, even if we're lucky enough not to be. He didn't seem to mind strange or dubious dealings and transactions. Maybe he found those were the moments defying expectation, convention, and received wisdom, when the learning begins — and not just for the paying customers. He knew he was viewed as flaky by many of his colleagues; it wasn't that he didn't care about his professional reputation. He just didn't care enough to let it affect his behaviour.

He seemed to have moved either beyond psychotherapy or back before it toward earlier models: gurus, elders, shamans, and others whose names and practices are lost because the written tradition took no note of them or there was no writing. Most societies have had a place for troubled souls to go, along with people recognized for insight, wisdom, experience, and a strong capacity to empathize. They might deal with individuals considered "sick," but not only with them. Sometimes they function to heal the trouble (and sometimes the magic works; other times it doesn't), but they may also lead the applicant further into the process, beyond the medical model or the cure for troubled souls. Maybe that's what exhilarated Freud when he almost jubilantly announced that the treatment he invented was bound to fail, for as he did so, a whole new country hove into view. It had to do with wisdom and growth. He needed to pass beyond the framework he'd been working in as Dr. Freud. Harvey was part of the current that challenged the medical model. He began as an MD because it was the groove of motion worn in our society for dealing with mental health. But he moved toward the older tradition: a wise, smart guy with an intuitive bent, he learned to trust. If I laboured to describe a feeling in a dream, he'd often toss me the precise word I was groping for, as if he'd climbed inside the dream with me and experienced it faster than I did, either out of impatience or empathy. I don't know how he did that — it's as if he could tune in to each cue and clue I emitted.

Once, after we'd had a spat about the 1995 Quebec

referendum, he apologized for mindfucking me. He said it was one of Perls's terms. It meant interpretation was forbidden, an odd stance for a therapist who was also an "analyst." But the point wasn't really a rejection of interpretation; it was about who did the interpreting. Until the patient provides the analysis on his or her own, it doesn't count. Until then, the therapist's task is to travel alongside, joining the journey — clarifying, sympathizing, proposing side trips perhaps — but not interpreting. What the therapist knows, or thinks he knows, is irrelevant, even if it's true.

There were also times when he didn't withhold interpretations, as if mindfucking the patient was no concern at all. "What else could it mean?" he'd say, after flatly announcing what a dream that might have signified anything undoubtedly represented. His confidence was so great that I didn't dare ask why this and no other possible meaning. It was his intuition at work; he'd never have imposed his mere judgement or intelligence. He was in elder, or shaman, mode. When he was that far inside my head, he just knew what I thought and felt. It wasn't based on his certainty but on mine — on knowing my soul better than I did myself. Of course, it could just have been arrogance; he could have been wrong. You have to decide whether to trust the guy at a time like that.

He told me he had occasionally tried writing but found it a wretched grind that didn't work for him. He had many colleagues who wrote — books,

TV series — and who often paid him tribute in their work. He was a voracious reader (and must have been astounded when his daughter married Bellow), but he didn't seem to have it in himself, even when others urged him to put down in print whatever it was he knew. Buber wrote a short essay called "Productivity and Existence" in which two friends talk about a third, who has just walked away. They agree his insights are extraordinary, yet he has never written. Isn't it a shame? they say. But then again, they add, maybe not. Because some versions of insight and creativity might be meant to be lived out in the actual presence of others rather than published and read. Such people leave their mark, except it is unmarked. He told me that his son, when Harvey was once lamenting his inability to get "it" down, said, "There are other forms of wisdom, Dad. You're in the oral tradition."

Innis too was a great voice of the oral versus the written, even though, or because, he was embedded in the latter. It survives in forms like teaching and therapy, where no one has yet figured out how to replace it, despite online courses and the self-help section at the bookstore. And in the thought process itself, which the oral tradition mirrors so faithfully. Harvey was an adept in the oral; he knew how quicksilver it is, and even though he loved literature and loved the thought of writing something himself, what he was made for and lived for, was the process of flowing dialogue that therapy trucks in.

Freud embodied both tendencies — the rigidity of conclusions and the quicksilver of actual thought — and exemplified them herky-jerky. He feared the practice he invented might be used to foreclose the process of living a life by fixing its meaning once and for all through a completed "analysis." But there's also his multivolume written side, which can be sententious and know-it-all. The *practice*, though, tilts clearly toward the oral. Adam Phillips calls psychoanalytic treatment a "to and fro between oral autobiography" — the patient talking — "and oral biography" — the analyst tossing in his two cents. It's no surprise that this conflict plays itself out not just in individual therapists who write as well as treat, but also in treatment models: between approaches that have a kind of written bias — analyze, cure, terminate, close the book — of the sort I had with Peck and the more open-ended, inconclusive experience I had with Harvey.

According to John Seeley, ruminating on the occasion of his 80th birthday, only three things remain of Freud's legacy: the role of the unconscious, the importance of dreams, and, above all, the method of free association. Writing feels to me like the enemy of free association, while conversation is its kin. People associate freely and switch topics or tones in conversation all the time. No one listening despairs. Anyone can stop in midsentence and start somewhere else, and everyone will follow. I bet full sentences are a rarity in spoken life; someone should do a study. But editors still arch an eyebrow if you omit a subject or predicate on the page. When writers attempt it deliberately — free fall (as W.O. Mitchell called it), or free association, or automatic writing — it always seems self-conscious. It's affected and self-dramatizing when you follow the same spastic, associative pattern in print that you do in normal chit-chat, like an attempt to fly outside the norm that flags itself by its preciousness. As a reader, you labour over those "experimental" styles (at least, I do). What straining it takes to be free as you write, yet it takes none at all to associate freely as you speak. Maybe Harvey or the man Buber described, who never wrote down the worthy things he knew, wasn't willing to expend their energy merely to transfer some of the freedom that comes so naturally in what's spoken over into written form. Maybe they knew it wouldn't work and would do more harm than good.

I think of Plato that way. He didn't try very hard when writing his dialogues, those early attempts to convey the oral via the written. They feel desultory, as if he couldn't be bothered to accurately replicate the living speech he'd been present for. They're unbearably stilted. "Oh, Socrates, how right you are in what you say." No one *talked* that way, not even in ancient Greece. Students wince when they're forced to read it. Plato was, at most, willing to sketchily *indicate* the content of those lived encounters; anyone who wanted to know what was actually said (gestured, muttered, hissed) could wander down to the Academy and join the discussion in person. Surely there would always be an Academy to wander down to.

Even if you labour like a Hegel or a Heidegger over weighty thoughts and strive to convey mountains of nuance, the resulting text will probably have more in common with a tabloid front page than with the average exchange between two neighbours chatting over a fence. The most mundane conversation can be indescribably loaded: think of the plays of Pinter — in performance, not on the page. The written form can make jumps and shifts, but it has to overcome its own impulses to do so. Writing would prefer (has a bias) to stay on the spot, to finish its thoughts and sentences, before moving along. Writing is lazy in that sense. If writing were in therapy, it would say it doesn't *wanna* free associate. It would threaten to quit, which the therapist would label resistance, and you'd be at the classical impasse. Even when it does manage to execute a few of those shifts and leaps, writing, at its most dazzling, can't begin to match the swift, unpredictable fluidity of almost any conversation, anywhere.

*

IN MY OWN CASE, I BECAME A WRITER, I SUSPECT, due to early encouragement from teachers, which was fortified by a certain prestige it had. It was also a way to make a virtue of traits like social awkwardness, a sense of alienation, and self-absorption. As a writer, you get rewarded for those. Suddenly you feel as if you have been their master all along, rather than their slave. You hang back in social situations with a sense of superiority now that you're a writer, observing. You nod a secret nod to other writers. Harvey, who had met some of the famed authors of his time through "that son-in-law of mine," told me they were all "undoubtedly brilliant" people, but some of them were also "assholes." By that he meant they avoided their actual experience, the life in front of them, in order to cadge it as material for future use. They weren't fully a part of the conversation, the ongoing one that surrounded their lives; they were at least partly withdrawn, taking notes.

But, like Innis, we all have little choice about the circumstances we're given, which shape our options, choices, and the lives we live. Long after, in the light of the dimension that's been added (which I'm slotting under the term *therapy*), we can try to get a handle on the process in retrospect with some limited, belated understanding, singing in our chains like the sea. You're always playing catch up with your choices, which outpace you, but it's better than not catching up at all.

In those nonterminating, non-curing versions of therapy of the sort I had with Harvey, what would it be *for*? And what, if anything, might constitute success? John Seeley said he "once asked one of the greatest men in the field how he knew when he had succeeded with a boy. In a language typical for him, he said cryptically and profoundly, 'Vulnerability, I suppose.' . . . A boy who was better was a more voluntarily open boy, a boy not frozen or carapaced in rigid defenses, a boy who would be willing to be wounded again for the sake, presumably, of a good greater than mere security." That's an inconclusive, open-ended aim, to jibe with a comparable process. It also sounds like Seeley.

When I was 19, I walked into his office at York University on Queen's Park Crescent in Toronto, and asked him to be my tutor. We didn't really know what tutors were, but York, then in its first year, said its goal was to become "the Oxford of the North," and we knew Oxford had a tutorial system, whatever it was. He asked what I was reading. I said *I and Thou* by Buber and *The Lonely Crowd* by David Riesman. He suggested I write an essay on them. So I did, and marvelled at how I found a kinship between the authors. His proposal made me feel my own thoughts were worthy of my attention and could, as it were, birth themselves, without mediation from an authority like a course, a prof, or a book. I think now it was like his approach to therapy, which he taught and then practised till his death in 2007, or his basic advice on parenting — listen to your kids — whenever he was asked. Sometimes, giving a public lecture, he'd simply say that and sit down.

He used to wander the halls of York in those years, telling students, many of them troubled by the gulf between the scholarly intimacies the university had promised and the bloodless collection of buildings rising around them, to lean against the walls and see if anything held them up. After three years, he sided with the students against his friend Murray Ross, the president of York, and went public with his opposition to the direction York had taken. In their last conversation, amid the bulldozers and half-built dorms, Ross said, "I may be a liar, and I may be a bastard. I may be everything you people say I am. But I'm here like those buildings are here, and anyone who doesn't like it can get out." Maybe that should be engraved on the front of the Ross Building at the Keele Campus, instead of some turgid Ross phrases about education set in the stone.

After he left York, Seeley went, coincidentally, to head the sociology department at Brandeis, in Boston, where I'd gone to study after my year at York. He soon came into conflict with the president there too in a battle about student rights. He left Brandeis and moved to California as dean of the Center for the Study of Democratic Institutions, founded by Robert Maynard Hutchins, legendary liberal and president of the University of Chicago when it created its Great Books curriculum. He wound up in conflict again and left in a dispute over similar principles. He'd ascended to a considerable height in his fields because others in intellectual or academic authority, like Ross and Hutchins, recognized his brilliance. He consulted often with people in the Kennedy White House. He spoke sometimes on platforms with figures like Anna Freud and Jean Piaget.

But the conflicts over authority and privilege mounted and were battles he could not, or did not, win. Eventually, he moved his family to Los Angeles and practised therapy privately. He was still doing it in his mid-90s, working mainly with troubled kids and people who had multiple personality disorders, each of whom he treated with characteristic respect. He always loved Toronto; it became his home after he was shipped out from England in his teens during the 1920s to work, in effect, as an indentured farm labourer. He yearned to return to Canada. But he'd crossed the authorities in Ontario years earlier, during the battle of York, and they have long memories. They intervened to keep him out.

I tried to eliminate him too, in my way. During my years of Marxism and revolution (or of talk about those things), I more or less situated him on the other side, where the bad guys were. Once I invited him to my apartment in Toronto when he was on a visit and asked him to explain why he'd never been a Marxist, as if I had the right to conduct an inquisition. "It may have been autobiographical," he said. "None of the people I associated with or learned from were Marxists." It was a nondefensive attempt at a sincere response to an inquiry that didn't deserve such respect, keeping faith with me, though I'd hardly done so with him. It was a sign of his vulnerability.

He never gave up on me. I think he believed in me as Milton Acorn believed in Canadian youth when he wrote, "Not as you are . . . But as you should be . . . I believe in your happiest wishes!" When Seeley was 80, he came again to Toronto and we went to Dooney's on Bloor Street. "One reason I made this trip," he said, "is I wanted to tell you in person that the years after 65 really can be the best of your life." He didn't promise they will be or must be, but that it's possible. About ten years later, when I turned 65, I asked if he remembered saying that, and he answered, "Of course, though now I'd say the years after 90."

He'd done a lot of writing, long before. In the 25 years after the war, he turned out many papers and some outstanding books, including a classic of sociology called *Crestwood Heights*. It was a study of Forest Hill Village, the community I grew up in. I remember what a scandal it caused. He moved away from Toronto for several years, as was common practice among scholars who did that kind of research, to let the storm subside. His last book was a collection of essays called *The Americanization of the Unconscious*. It was, in a sense, a halting book, expressing his many doubts about the nature of studies and conclusions in the social sciences, but it was extremely confident in its haltingness. It had the passionate conviction of

Otis Rush singing "Uh-oh, uh-oh, I don't know!" in "This May Be the Last Time." He told me much later that he felt he'd said by then pretty much all he had to say — at least in written form.

It didn't mean he stopped learning — he probably speeded up — since real understanding has a quicksilver quality that's risky to try to slow down and capture in a fixed snapshot. He continued doing psychoanalysis till almost the day of his death in December 2007. He was 94.

Near the end, when he was bedridden, he read a magazine piece of mine — it's in this collection — in which I said it's okay to tell kids that lying can be permissible, and sometimes it's even right. He told me he disagreed and proposed telling them instead that lying is always bad but occasionally unavoidable. I passed Seeley's view on to my seven-year-old at the time, who'd caught me lying in the case at issue. "No, Daddy," he said firmly. "You were right." I passed that back to Seeley, who knew Gideon and admired his judgement. He gasped in recognition over the phone from Los Angeles. "I just realized," he said, "that my mother never let us lie when we were children in the 1920s, yet we heard her tell white lies all the time for her own convenience. She just never gave us that out!" He seemed thrilled at the chance to revamp his sense of why he was as he was, and what he thought.

3

JONAS AND ME

When I was a grad student in New York during the late 1960s, I went to see Hans Jonas in his office at the philosophy department of the New School for Social Research, now known as the New School. It was founded in the 1930s as a refuge for German Jewish scholars fleeing Hitler, though I don't think I assumed anything about Jonas's own background. I told him I'd finished an M.A. in religion as well as some rabbinical studies and a year of university in Israel. I may have implied that I viewed a Ph.D. in philosophy as a sort of soft landing on my way out of religiosity.

He was helpful but warned there could be a problem, since they had a small faculty and some required courses might not be offered every year, so it might take awhile to get a degree. I told him I felt embarrassed to say so, but my chief goal wasn't a university career; I was more interested in, er, exploring, the, um, truth. He gazed at me over the top of his glasses and said kindly that he didn't think a philosophy student should have to apologize for being interested in the truth.

That was as personal as we got while I was there. I took his courses on Hellenism, Gnosticism (for which we used a fascinating book by him based on his doctoral thesis, which had been supervised by the superb philosopher and vile Nazi Martin Heidegger), and early modern science, which was an eye-opener for me. I read a book of his called *The Phenomenon of Life: Toward a Philosophical Biology*. It seemed out of character for someone of German existentialist training. It was the kind of science- and nature-based thought I knew more from Anglo-American thinkers like Alfred North Whitehead, which I'd encountered in some Protestant and Catholic theologians. I felt it might have been a quirk based on a line of thought he'd perhaps encountered in Britain on his way from Nazi Germany to the U.S. Emil Fackenheim, who'd sent me to Jonas, went that route, studying in the U.K. en route to Canada.

Those were times of political upheaval in the U.S. We, the students, occupied and shut down the New School to protest the Vietnam War. We were eventually rousted by the police and charged and convicted for it, a process backed by most of the faculty, who also requested a "sanitary cleaning" to expunge, I think, what they pictured as gobs of sperm on their office walls. Most of my department strongly encouraged the arrests, but I don't recall Jonas being involved. Perhaps he was on sabbatical or just stayed out of it.

Then, a few years ago, I wandered into the Bob Miller Book Room on Bloor Street in Toronto to get out of the rain and spied on a shelf a collection of essays by Jonas called *Mortality and Morality: A Search for the Good after Auschwitz*. I've had luck with this kind of serendipity, so I took it home and read it, and then I read an autobiographical book of his called *Memoirs*. I was stunned to learn how wrong I'd been about the course of both his life and thought. I was also puzzled that he'd never mentioned any of it during the years I was his student, though he must have known that portions of it would resonate.

*

HE WAS BORN IN 1903, SON OF A WEALTHY GERMAN Jewish businessman. He lamented the smug and boring quality of his community, as if nothing interesting would ever happen in his life — a bit as I felt in Toronto's Forest Hill Village in the 1950s. In his teens, he committed to Zionism, learned Hebrew, and spent time on German farms, as part of the Zionist program to create a more "normal" life for Jews than they'd known in Europe. He also studied philosophy, particularly with Heidegger, a superstar. He began a lifelong friendship with fellow student

Hannah Arendt (whom he'd been instrumental in bringing to the New School). He told how they once almost made love, but she stopped him, saying she was already the lover of Heidegger. He makes his sexual and emotional involvements an integral part of his memoir. He doesn't say why. It's more as if he assumes they're a crucial part of who he became.

After Hitler's seizure of power, he immigrated to Palestine. He didn't go to live on the land. Instead, he became part of a group of young intellectuals in Jerusalem, including Gershom Scholem, the colossal scholar of Jewish mysticism. Jonas did join and train in the Haganah, the Jewish self-defence force, and stood guard at Jewish communities. When the Second World War broke out, he was among the first to advocate for a "Jewish army" to fight alongside the Allies. He joined the British forces as an artillery officer, and when they finally agreed to create a Jewish brigade in their own ranks, he entered it, fighting through Italy till the end of the war. His efforts to rescue his mother from Germany failed; she had given her exit visa to her other son, already in a Nazi camp, and eventually died in Auschwitz. It was Jonas's most enduring source of pain.

At the end of the war, his unit was in Udine, Italy. Almost 50 years later, in 1993, he delivered a lecture at the university there and described an encounter he'd had at that time. He said it was the reason he agreed to take one last transatlantic flight, in a frail state.

He and a friend had gone into the public square, proudly wearing Jewish stars on their uniforms. They were hailed by two Jewish women, whom they urged to immigrate to Palestine, as they did with any Jews they met. The women said they could not and explained why.

They had fled here, to Udine, from Trieste when the Fascists began rounding up Jews there. They were smuggled onto a train by a friendly conductor they didn't know, under the eyes of Fascist officials. In Udine, they rented a bleak garret, but within days, a wagon arrived loaded with furniture. It had been sent by the bishop of the city along with a message: he'd heard about their plight and wanted them to be comfortable. Later they went shopping and bought a pound of lard at exorbitant black market prices. Soon, again, the boss of the black market arrived at their door to return their money, apologize, and give them a large supply of food. So, they explained, it should be clear why they could never leave this place, even if it was to go to a Jewish homeland.

Jonas also described a companion event. When his unit moved north after the Nazi surrender, he travelled through occupied Germany. He went to visit the renowned New Testament scholar Rudolf Bultmann, with whom he'd studied and who was on his thesis committee alongside Heidegger. Jonas appeared unannounced (communication was chaotic or nonexistent) in uniform at the door of Bultmann's house. He was shown into the study by Frau Bultmann. Bultmann looked up in surprise, rushed around his desk, and looked happily at Jonas and the package he carried — clearly containing a book — which he'd been asked to deliver. Bultmann said excitedly, "May I hope that's the second volume of your work on Gnosticism?" Jonas writes, "At that moment something changed inside me . . . the terrible bitterness gave way and a sort of peace filled my heart. The evidence of this man's loving loyalty, which had outlasted the liquidation of an entire world . . . and had clung to the hope that his student Jonas might yet finish his Gnosticism project let me feel for the first time the possibility of reconciliation . . . the restoration of trust in a person of German origin."

I read those accounts as a person who has been immersed in elements of the Holocaust all my life: in people who survived it (or did not) or who testified, memorialized, theologized, and novelized it. But I'd never encountered anyone who lived through much that was at the heart of those events and yet remained so resilient and prepared to hope. He may seem naïve, but it doesn't strike me that way. The resilience and hope also relate to his thinking as a philosopher, which I'll come to.

After the war, he returned to Palestine, soon to become Israel. With his military experience, he fought in the war for independence there in 1948. Afterward, he declined a post offered to him at Hebrew University, offending some of his close academic friends, including Scholem. He doesn't explain why or say if intimations about the Zionist future may have deterred him. But he moved with his young family to North America — to *Canada*, in fact, though he, again, never mentioned that part of his life to me.

He says he found Canada strikingly decent, in contrast to the way displaced or new populations were generally treated in Europe. On the train platform in Montreal, when he and his family arrived, women moved down the line of cars asking if there were newborns inside who needed milk, diapers, or the like. He taught in Montreal and Ottawa. Then, in 1955, he took a post at the New School. He settled in New Rochelle, a placid suburban community outside New York where other intellectuals lived. For the rest of his life, he taught, pursued his studies, and wrote. He became a distinguished, internationally known scholar and, toward the end, a sort of intellectual hero during environmentalism's rise. He delivered the Udine lecture in 1993 and died that year.

*

As for his thought, it was not the aberration from the continental and Germanic tradition I mistook it for. It grew directly from a deliberate choice to challenge one of the core elements of that Western intellectual tradition: the dualism "that has characterized Western thought since its origins in

Platonism and Christianity." Jonas felt philosophy had been typified by "a certain disdain for nature," meaning the material world, to which the human "mind or spirit felt superior." Because human beings are self-aware and can think, they drew a strong line between themselves and the rest of reality. He set his mind on a "reconciliation between our presumptuous special status as humans and the universe as a whole," which, he added, "is the source of our life." *Nota bene.*

Jonas, in effect, went the reverse route of Platonism and idealism, which claimed that humans have consciousness and thought and are therefore distinct from nature. He argued instead that because people are aware and think *and* are part of the world, then the world itself must partake in some way of those elements in us that show up as awareness and thought. The presence of thinking beings in nature argued for a relationship, not a separation, in his view. Then, instead of concluding that the world is a big mind, or the mind of God or other variations on that theme, he derived the relationship from *biology,* starting with the single cell. It's a pretty breathtaking move on the philosophical chessboard.

The emergence of even unicellular organisms, he said, amounted to a "revolution in the history of existence," because they are characterized by existence in time as well as over time, as they change through their metabolic exchanges with their environment. This makes them fundamentally different from inanimate matter, which exists primarily in space and doesn't vary over time. From this microscopic beginning comes, in an utterly rudimentary way, the origins of selfhood, as something "in opposition to the otherness of what is outside" and even as a dim anticipation of consciousness, eons down the road. You can already see the vaguest intimation of self-awareness in a one-celled organism's "irritable" response to external stimuli. These tendencies unfold and expand vastly as life itself develops into more complex forms, but the potential is there from the start. Survival is not assured by mere organic functioning but by a certain "effort" to resist encroachment and a very primitive form of awareness, in which further developments of self and consciousness are implicit. Yet all the distinctions he draws between life and inanimate matter depend not on their separateness, as is the case in the Christian-Platonic tradition. They spring from a common source — nature — out of which something new emerges. I'm not doing justice to the argument, but I guarantee it's worth a read.

What he does along the way is restore respect for matter, even inorganic, inert, inanimate matter; he rehabilitates it from "mere matter" in the Western tradition because, somehow, from nonlife emerges life, which is an "ontological revolution." Yet nonlife remains the realm to which "life *with* these reversals still necessarily belongs." So it is a genuine revolution in the modern sense, a transformative upheaval from within the bosom of what was before, which creates something truly new and different. This may be materialism, he says, but materialism is more mysterious than people think; there is nothing mere about matter. In human beings, eventually, this vast unfolding process of individuation takes its form in thought, awareness, a sense of self, and speech.

Why then, in the Christian-Platonic tradition and others, do humans insist on separating themselves from the world from which they emerged and of which they remain a part? It's because we are "a piece of the world itself, but at the same time possessing all the world as objects and endlessly retrieving these objects" in our thoughts. So we mistake ourselves for other than what we are — pieces of the world — due to the unusual manner in which we are a part of it. This accounts for the peculiar and wrong-headed dualism that was the starting point of his contrarian search for meaning and which he aimed to refute.

As to what accounts for the revolutionary transition between nonlife and life, he seems willing to leave that mainly to science and perhaps the mysteries of the electron, "in the constant preservation of its particularity against the levelling powers of energy" — an intriguing suggestion that some qualities of life may extend even further back into nonlife. He also indulges in some theology — which he acknowledges as an indulgence — based on the kabbalistic myth of an original all-in-all deity, who constricted himself for the sake of allowing (or creating) the diversity we see in the world.

But, mostly, Jonas simply can't see the world in any other way than as a multifarious totality in which humans belong. They are at home in this world. It's a given; it's what he came out of the womb as. "To me," he wrote after the Holocaust, the loss of his mother, and the rest, "even though terrible things happen, of course, the world has never been a hostile place. . . . Ultimately, affirmation is implicit in any sentient and conscious existence. I've never been able to share that sense of alienation that's based on the idea that the human being is cast into this world without being asked and sees himself confronting an alien, hostile, or even absurd universe." Heidegger and other existentialists, among whom he came of age, took the alienation stance, the one he rejects. At least he puts the arbitrary and subjective nature of his basic attitude out there frankly. It seems to me this kind of intrinsic, innate personal disposition is at the bottom of even the most sophisticated "systems" of thought. And it's up to all of us to accept the inevitable differences between our views and then live fruitfully with the variety.

There remains one other intrinsic autobiographical component that he had to embed in his thinking alongside that unitary, basically positive, view of the world: his experience as a Jew during the Nazi years. He says he found the key to remaining hopeful in the fragmentary writings of Etty Hillesum, a young Dutch Jewish woman who chose willingly to go into a concentration camp although she had an exemption. She went in order to be of service to others she loved, and people she didn't know, or just to the world or God. (She says in one of her "prayers" that she doesn't know what she really means by God, perhaps just everything that is or the basis of it.) It doesn't matter when you die, she wrote, since we all will; what matters is how we "serve" while we are alive.

There is an unspecious tranquility in her writings. Jonas found in them not so much specific affirmations or arguments as general encouragement to add an ethical component to his thought. That element was especially important in some of the traditions he revered. We belong to the world — it gave us life — and we owe it to the world to aid "it," as it were, whenever it falls into a harrowing state. He expressed this sense of the relation between ontology and ethics in his book, *The Imperative of Responsibility: In Search of an Ethics for the Technological Age*. Hannah Arendt called it "the book the good Lord had in mind for you."

Let me digress a moment over the 2012 feature film, *Hannah Arendt*, about Arendt's book *Eichmann in Jerusalem* and the conflicts between her and Jewish communities in New York and Israel about it. Hans Jonas is a major character in the film. It's true he and

Arendt broke their lifelong friendship over those views, but the film leaves the impression the rift was permanent. Jonas himself says the rift healed two years later, and they resumed their closeness till her death in 1975. In the years I knew them both, the break was behind them.

This leaves the not-very-urgent question of why he kept a distance from me and other students. He knew, for instance, that I'd studied with Abraham Joshua Heschel, whose book *God in Search of Man* to some degree reflects Etty Hillesum's views and his. Or that I'd done my M.A. at Columbia with Jacob Taubes, whom he knew and considered an intellectual fraud — but one with good judgement, since he'd stolen half his best book from Jonas and the other half from a friend of Jonas's. Or that I'd been to Israel and was preoccupied with the Holocaust. Or that I came from Canada, where he'd lived too, and had been sent to him by Emil Fackenheim. He also stayed apart from the stormy politics around us, though he'd been highly engaged in earlier years. I didn't sense anything hostile in his detachment, unlike others from his background. Some members of the philosophy department, for instance, not only supported the arrests over antiwar protests at the New School but also formally requested that the police beat me up in particular, or so a faculty member told me. I grant I'd provoked them by threatening to "torch" the Husserl Archives in the New School basement if the cops came. I don't think I meant it, but those were testy times. Jonas simply didn't get involved.

I think now that he had good reasons. He had to get on with his real life's work, which was his thought, through his books. He was 52 when he finally settled into place as a scholar at the New School, 20 years later than many of his peers. This wasn't just a matter of a late start to a career. It was a matter of his contribution to the needs of the world, as Etty Hillesum had made hers. He had to complete the gesture of his life, which consisted mainly of hope and resilience — as he'd found those qualities in Udine and Bultmann at the war's end — and which he could only *justify* through his writing. So he stayed away from our politics, and me, and now I'm glad he did. He's given me far more in those books than I'd have gleaned from some chats. I still have a preference, like Innis, for the oral over the written, but not always and not all the time. That would be silly.

His writing provides a deepened understanding, for instance, to our sense of what we can contribute to the world in our lifetimes. He acknowledges the familiar duty of ethical and historical striving that is laid on us — of which he did his share — to play our part in the history of our time. But whatever is accomplished in that way "eventually dissipates," like all historical achievement and, probably, like human existence itself, in the long or short run. But he sets alongside that a "simultaneous" form of duty "in terms of its impact on the eternal realm, where it never dissipates." This may sound hopelessly hopeful and ethereal. But if we truly are pieces hewn from the world and returning to it, then our impact is also felt on some subpersonal (versus supernatural) level. I don't think that's implausible, though it's unknowable.

For example, several years ago, a cottage I had bought and dearly loved burned to the ground in a lightning storm. So I had it rebuilt, with the help of my son, architects, and contractors. Now I swear it is better than ever, and I feel, somehow, that I have made a contribution more my own to the world, both for those who come to visit and merely as a thing or place in itself. Of course, it will not last forever, but it is my infinitesimal addition to a richer reality. Make of that what you will, but Jonas helped *me* make sense of it.

Still, there are things I'd have liked to discuss with him, in retrospect anyway, especially when I sit on my dock. For example, I'm less taken by the phenomena of life than he is and more by the rocks around me. I know he argues that life is "ontologically richer" than inanimate matter, and he makes a strong case. Yet, to me, mere inert matter seems similarly awesome. His arguments on behalf of life are impressive, but so is the Canadian Shield, in (or on) which I sit — not in some Heideggerian sense that it simply *is*, qua abstract being, but in the sense of *these rocks*, out there, to my right. After all, *they* made possible the frail pine trees that straggle out horizontally from them. (And Jonas did make that appreciative aside on behalf of electrons.)

Or maybe it's just the Canadianness in me.

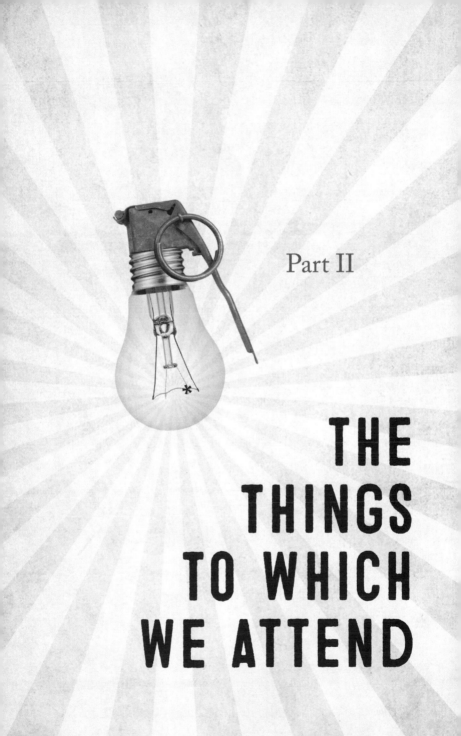

Part II

THE THINGS TO WHICH WE ATTEND

4

NATIONAL CULTURES IN THE AGE OF GLOBALIZATION: THE CASE OF CANADA

PRELUDE: ON BEING CANADIAN AND JEWISH

"When I sit down to write," said Israeli author Aharon Appelfeld, "I feel I am sitting on a mountain of Hebrew books fifty miles high." Aharon is small and elfin and looks like he might slip right off such a tippy height. We were at the Bagel, RIP, on College Street. I said I understood; I thought hard about moving to Israel and becoming a writer there myself, back when he taught me Hebrew during my student year in Jerusalem, in the 1960s. It would have meant trading English for Hebrew, but I adored the language and literature. I was acquiring my own little mountain of Hebrew books: biblical commentaries, love poetry from medieval Spain, the novels of Agnon. Each time I purged my bookshelves over the coming decades, those didn't get tossed.

We'd been to Tip Top Tailors at College and Spadina to buy gifts for his family. When we finished, he said, "Now I want to go where I can see Jewish people." So we crossed College to the Bagel. It had been taken over recently by a Japanese family.

Aharon is a café kind of guy. He appears in Philip Roth's novel *Operation Shylock* as a character named Aharon Appelfeld who meets a character named Philip Roth in Jerusalem cafés. In my student days there, I'd hear him hail me by my Hebrew name, Yisrael, through a café window as I roamed the Orthodox parts of Jerusalem after class. He was like an 18th-century character from *Bilvav yameem* (*In the Heart of Seas*), an Agnon novella we studied with him, a simple tale ideal for learners; its style mirrored the purity of souls on their way from Eastern European shtetls through the heart of seas to the Holy Land. Aharon himself survived a Nazi camp. He was 8 when he went in and 16 when he got to Israel. All his novels deal with that lost world. Come sit, Yisrael, he'd say. Thirty years later, he was in Toronto to read from his latest novel.

"What I *don't* understand," I said, "is why I chose to be a *Canadian* writer instead."

"I understand," Aharon said with a flutter of his hand. "In the modern world, every choice to be Jewish is a complex choice." That's all he said, but I knew exactly what he meant.

What drew me to Jewishness as a choice in my

adolescence was its eccentricity, its marginality, how much it had to do with being an outsider. That fit what I felt. I became an outsider (I suspect) when I was nine and we moved to Forest Hill from downtown, due to social pressure on people like us to gather in the "gilded ghetto" that became the subject of John Seeley's study of a wealthy suburb. Why there? Because it had a great educational system, by common consent, and education was the parental grail. Since we couldn't afford the move, we were the only family I knew who rented rather than owned and didn't go to Florida each winter and a private camp in summer. Had we stayed downtown, across from Christie Pits, I'd have felt like everybody and probably become neither a writer nor intensely, theologically Jewish. Maybe I also intuited that outsider status had cachet in the modern frame, starting with Jews like Spinoza or Disraeli. Adolescents are aficionados of being both inside and outside.

So, making a virtue of necessity, I embraced not belonging as if I chose it. I became a social critic of the smug, materialistic community I felt excluded from, a nonconformist — the term at the time for troublesome outsiders. I asked student council to condemn reading the Lord's Prayer each morning — though by then I'd found God and become observant. That didn't seem a contradiction, since it was all about scandalizing them, making a positive from a negative. I demanded replacement of the Union Jack on the school flagpole with a distinctive Canadian flag. (Canada still flew the red ensign.) I refused to pay my student activities fee because it was "taxation without representation," as we'd learned in American history. And since I was Jewish, as they were, I scorned their secular, insular version of Jewishness and sought to outrage them with my piety, like the suburban Jew in Philip Roth's story "Eli, the Fanatic," who expresses his estrangement by parading through *their* neat suburban streets looking like Barbra Streisand in *Yentl*. Some of it was about being Jewish and some wasn't. The draw of being Jewish had to do with that kind of stand-taking against the majority, any majority. Come to us, the majority taunts. Convert, join us, or strive to, since we may not let you in. Come over, Red Rover.

But by the late 1960s, Philip Roth and other Jewish writers were pillars of literary respectability, and so was the Jewish experience. Before, it felt anomalous and thrilling when something identifiably Jewish appeared in a book or film. Elizabeth Taylor as Rebecca in *Ivanhoe*. Someone says *oy vey* in a movie. As if those references snuck in, like gatecrashers at the country club. Then the intruders became paying members or joined the board: Leon Uris's *Exodus* and André Schwarz-Bart's *Last of the Just*. In Canada, Leonard Cohen and Irving Layton. They still traded on gatecrasher status; it was their ticket in, the way Disraeli used it to become Britain's prime minister.

But the underlying conditions changed. As a Jew, you grasped this slowly, as if you weren't sure it was something you wanted to know. Anti-Semitism was now a minimal threat, though it continued to be feared on the principle that the less you see it, the more wily those anti-Semites have become. But you didn't just fear it; you'd come to rely on it in order to verify your heightened sense of existence, aliveness, and awareness, largely based on your historical marginality, now slipping away. An early case of embracing victimhood, which became widespread later. Jews were rising to the highest levels of the economy. There were fewer Jewish workers and union members; then there were none. They were bosses and professionals or union *leaders*. Areas once excluded opened up, like the restricted neighbourhoods where Jews had been unable to buy homes and cottages. Jews were shifting politically, from left to right, becoming the leading neoconservative thinkers in the U.S., France, and eventually Canada. The new conversion of the Jews. It became a stretch for Jewishness to equal outsider.

But Canadian could. "Come over," wheedled the Americans and our own Americanizers, when they talked about free trade, for instance. "We are big and powerful," they said. "No one is more so, while you are puny and a source of amusement or contempt. How dare you defy us? Be grateful we notice you (trade with you and extract your resources, including your comedians and singer-songwriters). But if you provoke us, we will crush you." I think it was my way of staying Jewish after my faith slipped away. Being Jewish no longer filled the need or my acquired taste for marginality. Canadian was my new Jewish.

At least that's part of the story of becoming a Canadian nationalist. Some of it, on the other hand, probably had nothing to do with Jewishness at all.

*

(NOTE: THIS PIECE IS DERIVED FROM A TALK GIVEN in various parts of Europe in 1997.)

*

LET ME BEGIN BY EXPLAINING WHAT I MEAN WHEN I use the term globalization — and what I don't mean. I do not mean globalization in the sense of the communications revolution, the information highway, the internet, and other breathless coinages. Every advance in communications technology over the past two hundred years has been hailed as unprecedented and transformative, inaugurating a new version of human nature, extending democracy, and so forth. During the French Revolution, the introduction of semaphore, of all things, was hailed in this way. It was going to make the nation state obsolete and lead to the integration of all humanity. Similar claims were made for the telegraph, film, radio, television, and, of course, the internet.

The sense in which I do mean to use globalization refers to the global economic reach and power of corporate capital in our time. This is certainly not the only form of globalization or even the only possible form of economic globalization. It is capitalist and corporate; it subjugates all human values and social possibilities to economic calculation and the profit advantage of a few huge players — and they are growing ever fewer. In the time it has taken you to read the last few paragraphs, the number of major corporate actors has probably decreased due to mergers and acquisitions. This is concentration of wealth on a level that makes feudal accumulations of property look shabby and decentralized. It is not globalization in a general sense but in a very limited and particular sense. In this light, the central contradiction of our time is not between global and local realities but between corporate capital as a centre of power and all other possible sources of power.

Globalization, in this sense, is a terribly serious threat to the cohesion of societies and the welfare of individuals, and it seems to me comparable to the situation in Europe before the First World War. A savage, destructive global conflict is having massive deleterious effects, and so far we have only seen their beginnings. The little progress toward social justice and equality that had been achieved is being rolled back — in the Third World, in the cities of the First, in the immense and shameful gap between rich and poor everywhere. Globalization, in this sense, is a social calamity for the majority, for structures and institutions (from nations to communities), and for the assumptions around which they often organized their sense of self.

One of the striking traits of our age is the increased importance of national cultures in the midst of this phenomenon. Given the great disruptions that globalization has caused in lives everywhere, it is predictable that people should turn to traditional sources of stability and identification. Whatever provides such a resource will be valued, clung to, and, if necessary, resuscitated. We see this with the renewed attachment to religion in our time — from Islamic fundamentalism to the born-again Christians of the U.S. and Latin America. In his series of novels about the end of British rule in India, *The Raj Quartet*, Paul Scott has a character speculate that the rise of Hindu and Muslim militancy in India during the later years of British rule was due to the "comfort and support" religion provided in the face of British imperialism. "Hit a man in the face long enough," writes Scott, "and he turns to his racial memory and his tribal gods."

In other words, modern imperial politics revived religion. In much the same way, you might say that modern global economics has revived national culture and ethnicity, along with religion. What I want to stress, however, is the intimate relationship between economic distress or catastrophe, and cultural responses. I'm thinking here of an argument made by economist Karl Polanyi in his book *The Great Transformation*, published in 1944. Polanyi — a socialist but not a Marxist — wrote:

> Actually of course a social calamity is primarily a cultural not an economic phenomenon . . . the disintegration of the cultural environment of the victim is then the cause of the degradation. The economic process may, naturally, supply the vehicle of the destruction, and almost invariably economic inferiority will make the weaker yield, but the immediate cause of his undoing is not for that reason economic; it lies in the lethal injury to the institutions in which his social existence is embodied . . . Nothing obscures our social vision as effectively as the economistic prejudice . . . which tends to hide from our view the even greater issue of cultural degeneration.

Polanyi argued that when people feel great economic pressure, they naturally seek some confirmation that their lives make sense, and they look for this within their families and communities. If they can find such reassurance, they are able to withstand remarkable levels of economic deterioration and catastrophe. It is culture to which they turn because it makes sense of their lives in relation to their community and its history. On the other hand, argued Polanyi, if cultural bonds deteriorate, then even if the economic situation in some respects improves, the human results may well be disastrous.

The examples he used were striking. He argued that for Africans sold into slavery, "their standard of life, in some artificial sense, may have been improved." But this was far outweighed by the cultural impoverishment the slaves suffered. A similar fate befell American native peoples when they moved onto reservations. Even if they benefitted "individually, according to our financial scale of reckoning, the measure all but destroyed the race in its physical existence." There's certainly far more information available today on those particular cases, but his general point stands: culture — that which makes sense of our lives — matters to the quality of human existence more than purely economic "factors." So, in an age of severe economic disruption, it is natural for people to turn to their cultures, including national culture, as a resource.

Our own Canadian culture is particularly threatened in the present age of globalization. The very nature of national culture in Canada (especially in English-speaking Canada) and the special role of institutions in that culture make it vulnerable. I'm thinking of both institutions that are specifically cultural, like the Canadian Broadcasting Corporation, and institutions that are noncultural, like the health care system. Some institutions, in fact, are both cultural and noncultural. The railway was originally a means of transportation that created a national reality in the 19th century, but it also became a cultural icon described in works of nonfiction, like Pierre Berton's books, and works of art and music, like Gordon Lightfoot's "Canadian Railroad Trilogy." This matters because the kind of nationhood expressed in Canada has always been simplified; we're a sort of no-frills country — in many ways, a stripped-down, minimalist nation. It's typical that we'd double up on institutions that are both practical and cultural.

Most other countries have expressed their sense of nationhood in more elaborate, sometimes murky, and mystical ways. But we lacked the kinds of glues that characterized other national societies and held them together: glues like a distinct national language, a long history, a deeply embedded culture or folklore, and a national mythology (the American dream, 19th-century England's "white man's burden," the French *mission civilisatrice*). Nations can survive severe political or economic dislocations when they possess that kind of glue. Harold Innis once noted that France puts on and takes off constitutions without the French ever wondering for a millisecond whether la France itself might cease to be; that is unthinkable. The French nation's language and culture guarantee its survival. Poland didn't exist on a map for 125 years, but its reality for the Polish people remained firm and strong.

It is true that we Canadians (I should repeat that I am speaking mainly of Canada outside Quebec) have a few symbols: a beaver, a cop on a horse, a game played on ice. But we lack a language uniquely our own, a long history, folklore or myths, even a cuisine, which should not be underestimated as a source for a national sense of self. I'd say one thing we've counted on in the place of all these is a set of socially constructed institutions: the railway, the CBC, our network of social programs, the post office. These are (or were) real, not mythical, entities, but they served a reassuring function, like myths and other glues. They not only deliver actual things like TV shows and pension cheques, they give us the sense that we are part of a cohesive society.

This also helps account for the peculiar role of artists in Canada. Many Canadian writers and artists, when they sat down to produce a work, have felt responsible not just for expressing themselves but for verifying that the country exists. That's not a burden artists feel in France or the U.S. If we had more culture in the sense of those glues, we might put less pressure on our novelists and filmmakers. I think this also accounts for Canadians' readiness to support the CBC even if they don't watch it or prefer to curse it. Someone correctly noted that Canadians are prepared to support the CBC as long as they don't have to watch it. That's because an institution like the CBC is evidence that we have something to express and that, therefore, we exist in a collective, national way.

Given the fairly mundane nature of the glues we rely on — institutions, individual artists — you can see why this has been a rough period for the Canadian sense of self. There has been a series of bloody assaults on those few national institutions that offer a quasi guarantee of selfhood, in the name of fiscal responsibility, privatization, and keeping up with global economic trends. As for the arts, I won't get into a debate on whether we'd be culturally deprived without our own versions of Broadway and West End hits — typical fare for our theatres in recent years — but those products certainly don't feed the kind of national sense that comes from original Canadian plays. In addition, the period beginning with the free trade debate of the late 1980s saw a series of political sneak attacks on our national sense of confidence. First came the trade deal itself: we were told we had to sign on or admit we were afraid to compete. Then the Meech Lake chaos: we were expected to swallow terms we found offensive or the country would disintegrate. The Charlottetown Accord carried the same threat. It's been a period of serious psychological nation abuse.

This may sound like the start of a big whine, but I actually rather like our difficult, occasionally dire, way of being a country — including our emphasis on institutions as the basis for our national glue and sense of self. For one thing, it makes us unusual and perhaps unique. For another, the trouble with basing your country on all that myth is that it's mythical. I wouldn't want to believe, like Americans, that my country was "the greatest country in the history of the world," as all U.S. presidents aver. It might make you feel good, but you also pay the price of sounding stupid and being self-deluded. Personally, I prefer things like a railway or our social programs as the basis for a national sense of self exactly because they're not mythical — they're concrete; they represent things we've done together, consciously, for and with each other.

I'd like to state clearly that I don't believe nations need to live forever, nor institutions. All these come and go and justify themselves during their lifetimes, not by being eternal. At the same time, living in the after-shadow of free trade and NAFTA has given me new respect for what Canadians accomplished in the past by merely keeping this rather self-effacing little (population wise) country going. I used to have much less respect for their achievement, but I can now see it was no mean feat. As for the current threats to our nationhood, I don't know what the outcome will be; in an era like this, when the Soviet Union disappeared and Nelson Mandela became president of South Africa, attempts at prediction are palpably stupid. But I can see certain reasons for optimism or, at least, wary hopefulness.

For instance, the mournful procession toward political, economic, and social demise can lead to cultural success. This is because the prospect of death concentrates the creative mind in a way that leads to a deeper sense of the richness and meaning of life — individual or collective. Picture among other examples the flowering of culture and the arts in Poland or in Ireland under severe conditions of political or economic disintegration.

In a cheerier vein, may I point to some rather surprising areas of current Canadian cultural success? I'm not referring to the quite-respectable Canadian showings lately in the reputable realms of literature, like the novel. I'm thinking instead of popular music and also of satire, especially television satire. What is this success based on? It seems to me it has to do with the prevalence of American pop culture on a global scale, during the age of globalization. That becomes the content everyone has to stand up to and define themselves against — as the French and others have discovered during various rounds of world trade negotiations. Well, to the extent that taking the measure of — and the piss out of — American popular culture has become a universal experience, we in Canada are far ahead of the rest of the world, and we always will be. Think of The Band, Neil Young, Leonard Cohen: all are examples of Canadian artists shaped by their encounters with American popular culture. Young and Cohen have lived in the U.S. for decades, but are, in my opinion, verifiably Canadian in their sensibility. When Cohen sings, "Democracy is coming . . . to the U.S.A.," it has an ironic detachment that I don't think Americans are generally capable of with regard to their own mythologies. Americans deeply identify with those mythologies; so when they turn on them, they tend to do it with rage, as in the music of Bruce Springsteen. A satirical or ironic mode is harder for them; a great deal of the political and social satire in American media during recent decades was produced by Canadians.

Finally, in a time that is largely and even tediously characterized as one of information and communications, Canadians may be especially well equipped. Throughout its history, this country has been about communications: from the far-flung connections of the fur trade, through the meshing role of the railway, to the broadcast system and the odd attachment Canadians have to it — and, then further, to the contributions Canadians have made to the theory of communications itself. This is a field more or less invented by Harold Innis and developed subsequently by Innis's successor, Marshall McLuhan.

In everything I've ever written on or based in Canada, I've faced the problem of the ending. I mean the challenge of how to be honest about how dire things are yet not cause your audience or readers to despair. For, if that's your effect, then why write at all? So I ended a play about the failed Canadian revolution of 1837 with one character, about to be hanged, saying to another, "We lost." And the latter replies, "No, we just haven't won yet." I even ended a play with the line "Cheer up, there's no hope." But I feel there is cause for cautious enthusiasm in our current national and cultural struggles. This is due to the collapse of the hoary, old shibboleths of the left and what I'm convinced will be the imminent demise of those of the right. A vacuum of shibboleths creates an opportunity — also a need — for creativity.

My recent novel centred on an actor who, in his youth, worked primarily in the theatre of improvisation and collective creation, though later in his career, he became a successful film and TV star. But he looks around and sees the country in a mess, while all the old political scripts, those of the left and those of the right, are useless and irrelevant. There is therefore no alternative as a citizen and a Canadian to improvising — collectively.

5

EXTREME GIVING:
THE POTLATCH

ON A 2005 TRIP TO HAIDA GWAII, FORMERLY THE
Queen Charlotte Islands, I learned that the potlatch,
an ancient, intriguing ritual of wealth redistribution
among Pacific Northwest Coast First Nations, had
survived. Memories of intro to anthro in student days:
a culture where prestige came from giving, not acquiring. The subversive French situationists, who staged
happenings in the '50s, named their journal *Potlatch* and
gave it away to make a point about their commodified
society. American author Lewis Hyde argued that
all art embodies the potlatch spirit. As for me, in the
face of a braying, globalizing capitalism, I clung to the
potlatch as an alternate economic model. And here at
the top of one of Canada's most remote archipelagos,
amid amazing vegetation and a Haida majority, it lived.
I wangled an invitation to one. Or so I thought.

*

THE DAY BEFORE I LEAVE HOME, I GET AN EMAIL from one of the Haida. "I don't think it's a potlatch," he says, "just a deceased chief's headstone dedication." I don't want to hear it. I've bought my ticket, spoken with the chief's family, and booked a guide named Dick Bellis, the late chief's son-in-law. I'm hot on the trail of the elusive potlatch. But when I arrive there the next day, a Thursday, there's another email saying that, as he thought, it isn't a potlatch. Shit.

I call a friend, someone who lives there and helped me arrange this botch. She is reassuring. She visited Alma Bellis, the chief's daughter, whose house is crammed with preserves of smoked salmon — for the potlatch after the headstone ceremony, Alma told her. You should write about this, says my friend: how things in Haida culture are sometimes complicated. Hmm. On the flight in, I read a memoir by Florence Edenshaw Davidson, a Haida woman who had a potlatch to mark her first period. An Indian Affairs agent said they could range from "an invitation to dinner up to a frenzied carouse, leaving the hosts absolutely penniless." Sometimes they called it a memorial, or memorial potlatch. It was a thing in flux, not a definition to memorize for the course final. I say potlatch; you say notlatch.

Later, at one of two Chinese restaurants in tiny Queen Charlotte "City," just up the highway from the Skidegate reserve, I stare at the harbour, the mountains, the ever-present mist. I haven't reached my guide, Dick, Alma's husband. He said to call when I arrived, and I did. Is this "Indian time"? I fret. Gaze again at the sea, the sky, those ravens. The Haida have been here ten thousand years, in harmony with all this; why wouldn't they have a different time sense? At nine, Dick phones, apologetic. He says everyone has been busy getting the potlatch ready. Whew — he used the word. Or was that because he knows I'm primed, like the Samoans humouring Margaret Mead? "Here comes the anthropologist — let's tell her some good ones about sex." I ask if I can come see.

Dick whizzes over in his pickup, and we head back to Skidegate. He says he talked to the chiefs; they say I can hang around the prep work, though outsiders usually just attend the event itself, still two days off. The matriarch is a problem, he adds, but luckily she isn't matriarch yet. I wonder if he's using the title in quotes, as I might, but there are matriarchs here. It's a matrilineal society: women aren't chiefs but make major decisions. The matriarch he means is Barb Wilson, the daughter of the late chief's oldest sister; the next chief will be her brother. I've always found these kinship networks a headache in books or courses, but they're clearly clearer in real life.

We enter an old hall with a stage, like the rec hall at summer camp. It's bursting with stuff and people preparing the potlatch. "Ever see anything like this?" asks Dick. Yeah, I think, the Hadassah

Bazaar. Rows of tables groan under gifts; the artful (carvings and crocheted doilies) and the luxurious (blankets and towels) sit alongside dollar store fodder like deodorant and back-scratchers. There are colour-coded plastic bags for men, women, and kids and tall woven baskets for the chiefs. Ever since Charlie Wesley, Alma's dad and Dick's father-in-law, died nearly two years ago, his family and friends have been busy. They've made, bought, and brought what they could; now they're assembling the loot bags, as it were. Not quite as I pictured. What did they think when I said I wanted to write about a potlatch as an alternative to capitalism?

In the kitchen are huge pots of soups and stews, 150 pies, cakes. This won't be catered — it would depersonalize the gifting. This is super personal; each stew has its crew. They'll continue cooking tomorrow, then move everything to the new hall where the potlatch will be held. There are buckets of takeout Chinese. Dick says the matriarch ordered in for everyone. The giving is pervasive. She gains prestige from hosting the feast and gives food to the helpers. No doubt about it, I got myself a potlatch.

We drive to Dick's house. He says he's tired and tense and wishes it were over — like anyone having a big "affair," or simcha (among my tribe). Outside are two carvings, a raven and a Haida-looking Virgin Mary who eyes you eerily from every angle. Dick is a carver. He took it up late in life, as he did guiding, after a career as a heavy-duty mechanic in logging camps. The house is crowded with gifts, including the preserved salmon and jam and traditional button blankets Alma has made. There's hardly room to move. She comes in with an air of exhaustion and crisis, saying, "We need more gifts for the men." They sigh.

Driving me back, Dick says that in the old days, after the white man came, the Haida were rich. They'd have a potlatch with a Singer sewing machine for everyone, like Oprah giving cars to her audience. I've read accounts of one — canoes, pool tables, powerboats, dresses, sweaters, bracelets, blankets, gaslights, violins, guitars, basins, washtubs, teapots, trunks, gramophones, bedsteads, bureaus, flour — that lasted days. It happened after 1885, during the six-and-a-half decades when the practice was criminalized. Several people were jailed; everyone had to surrender etched "coppers" and other regalia that were forwarded to places like Toronto's Royal Ontario Museum. "You could give away everything but your wife and family," says Dick. "We made war in summer and potlatched all winter."

So it's a verb as well as a noun, with a range of uses. In her memoir, Florence Edenshaw Davidson says one of her sister's names was Lots of Things for the Potlatch. People here acquire names lifelong, which makes more sense than being stuck with the one given before you're born by someone who didn't know you yet. Her dad had ten potlatches, and the last name he received was They Gave Ten Potlatches for Him.

*

WHEN POTLATCHES WERE BANNED, THEY CARRIED on, cloaked in other names: *feasts*, *memorials*, *doings* (as in *affairs*, but diffcrent from our affairs). The ceremonies aren't just familial: they're communal and historic. They represent the nation ("The potlatch is our government," said one potlatcher) and link it to its past. It's not really like the Hadassah Bazaar. There, every item is on sale. Here, stuff is not allowed to be sold. And the focus is on gifts for the guests, who bring no gifts for the hosts, though reciprocal obligations are incurred that apply to future potlatches. This was once the basis of the Haida economy and society. Outsiders have often puzzled about whether it was about giving or exchanging, social or economic. But maybe it's a different kind of exchange or gift, in which each implies the other. You can give and not worry about loss since you know you'll get it back, not because of economic calculation or legal compulsion but due to a sense of trust and duty on both sides, which releases the innate, human giving-and-sharing impulse.

"Alma spent last night worrying about the men's presents," says Dick on Friday morning. "I said, 'I think I remember something in the crawl space.' We found five boxes, but none were men's. So the matriarchs are meeting to decide what to get." He says it can be almost anything, as long as it's useful. "It can't be totally junk." I wonder if potlatchers were as flexible and philosophical before the colonizers came. Maybe. Why not?

As we drive along the shore of Rooney Bay, Dick explains that every Haida is a Raven or an Eagle. Ravens can't marry Ravens, and Eagles can't marry Eagles. I ask whether it happens anyway, and he chortles at the ridiculous thought. They can marry outsiders, though; his mother was a Raven, and his father was a Welshman from Cardiff.

He pulls over by a clearing with wood sculptures of ravens, eagles, and other animals. The bush spreads before us. Behind us is a vast, littered beach; the tide is out. Dick says artists command vast respect among the Haida. The leader of their national council, who negotiates with governments, is Guujaw, a master carver. I ask, Why such prestige? "We didn't have to scrounge for anything," he says. "Clams, crabs, fish; most vegetation is edible. The forests are thick; we cut them down for houses. So there was time for art." There's an abundant quality in the air itself, all mist and rain. Everything grows and regrows. Due to this absence of scarcity, status wasn't associated with acquisition but with giving. Who would demand respect for accumulation when it came so easily?

Our next stop is the home of Dick's friend Eric Ross. He is about 80, white, and a widower. Dick says it's panic time at the hall, and Eric offers the food trolleys in his garage. Eric's late wife was a Native woman from down the coast. He says his father-in-law was one of the Native leaders who supported the ban on potlatches, because they led to destructive competition; some chiefs would impoverish their people "to build their name," as they still say. I knew Native people supported the ban, but I'd read they had been manipulated by missionaries or government. This sounds plausible too. Any institution can take contradictory shapes over time. In 1883, some chiefs petitioned against potlatches. Then, in 1885, Sir John A. Macdonald, who was his own Indian Affairs minister, introduced a law saying "Every Indian or person who engages in, or assists in, celebrating the Indian festival known as the 'potlatch' is liable to imprisonment."

The potlatching tribes resisted, but cagily. They asked to hold just a few more potlatches so they could pay what was owing from the last ones. Twenty years later, a government report said the Native peoples were "still so wrapped up in this deplorable custom that they give no heed to any advice for the betterment of their condition." They circumvented the ban for half a century. In the 1920s, an Indian Affairs agent wrote to his boss in Ottawa: "The potlatch is killed." Then, in 1931, "I am sorry to say I have reason to believe it has broken out again."

This effort to suppress potlatching may seem odd,

a bit like outlawing bridal showers, someone said to me. But official policy was to bring Indians "under the sway of civilization, as far as is practicable with any of their race." Duncan Campbell Scott, one of the "Confederation poets" who worked at Indian Affairs for 52 years, wrote, "Our objective is to continue until there is not a single Indian in Canada that has not been absorbed into the body politic, and there is no Indian question and no Indian department." Bureaucrats and politicians viewed the potlatch as a major obstacle to assimilation. Introducing orderly habits was "utterly useless" where the potlatch existed, Sir John A. was quoted as saying. Opposition leader Edward Blake called it "an insane exuberance of generosity." To the press, it was "the evil potlatch." The question is, why so grim over a few potlatches? One can speculate.

*

CAPITALISM AND CHRISTIANITY WERE THE KEY components of the civilization being imposed, and the potlatch was an anticapitalist scandal, "a distribution that renounces every profit," wrote one scholar. The 1880s, when the ban was enacted, were rotten with challenges to capitalism. Marxism, anarchism, a "revolutionary" labour movement — they all emerged during western expansion, and the resulting clashes with Native peoples, including the Riel Rebellion of 1885. Nor were potlatchers woolly minded, unmenacing dreamers. That would be as mistaken as thinking of Gandhi as timid because he was a pacifist. The Haida were war makers and slave takers. Their potlatches embodied intense, even vicious, competition. They disdained capitalism while embodying the very traits capitalists admired. By the end of the First World War, capitalism's stock had reached a low ebb. The Bolsheviks created a communist society in Russia. Uprisings in Europe mimicked it. A Canadian communist party had been formed. In 1919, the Winnipeg General Strike, with explicit anticapitalist rhetoric, erupted in the West. It scared the hell out of Canada's ruling forces. That's when Duncan Campbell Scott ordered the first serious attempt to enforce the ban.

Back in the truck, I ask Dick if there are still competitive potlatches of the sort Eric mentioned. He says they're all competitive, including the one we're going to tomorrow. Everybody wants theirs to be the greatest. Up in Masset recently, they gave out utensils that people kept. Normally, guests bring their own; it used to be that they got a spoon at birth and used it all their lives. "Remember that one in Masset with the cutlery?" people now say.

The boxes in the crawl space are on Dick's mind, so we return to load them onto his truck. "Moving potlatch gifts — about as hands on as you can get," he says, watching me lift. He worries Alma will be mad he wasn't around, but we don't run into her. Someone says she went to the dollar store in Masset, 90 minutes away, since, as everyone seems to know, there aren't enough gifts for the men. We swing by the old hall, where Eric's food trolleys have arrived and the stew is stewing on the porch. Then we go to the cemetery.

This is where they'll have the headstone "turning" before the potlatch. In the old days, they put up a totem, or mortuary, pole. Gravestones are among the accommodations to Christianity that worked better than outright rejection — like "accepting" an antipotlatch law but saying you needed to hold a few more. By 1910, the majority of Haida had converted to Christianity, and the potlatch, renamed "doings," went underground, its elements dispersed. By the '20s, covert potlatchers might have simply distributed movie tickets. It persisted tactfully.

The cemetery is plain, fenced, beside the ocean. A sign says "Only Natives Allowed." Dick explains that a smallpox epidemic (as if there was only one and all its victims are before us) devastated the Haida a century ago: "We went from ten thousand to six hundred." The survivors fled into the woods, abandoning the dozen or so settlements that had thrived, including Cumshewa, where Charlie Wesley's clan lived. Eventually, missionaries convinced them to return, but only to mission sites in Masset and Skidegate; now some former settlements are being reinhabited. Research says there were numerous smallpox outbreaks, starting in the late 18th century, reducing the population from a precontact level of over 10,000 to 588 by 1915. Today it has recovered to about 2,500.

On the way back, we stop to see Haida master carver Norman Price. I'd met him earlier at the garage where I was renting a car. He was having his Cadillac serviced. His face looks carved. I toy with buying something, till I learn that a little black pole 25 centimetres high made of argillite, a form of slate only found here, costs $12,000. Lewis Hyde calls gifts "models of the creative process": the artist received his talent gratis and passes its outcome to others. He has a gift; he makes a gift. Back when I wrote plays, I thought of them as gifts to my friends. It seemed to suit something as concrete as a play (or a carving) more than, say, a novel. Price asks if I know Haida artist Bill Reid's work. A bit, I say, and ask his opinion. "Too many details," he replies, like Emperor Franz Joseph II telling Mozart that he used too many notes. We go next door to his workshop, which has a shutter to slide the ends of full-sized poles outside. It's spare and clean, like his work. He's the Count Basie of carvers.

After dinner, we return to the hall to watch a kids' dance rehearsal. Dick wants to explain the dances in a way he won't be able to tomorrow night, when he's at the head table. The dancers aren't all Haida. There are some local white kids. A scary figure, the *hummia*, enters first and chases away evil spirits. A teenager in a wooden raven mask, which clacks as he tilts his head side to side, catches that raven quality and suggests how uncanny these dances once were. There's also a men's dance competition, which could have been ferocious in its time. Dick's grandkids come to have their masks, which he made, adjusted; it's sweaty under there. These dances were banned too; same terminology, same section of the Indian Act. Perhaps they were the cultural component of the challenge to the dominant patterns of the time. American anarchist Emma Goldman, who visited Canada often in the first half of the 20th century, liked to say, "If I can't dance, I don't want to be part of your revolution." Officials like Duncan Campbell Scott denounced the dances' barbaric — literally bloodthirsty, they claimed — nature (dancers biting into living flesh!). Anthropologists referred to its "Dionysian quality." The bans weren't repealed until 1951. After that, it was a matter of recovery and reclamation, which wasn't easy, given the decimation of the people, their culture and language, and the effects of residential schools.

When the rehearsal is over, we return to Dick's home to transfer more cases of jam. He's happy he and Alma are reclaiming their house. Driving back, we pass an outdoor pavilion where war canoes and totem poles are sculpted from giant cedars. It's late and dark, but someone is there alone, working by a single light, like a mechanic under the hood. Dick says it's Guujaw, who spends his days negotiating land claims and treaty rights; this is often the only time he gets to carve.

*

IT'S SATURDAY MORNING AND ALMOST TIME FOR the headstone ceremony. I collect my rent-a-wreck and drive to the cemetery. It's raining hard. As I enter, I'm hailed by George Westwood, a Scot who used to work at CTV in Toronto. He's been here 25 years. He's the undertaker. He gently suggests I remove my hat. Luckily I have an umbrella. He says it's a shame I never met Charlie Wesley and goes on to describe his funeral. There was an open casket with Charlie in full headdress, looking like a pharaoh — a government bureaucrat's term, he clarifies — on two-and-a-half-metre planks held together by copper rods through the wood that, George explains, will oxidize so the coffin won't disintegrate. We could have been the Athens of the Northwest Coast, he says — using the same "we" as Dick — if not for the smallpox. Wrapped in a gorgeous button blanket, he says he was close to Charlie and was adopted by the family a few weeks ago. As women of the family ceremoniously wash the headstone, Dick's son-in-law — a Maori from New Zealand, his face tattooed in the Maori way — joins us. Then everyone heads to the new hall for the potlatch.

I'm apprehensive about passing the hours till it starts. But it's no problem. People arrive and hang. It's today's activity: waiting for the potlatch. There are ranks of tables for six hundred, though there's no guest list or seating plan. In the bleachers, kids wait to see if there will be room at the tables.

I meet Robert Russ, a youthful man studying on the mainland, who emcees these events. He was spotted by a "mentor" and groomed for it. He knows the "protocols," a beloved word here: it concerns tradition and its recovery; it means how things are done, after being suppressed or forgotten. This one is unusual, he says, since it separates the mortuary potlatch, which we're at, from the chieftainship potlatch, which usually follows immediately but won't be held until spring. He has a deft administrative mentality. He says timing is everything in this rushed society (as people drift in and loll about); in the past, a potlatch would take days, but he aims to get everyone out of here by 9:30 p.m. "You need a thick skin for my job," he says. He collects protocols, mainly from people's memories, along with some recorded accounts. Then he sends them to the chiefs, who add their own clan versions, which vary, like customs, from one First Nation to the next along the coast.

I find a spot with a good view of the head table. Two women from India sit down; they've just arrived as tourists and heard about the potlatch. A couple of grumpy locals join us. They make sarcastic cracks but stick around for the gifts. Somehow the transition to formal event takes place.

The chiefs, wearing headdresses, are drummed in.

Guujaw is among the drummers, underlining the difference between the political leadership he provides and that of the chiefs, who represent continuity with tradition and the solidarity of the nation. This is a strange distinction for us, but it remains prevalent in places with strong traditional ties, like Iraq and Afghanistan.

*

RUSS TAKES CHARGE. THERE'S A BLESSING THAT YOU could describe as semi-Christian, involving the Creator, and the meal is served: finger foods first, followed by soups and stews from huge pots on stands. Most people have brought their own bowls and spoons. There are plastic bags for taking home uneaten food. The rule is: nothing shall be left. Then the dances start.

The *hummia* dances in and clears the hall of evil. The ritual isn't too ominous, since a kid is performing it. It's a challenge to attract adolescents to their traditional culture. Historical Haida dances have to compete with hip hop. It takes guts to try to revive ancient traditions in the face of the zeitgeist. When the colonizers no longer have the fleet and the cannon to impose their will, they bring out the cultural artillery, which positions itself inside people's heads — a dicier battle. (In the '70s, when a Newfoundland folk-rock band called Figgy Duff played traditional jigs and reels in clubs, the crowds loved it. But toss in a sea shanty or dirge and the crowd noise would drown them out. "Shut up," one of them once bellowed. "We're preserving your fucking culture.")

After the kids, an adult group from Masset performs. They do a powerful dance called Eagle Spirit, then a haunting new song. Individuals are now writing these traditional pieces, which isn't as paradoxical as it sounds. I've heard aboriginal singers in Toronto chant, "Meet me at Tim Hortons. Make it a double-double." It took awhile to make out the lyrics.

I run into Astrid Egger, whom I met on my first trip. She's from Germany; she and her daughter have been adopted into the Cumshewa clan. "Too bad this isn't a real potlatch," she says cheerily. Here we go again. Confusion over definitions seems to go with cultural revival. Everyone gets discombobulated after so much time has passed, so much has been lost, and reality itself has been skewed. I mean, what am I doing here? Isn't it because I got hooked by some university courses and books I read? Why did anthropologists like Franz Boas even come here a century ago? What gave them, and me, the right? The whole notion of interest belies detachment, leisure, and advantage. Would a Haida be commissioned by a national magazine to travel to Toronto to write about a bar mitzvah or an Italian wedding? There's an element of power and privilege indicated by who "takes an interest" in whom. Inuit don't go on ecotours of Montreal.

Everyone — outsiders, Native people, academics — thrashes around, looking for what they hope to find in the remnants and wreckage of these places and cultures. Thorstein Veblen, a sociologist, used the potlatch to exemplify his theory of conspicuous consumption. I knew an academic who claimed the "noble savage" of 19th-century anthropologists was a mask for the working class of their own age. They found what they wanted, and my academic acquaintance found what she wanted in their findings. I come seeking an alternative to capitalism, after the socialist models of my era vaporized. You take and you use. But the closer you get, the less simple it looks. "I know all about [the potlatch]. I know more than you do," said an Indian Affairs agent long ago to a Haida, who replied, "You must be older than I am, because I have lived all my life amongst them and I still don't know everything about it." Early social scientists like Boas meant to be sympathetic to their "subjects." Today the U.S. military hires anthropologists to work in Iraq or Afghanistan. All the outside interest and the ability to pursue it ends up as more data for more study; in a better world, everyone would get an equal chance to study everyone else.

"I remember a potlatch similar to this," says a chief, as the tributes to Charlie Wesley begin. (Charlie was 18 when he became chief and 87 when he died, so there's a sense of lostness; no one can recall when he wasn't there. He was born in 1918, and he lived through the bad years for the potlatch and its revival. Smallpox would have been a vivid memory, and memory here is a theme.) The chief looks around and says happily that the "protocols" are as they were in the past; he knows, because he's talked to the elders. Another chief, wearing a Métis sash, says, "I want to say *howa'a* [thank you] to the cooks; it was an awesome feast. I want to say *howa'a* to the dancers; it was an awesome dance." Then comes the gifting; verbs generally seem more apt here than nouns: they potlatch, they gift. It's about social interaction.

The matriarch-to-be gives out envelopes with cash for individuals who helped. She has a competent air, as if the men get to march in and speechify but the women make the decisions and distribute the bucks. Then they bring out the wicker baskets for the chiefs. They deliver Canadian Tire–type outdoor furniture to special guests. Through it all, there's drumming and chanting; it's a bit primal. Russ asks the Raven women to raise their hands until their gifts arrive. Dick hands cartons to people who have a lot to haul. It's kind of chaotic and acquisitive, a taste of a taste of what the missionaries may have reacted against. Russ is conscientious, an ideal man at the front. He asks anyone who didn't get a Raven print, specially created for this, to raise a hand. I've got mine. Someone hands me a bag and says, "Thank you for coming," a personal touch that feels nice.

Dick comes over and says, with a note of surprise,

that the current matriarch has agreed to speak to me. He means nani, Charlie Wesley's widow, a striking, serene woman at the centre of the head table who's been deferred to all night. I sit beside her and say I wish I'd known her husband. She says she misses him every day. I maunder a bit about how you think you know someone, but there are always new discoveries; she interjects: "There are things I wanted to say that I didn't get to say." I suddenly notice that they're starting the final prayer. I mistimed this. I thought they'd still be distributing gifts to the Eagles, but they've moved on. Russ's efficiency at work. Here I am at the head table with the matriarch at a solemn moment, so I hightail it out, and as I pass George Westwood, the undertaker, on the way back to my seat, he says, "Nice getaway, Rick." I mop my brow. It feels like a moment in a Bing Crosby–Bob Hope *Road to . . .* movie from the '50s, where the footloose Westerners barely escape a scrape with the natives, a scrape they don't know how they got into. *On the Road to Haida Gwaii.*

*

ON THE PLANE HOME, I THINK BACK TO WHEN I first owned a house and how I puzzled over whether to thank the tradespeople who came and solved my problems. After all, they got paid. But most people want to be useful and generous in their work, not just compensated. It's as if money exchanges obscure those normal impulses.

Novelist Joseph Conrad called works of art the signs of a "subtle but invincible conviction of solidarity," a strange way to describe supposedly individualistic acts of creation. Lewis Hyde said the engraved "coppers" given away at potlatches, sometimes broken into small pieces, expressed the group's solidarity and perpetuity, the need of all for all. "In the case of the mortuary potlatch," he wrote, "a material thing symbolizes a biological fact, the survival of the group despite the death of the individual. . . . At some level, biological, social, and spiritual life cannot be differentiated." Franz Boas, the original potlatch outside investigator, quoted a potlatcher: "This food is the goodwill of our forefathers. It is all given away."

The connection to the forefathers is like everything else in human culture (language, agriculture, culture); it contains the accumulated wealth gifted to the future from the entire past. That's not myth or metaphor; it's literally true. The social nature of wealth gets cleverly concealed in a market economy, with its commodity exchanges denominated by prices. But no one can truly own wealth if it is social in its essence, even if chunks of it can be, as it were, amputated, isolated, bought, sold, and mystified.

French anthropologist Marcel Mauss said the existence of obligatory gift exchanges like the potlatch among "primitive" peoples demonstrated an "eternal morality" in humans. I'd rather call it evidence for an eternal reality, the reality of unavoidable interconnectedness and mutual need. Due to this dependence on others, past and future as well as present, everyone gives to everyone; it can't be helped, even if it's concealed by myths or tales about self-sufficient individuals and private property.

This connectedness is what community is based on; it doesn't rise from some set of psychological "needs" to "feel" a sense of belonging. It's grounded on actually belonging to a collectivity or many — even if you never know it or experience it explicitly and the sense of it becomes attenuated or obscured. In Haida tradition, that reality is unattenuated. The potlatch lays it bare.

The night before I left, I attended a benefit concert on the "white" side of town, to support a community member who needed special care. It was a night of giving. But the Haida put that image in the centre of their society, not at its periphery. As Dick said, they made war in summer and potlatched all winter. It was their central institution, a social practice with many forms, occasions, and sizes. It flowed through life. You prepared for it and reminisced about it. It played a huge role in binding society and binding time — past, present, and future — into an enduring unity. It put social and economic interconnectedness on display, rather than hiding it, as economic theories and explanations in our society tend to. That's why the early social scientists, and so many since, were attracted to it. Because it revealed, rather than concealed, a central fact that drew them like moths to the flame: the grounding existence of social reality, not just around us and for us but embedded deep within each of us.

6

THE MYSTERY OF TEACHING

BEFORE I BECAME A DAD AT A LATE POINT, READERS sometimes challenged me when I wrote on kids: "You don't have any," they'd say. True, I'd say, but I was one. Teaching is also a topic anyone has a right to opine on, not because everyone has been a teacher but because everyone has been taught.

It happens that I have always taught as well, though never full time. I taught at my Toronto synagogue during my teens. We made lesson plans and used advanced audiovisual aids like film strips. During university, I worked at summer camps. It felt like an extension of teaching. Inspired by A.S. Neill's book about his free school, Summerhill, in England, I boldly moved to abolish cabin cleanup. For over three decades, I've taught a half course in Canadian studies at the University of Toronto. It still runs as a discussion, though it grew from 20 to 175 students. "That class was real '60s," said someone who passed through. I prefer to think of it as the Socratic method.

I liked reading about education because it seemed to focus big issues: human nature, relations between the biological unit of the family and social units like the nation, values that ground personal and collective behaviour, what is the good society, what does citizenship require. As a teen, I adored writers like Paul Goodman and Edgar Z. Friedenberg who took the novel approach of siding with the students and so, by implication, against the system ("the man," as my kid, Gideon, likes to mock). Living in New York in the 1960s, I noticed a magazine on the racks called *This Magazine Is About Schools*. I knew instantly, from the self-effacing name, that it hailed from Canada. When I returned home, I joined its editorial board, though by then they'd given up on schools as the fulcrum of the revolution (against the man) and become left-wing Canadian nationalists.

My own kid's arrival resuscitated that interest. He went to a daycare in a private home when he was ten months old. I was distressed and guilt-ridden; I felt it would scar him and cry out my own failure as a parent. But he thrived there. The daycare itself broke all the rules for normal certification: adult-kid ratios, age ranges. The kids looked after each other, and since mine was an only child it compensated for the absence of siblings at home. Starting with his first day there, he formed intense friendships with other kids, some of which persist.

From this I deduce that you can't be sure what value a kid will glean from a teaching or quasi-teaching context. In that way education is like dating: no one knows what they really want until they get it. For his kindergarten years, he went to a Montessori school. There, each kid worked separately on skills like math and geography or a physical task like pouring. The teacher dealt with one at a time, teaching a skill till the kid grasped it; then the kid continued, alone or aided by another kid, till it was mastered; then on to something new. The teacher glanced around constantly to check the others. It looked exhausting. There was no lockstep learning: it was total decentralization, both collective and individual, like anarchism at its best (in theory). Kids respond positively to it, and I see no reason that the approach couldn't be applied to public systems, as Maria Montessori meant it to be, in the Italian slums where she developed her method. Yet there's this: Gideon loved his first year at Montessori but not the second; the difference was his reaction to two different teachers. Other kids had the reverse experience with the same teachers. From this, I deduce that regardless of method, the teacher is central. I mean this as more than the pablum it sounds.

He went to Clinton, our local public school, for the elementary years. Some of his old daycare friends were there, and financial considerations were involved, but the main motive was educational. What you learn above all in the public system is what the society you live in is like and that you are a part of it. That's because the public system must let everyone in. But it was also Gideon's choice; he initiated the move. I think he sensed that Clinton was a "real school," in the sense of an institution that was a part of the bigger world he would eventually join. Montessori had been a kind of sheltered hothouse, and the kids there sensed it. He strutted a bit through the halls at Clinton in a way he hadn't at Montessori. It was something I didn't expect.

But the mystery of teaching was most striking for me at his karate classes. I sat through hundreds at Northern Karate Schools twice a week, never bored, rapt each time trying to figure out why the teaching was so effective. He'd been briefly to another karate school that was quasi-military — lots of "Sir, yes sir" — but it didn't take. Northern Karate had none of that, though it was disciplined and highly structured. He could attend any of several classes any day of the week. Teachers varied along with the composition of classes, which were brief. Drills shifted often, so attention didn't flag. But at bottom, it was again about the teachers, though they had strikingly different personalities and approaches. They were well trained in teaching specific karate moves, but, said one, they each had to work out a method for themselves. It was the kind of teaching where teachers are taught to find their own way. They paid the same attention to three-year-olds as they did to advanced black belts. When students were taken through moves, stances, or full routines (*katas*) that they'd done thousands of times, there was always something to learn and the teachers seemed intent on finding it each time. When school founder Cezar Borkowski, a ninth-degree black belt, attended or taught class, even for the littlest white belts, he had an uncanny way of peering at what the kids were doing, as if he'd never seen this done before. Noam Chomsky was once asked on CBC-TV if he ever got bored repeating the same points about politics year after year. He chuckled, adjusted a pesky earpiece, and said, "No, after we finish this interview, I'm going into a linguistics seminar where we'll discuss issues I've been thinking about for a lot longer. There's always something to learn." Teaching is one of the most basic human activities, like breathing and walking. There's no end to it, just deeper depths. The best part about watching Gideon's karate teachers was that I couldn't nail down why it worked. *It's fun*, I'd think, but there was more to it. Or, they like kids. But the nub kept slipping away.

That's what made it teaching, an activity that reveals itself in the doing and constantly reshapes according to context. This doesn't mean that method is irrelevant, and content or curriculum is frequently attached. But there is a deeper independent variable:

the relationship between teacher and student. So there is no ultimate end or goal in teaching any more than there is in a friendship, a marriage, or therapy. The relationship can stray somewhere unexpected; it can simply stop or it can unfold further. Teaching is essentially open ended, because it belongs among those human activities that are embedded in time and can't be extracted from their unfolding process and formalized. It is in the nature of these relational activities that any human being can do them, and in some form, everyone does. There is no secret to teaching, but there is an accessible mystery.

Think of a teacher you've had who you recall in a good way. Most people have had at least one, though it's sadly possible to miss that experience. Do you actually remember the subject matter they taught? What almost always stays with you is a sense that they valued you as someone with a mind worthy of attention. The content they poured into you is secondary at best. What lasts is that sense of being valued. It kindled whatever in you is a student. They may or may not have been warm. Warmth is optional. It's the intellectual respect they conveyed that's basic. There is no formula for this; it can be accomplished in myriad ways depending on the teacher and student involved. That's why it's mysterious. Because it can happen in so many ways.

But here's what I want to say: that mysteriousness

is under attack — the mystery itself is being denied and the secret is said to have been revealed.

Since formal systems of education came into being a long time ago, there have been experts and authorities claiming to know that secret, the one and only one way to most effectively drill content into students. It seems to make sense. There may be many methods, but surely someone can discover the best. Then, once it's been discovered, you won't need real teachers any more, though you may still call them that. You can make do with technicians, mechanics, instructors, or, in a cyber era, programs that the students run themselves.

The ranks of secret-revealing mystery deniers in the field of teaching are proliferating. That's because there are vast amounts of money to be made by declaring that you possess the secret of teaching kids what they need to know in order to survive bad economic times. It's also because the money lords have found it harder to increase their profits by normal entrepreneurial means in such times but have realized there are hordes of wealth still buried in realms like public education. So the raid is on. Their cover story is: we can do it better than teachers, principals, or old-fashioned educators and school boards. We have found, through copious investment and arduous research, the Way to Teach. They have a product to sell, and no one ever did that by saying it's just one among many equally good options. You always claim to have the one and only.

The products they're selling aren't only methods for use in the classroom — where the teacher should stand, questions to ask, the right order to introduce topics, homework assignments. There are technologies too, chiefly online. And techniques like "flipping the classroom," which prioritize online courses that must, inevitably, be purchased. In addition, there are massive testing programs that assess the success of the teaching methods bought and implemented and indicate what further techniques need to be acquired to improve those scores, which will then be tested again. And again. This is a bottomless mine.

But what if there is not one correct way to teach (either in general or for particular subjects), which can be bottled and sold? What if, due to the mystery of teaching, all teachers can and must discover how to teach in their own way? Then the mighty payoff doesn't even exist.

If the claim is merely a scam, who will expose them? Where are the whistle-blowers? Why are all these products that jostle crudely for profit share in the marketplace, where most of the funds are public, treated so seriously? Sadly, many people who could blow the whistle are also caught up in the chase. It's hard to find professors at education faculties who aren't consulting or setting up their own companies to dig for gold. Principals, education directors, and government bureaucrats in the field are planning to shift over later in their careers. Many of these people are insightful and experienced. Out of one side of their mouth, they'll tell you that the only thing that truly matters in teaching is the teacher-student relationship and it can take many forms. They acknowledge that almost anything can and does work, provided the teacher is truly committed to the student and to sticking with the process. But since they're also probably consulting for the private firms pitching to the public systems, planning to set up their own operations in addition to their day jobs, or to eventually drop out of the public sector and work for the corporate guys, they also frequently hedge what they have to say. As a result, the poor public, whose kids are subjected to one method or technology after another claiming to have the answer, are simply confused as they cling wanly to their faith in the experts.

Here's what makes it even murkier for parents, kids, and teachers. The people pushing these faux solutions know what you're not allowed to say outright: "We will make teachers irrelevant or demote them to the level of techs and assistants." They still have to deploy the rhetoric of teacher centrality. So it's all broached as "Everything we're selling you here exists only to aid the teacher, who remains the centrepiece of the educational process." Once they've made that pro forma declaration, they move on to downgrade teaching to such a technical, fill-in-the-blanks activity that many of those with a true teaching gift despair and leave the field. Increasingly, especially in the U.S., students just out of university or retired business people (in programs like Teach for America) pop up in the classroom. The work they do there under the new regimes requires very little experience or craft, much less a sense of vocation. Some people work on their novel when they retire or lose their jobs. Others "teach."

What will go missing if this commercialized, standardized process paves over everything that used to happen in school? Only the experience you had with that teacher who made you feel special because he or she saw in you a mind worthy of thinking about the way the world works and your place in it. You might have got there anyway, but for most of us, teachers — the rare ones who resonated with you, just as other teachers resonate with other students — were crucial. Their encouragement and faith in your mind — that you had one and it would benefit you and others to apply it — led you on to discovering how to think for yourself wherever you chose to do that: in the workplace, in relationships with your friends or your kids, in the public square, or in the next election.

So if there is no essence of teaching that can be refined in a lab and put out on the shelf with a price tag, what is there to teach to teachers in their teachers' colleges and programs? Good question.

Finland has the most successful public schools program in the world by the most venal, conventional standards — by which I mean standardized testing. Finnish students score at the top, always, of the literacy, math, and science tests administered globally under the Programme for International Student Assessment. But Finland itself does no standardized testing at all, until students finish high school, when they all test for the purpose of admission to their (free) universities. There is virtually no curriculum, no standard methods or approaches, and relatively little homework. They spend a year and many hours less in school than comparable countries.

What they have instead is ruthless emphasis on the centrality of teachers. In attitudinal surveys, teachers rank socially higher than doctors and lawyers. It is harder to get into a teaching program than into law school. They don't make more money than other professions and are in the middle of teacher income scales among comparable countries. It's all about the respect for and self-respect of teachers. They are responsible for the success of their students, not experts or bureaucrats. They use their spare periods in the staff room to discuss student problems or teaching ideas. I've seen it. It stunned me. You simply don't find that in Canadian staff rooms, where teachers go for relief from classroom realities. When I asked

Finnish teachers what they do about bad teachers, they almost guffawed — a rare mode among Finns — and said, "We have very good teachers." Parents are far less involved in school matters than in other countries because they trust their kids' teachers.

I spent a day with an education prof who does hands-on supervision at one of the faculties in the town of Kokkola, near the Arctic Circle. We went from school to school, sitting in on classes where student teachers had week-long practice teaching assignments. Some aspiring teachers were comfortable with the kids, who sat attentively; others didn't seem to have a handle on it. I asked the supervisor what made the difference. "It's always the chaos in the head of the teacher," she said. "The children feel it." What she teaches to teachers is the mystery of teaching. Accept it, explore it, find your way in it.

One other point. This isn't just about teaching or education. It's about the nature of thought. The successes of the hard sciences in the early modern era — Copernicus, Galileo, Newton — created a model for thinking that was based on clear questions that had clear, unambiguous, and mathematical answers. For every question, there was one and only one answer. The social sciences tried applying that standard to society, the psyche, history, and human nature. It also became a model in politics, where it had apparent success in 20th-century events like the Russian and Chinese revolutions. Leninism and Maoism were based on the "scientific" assumption that, for any political problem or conflict, there is one and only one correct analysis. Earlier epochs too had their certaintics and solutions, based on faith, dogma, and divine revelations.

But the physical sciences have long since embedded uncertainty in their foundations. Politics and the social sciences should do the same. The Russian and Chinese revolutions wound up leaving many unsolved questions and no definitive answers. The cocky political and economic screeds of the past century look exhausted, and, happily, few new scripts are on offer. The one-and-only-one-solution mentality seems antiquated. A politics of the future, if there is one and if we have one, will be more improvisational than scripted, always tentative and open ended. If new kinds of political and social thinking are to develop that are more adequate to the shifting, unstable reality we inhabit, then the old kind of teaching, with its mysteries and relational core, is well poised to play a part. That's because, in teaching, the mystery never really went away.

Part III

WISDOM FROM A SHORT PERSPECTIVE

7

GOOD GUYS,
BAD GUYS, AND LITTLE GUYS

ODD. THERE ARE PEOPLE IN NOTTINGHAM WHO don't seem to have heard of Sherwood Forest. The clerks at the hotel stare as if no one ever asked how to get there. They call a number and say a cab will cost 30 pounds each way. Wow. I thought Sherwood would be a big theme park, with the region focused around it, like Orlando. But it is a nature preserve, with a short Robin Hood Festival each summer. We planned to get here on its final weekend. I was sure there'd be regular tourist buses.

Gideon has been engaged with Robin Hood since age four; now he's almost six. Pin it on Ross Petty. The actor-entrepreneur produces an English-style pantomime in Toronto each Christmas. That year it was Robin Hood. Ross played the sheriff of Nottingham. In the music hall tradition, the audience is encouraged to boo and cheer. Gideon was enthralled. From there we went to movie versions, such as the 1938 Errol Flynn film, with its robust music and rollicking jokes. Those tales met the main condition for capturing his four-year-old interest: they were about good guys versus bad guys.

Maybe it sprang from the rich, fraught world of daycare. The big kids get their way over little ones: on snacks, access to swings, and other desiderata. It's not fair. Or maybe it was about the relationship to parents and other adults, who get to set the rules, often just because they say so. Or both, one injustice reinforcing another. He started dividing the world between good guys and bad guys, as if it were an innate impulse. The Robin nexus added an intriguing complexity. Robin was an outlaw but a good guy. He did bad things, like stealing, but for good-guy reasons. So that seemed to make it all right. Only the bad guys objected when Robin lied or stole. It made life even more interesting than it already was. "Are bad guys nice to each other?" he asked one day from the car seat. And, "How did the sheriff of Nottingham get to be a bad guy? I think all the time about it." Surely the sheriff had started life as just a kid.

What I knew about child development went back to my days as a philosophy grad student in New York in the late 1960s. My friends in psych all made pilgrimages to Geneva to study with Jean Piaget, the grand master. They talked about the narrow range of kids Piaget based his studies on, especially his own children. He spent most of his career studying the development of cognitive process: how abstractions and categories form, where logic originates, etc. But late on, in 1965, he published *The Moral Judgment of the Child*, tracing the rise of a sense of good and bad in a way that was similar to his model for intellectual development. Emboldened by the notion that your own kid can serve as a model, I began to wonder: why make cognition the main focus for understanding kids' development? For kids themselves, it is often moral issues that underlie their experience of the world.

It isn't just that kids divide the world into good guys and bad guys. It's the fertility of those categories. When we climb into a canoe at the lake, Gideon becomes Cottage Robin (like Rocket Robin, on the retro toon shows), paddling through Sherwood Marsh to save the people of the lost city of Atlantis, which he watched the night before on DVD, emphasizing the theme of rescue, though the film didn't. Or how he brought the moral quality of the "force" (after seeing *Star Wars*) into a race on his bike — *Gideon, the force is with you* — and added Obi-Wan Kenobi to the *Justice League* action figures on the living room floor, where large realistic characters interact with a dinky metal plane that stands for Darth Vader, no questions asked. The key to the truly motley concoction is not an indiscriminate mingling of real with represented, tiny with huge, but the underpinning moral theme — good guys against bad guys — which draws it all together.

*

"How about we go to our room and watch a DVD on your computer?" says Gideon, who is bushed after the overnight flight and two-hour train ride to Nottingham. So we do. We fling ourselves on the bed and watch some *Looney Tunes*. The desk calls. There is indeed a bus, they say. Comes right by the hotel. *Aha*, I think, *the tourist run*. But it's just a local; it stops across the street or is supposed to, says the clerk, still sounding doubtful. It's due in seven minutes. I tell Gideon we can run for it. He's not interested. He lacks the adult sense of mission and duty while travelling. For him, there's no contradiction between coming all this way, then watching a cartoon because you're tuckered out. All the components of a life nestle together, the way Robin and Darth Vader and even Harry Potter coexist in the games he plays.

That goes for morality too. It's an adult cognitive trick to compartmentalize the moral sense in a term like *ethics*, which you can then write books on or take a degree in. Out in reality, the moral elements are imbricated in the flow of life and can be separated only artificially.

Later we wander into the centre of Nottingham and visit Tales of Robin Hood. It's a theatre with montages of Robin Hood episodes you ride through in a sort of medieval iron tub hung from a moving chain. It's okay but hardly different from, say, watching the Flynn movie or Ross Petty's play.

After supper at Pizza Hut, we stumble onto the outer wall of Nottingham Castle. That's better. It looks exactly right, even with picnickers strewn around. There's a great statue of Robin. We follow the wall, a massive structure, down a hill, and as it bends around a corner, we find before us the Ye Olde Trip to Jerusalem, England's oldest inn, says the sign. It dates to the First Crusade. It's built into the wall of the castle, and there have been no unnecessary renovations. When we finally go through the castle gates, there's no castle there. It came down long ago, though there's a 19th-century manorial pile in its place, which we have no interest in entering. Anyway, it's already closed.

*

NEXT MORNING WE CATCH THE BUS. IT'S CALLED the Sherwood Arrow, makes a million stops (mostly on suburban streets), circles lazily, and finally arrives in the forest. It's a bit reminiscent of taking the scheduled bus to Auschwitz from Cracow: it stopped often on the country road to let people on. Is this the bus to Auschwitz? they'd ask. Yeah, yeah, said the driver. Climb on. They didn't mean the death camp, of course; they meant the city, which existed before the camp and remains after. In ordinary lived life, everything is part of everything.

There is a reception area, food stands, and a kiosk selling Robinalia. The vendors call us "sire" in a way that sounds normal. I resist buying a plastic crossbow and foam arrows, which I say we can find anywhere. We get a Lincoln green cap, a collar, a sword, and a dagger (beechwood from the forest, they say). Then we start down a path that says "To the Major Oak." We assume it's what we know as Gallows Oak, from the Flynn flick, where Robin rallied the peasantry to join him against Prince John and for good King Richard. (Another complexity: is Robin a rebel against authority or a loyal royalist?)

And this is where the magic begins.

It's a thick, old English forest; the sunlight struggles through in patches. We pass minstrels and other tourists, but the forest dominates. Many trees seem ancient and could pass as major. They fold off the path into a tangle only Robin or his men could find a way through. No wonder the sheriff's minions avoided Sherwood. Gideon is playing Robin, and I am Will or Little John as needed. He carries Paddington Bear on his shoulders. (Gideon brought him from Toronto so he could visit his home, Paddington Station.)

Being Robin, here in Sherwood (the actual Sherwood), is a unique moment in his relationship to Robin. It's way better than the tableaus in Nottingham or the enactments they do near the gate. Those are representations, like Errol Flynn and Gideon's Robin games with his friends. But this is actually walking along inside the myth of Robin Hood. It's that myth that excited him from the start, not any particular representation or version of it. Those came after. A myth grips you not in any specific details but precisely because of its malleability and adaptability, the many meanings and situations it can include. You gather a sense of it, connect it to your own sense of the world, then explore and expand it, as required or desired.

I'd say this is similar to what a moral sense is about: not learning good from bad or right from wrong in particular cases but feeling that the world itself is limned in those terms. That is the human birthright. Notions about what specifically is good and bad are secondary to that basic sense of a world imbued with moral quality. The thickness of that moral sense in the Robin myth is what attracted Gideon. It reflected his own powerful sense of good guys and bad guys everywhere; he felt at home in it because of its underlying moral presumption in all the stories and versions. It's because of this foundational, proliferating quality that I think of his moral sense as complex rather than ambiguous. Are bad guys nice to each other? Sure, sometimes. Does that make them good guys? In a way. It depends. His moral sense is not ambiguous: it's rich and tangled, like the forest.

The major oak is about 30 minutes' walk in. It's massive and anthropomorphic, like the gnarled trees in *The Wizard of Oz* and *Lord of the Rings*. It's protected by a fence; its branches are buttressed, propped, and trussed like an old cathedral. There are some stands and kiosks. We buy a beechwood bow and arrows to go with the rest of our gear, and there he is in the heart of Sherwood, romping around the big oak or its brethren, shooting away.

I relent on the plastic and foam items because he's right and I'm wrong. Why insist on prissy adult distinctions about what is authentic or worthy and what isn't? It's the flexibility of myth.

*

IN MY TEENS AND EARLY 20S, I TAUGHT A LOT OF Sunday (or Saturday) school at synagogues. The curriculum often involved teaching moral values. It's a fad that races through the pedagogical world regularly. Piaget too wrote that the point of his studies was not just to discover "how young people learn to distinguish right from wrong" but, "most importantly, how can we induce them to prefer the former over the latter." To me that sounds disrespectful: pushing free moral agents in a particular direction and teaching them which goals to value and pursue. Either they make their own free choice or one is imposed on them, and if the latter, you deprive them of the dignity that makes them moral agents to start with.

But thinking about our walk into the heart of Sherwood I'd say there's also something superfluous about teaching moral values. The broad sense of right and wrong is endemic. It goes with being human; it's virtually the same thing. (Two things fill me with wonder, said Kant: the starry heavens above and the moral voice within.) That's why I find Gideon's tendency to see the world as a playing field for good guys and bad guys compelling and, in its way, sufficient. He's voicing the inherent moral quality of human existence. To think it has to be instilled or developed is like saying breathing or speech must be taught. At most you can aid or hinder it as the child discovers and cultivates it in himself.

This brings me again to Piaget. He discerned "two moralities of the child" that occur in sequence: a morality of "constraint," imposed on kids by adult authorities, and then a later morality that emerges between nine and twelve, built on cooperation between peers. It gets internalized; it judges on the basis of intentions and motives rather than external consequences. The first teaches mere duty; the latter, an inner sense of good. According to Piaget, the transition between the phases corresponds to a historical transition from primitive, superstitious communities to complex, differentiated societies marked by a sense of individual responsibility. This evidences a "qualitative" advance — in kids and societies. So the development of moral judgement in the child builds smoothly and inevitably to the better, more abstract, more truly moral viewpoint of the older child and then to the adult — as history might be seen to progress inevitably toward equality and democracy.

Now even if there are different versions of morality, it seems to me risky to link them sequentially (Morality 1.0, Morality 2.0). Think about people you know who behave according to fine principles that they articulate — say, serving the poor or oppressed — but are not very nice to others in their own lives and lack empathy. Or others you know who propound loathsome moral and political views, yet you somehow know they would stand loyally by you in a crisis.

But what really bugs me is not Piaget's tidy schematism. It's the way his approach denies to both small kids and primitive peoples the possibility of exemplary moral behaviour. I am at least as likely to learn from Gideon as the reverse and have always found this with kids. The requirement to advance doggedly through set stages is condescending and arrogant toward both kids and earlier generations. Those primitive moralities aren't always so primitive.

Why can't humans transition from highly insightful to shallow and mistaken as history thumps along? Take George W. Bush's dualistic view of the moral universe: you're either with us or with the terrorists. I wish he would ponder Gideon's question about whether bad guys are nice to each other. You can invert Piaget's schema and argue that moral complexity and sensitivity get off to a good start in small kids, then deteriorate. This model is easier to see in the arts, where creativity and imagination are common in kids who then have those qualities baked out of them, so that the task of artists — often seen as childlike — is to recapture and cling to those early impulses and resources. I know kids aren't inherently nice and can be brutal just like other humans. What I'm arguing for isn't their niceness, it's their moral acuity, that surprisingly sophisticated sense of good and bad.

*

THAT NIGHT WE WENT TO LONDON, AND NEXT DAY, by rail, to Legoland near Windsor Castle. It's a theme park, with almost everything built from Lego. It began raining hard, and we came to the Traffic ride. Little Lego-like cars with their own controls. There were lights and stop signs, and Gideon was salivating. At the front of the line was a notice: "Six and up only." "How old is he?" asked the attendant. Six, I lied. She let us through to watch a training video with other kids. "Daddy, you lied," said Gideon. "Yes," I said, "because they won't let anyone under six in a car and you're almost six and really want to do it, and sometimes it's all right to lie if it won't do any harm or even, sometimes, it might do some good. For instance, if it stops someone from being hurt."

He drove beautifully. He obeyed the stop signs and made the turns even though it was English on-the-left driving (not a real source of confusion for a five-year-old Canadian); when older kids crashed, he swerved around and kept on trucking. We were both proud. That night in bed, before he dropped off, he said, "Daddy, I liked it when you lied."

He seemed to find it a relief — and maybe a delight — to have some account of the problematics of lying. That's different from trying to instill a moral sense or values. It's more like tips on how to think about these things. Perhaps he had been working through similar thoughts and found it useful — a bit like Piaget's notion of moving from external moral realism (all lies are bad) to considerations based on intent and context. When I was a student at Union Theological Seminary in New York, that kind of moral calculation was called situational ethics and treated as daring, though it's how most people behave most of the time, whether they admit it or not.

The way out of the park took us, by design, through a big Lego store called, I think, the Big Shop, where I had my main parental meltdown on the trip. He wanted to buy a Bionicle — a pricey one — to go with his collection back home. I felt a surge of resistance about the cost and responded with a little blast instead of a regretful no. Maybe I was feeling underappreciated, after providing this grand trip. Isn't anything ever enough? His eyes teared up. Had they not, he might have argued that we'd flown all the way to England; travelled two more hours by tube, train, and bus to get here; paid a big entry charge; and roamed happily around for hours — surely this proved the importance of our attendance at Legoland. Why shouldn't he buy, as a memento, something grander than the toys he gets all the time at Kidstuff on Bathurst Street in Toronto? If he'd said that, I'd have had a hard time not conceding that he was right and I was wrong, which I did anyway. We compromised on exactly the Bionicle he had chosen and headed for the cash.

As we inched forward in a long line, I became aware of a cacophony of voices, howls really. Listen, I said. Every kid seemed to be yelling for something, and each parent was barking back in reproach. This place is wild, I said. Everyone in it is out of control. You got stubborn; I melted down; everybody is bouncing off the walls.

He started to laugh. We've talked about how these stores make you crazy, as if that's their mission in life. Nobody ever sounds happy in a toy store. Their goal is to drive you to buy beyond your needs or means. By the time we got to the bus stop outside the park, he was making faces to show how I looked when I had my dementia. I couldn't decide if that meant it had all been a good or a bad thing. But come to think of it, Piaget says something useful about this.

He offers advice for helping kids to depend on their own sense of moral judgement rather than outside authority.

> One must place oneself on the child's
> own level, and give him a feeling of

equality by laying stress on one's own obligations and ... deficiencies ... to draw attention to one's own needs, one's own difficulties, even one's own blunders, and to point out their consequences, thus creating an atmosphere of mutual help and understanding. In this way the child will find himself in the presence not of a system of commands requiring ritualistic and external obedience, but of a system of social relations such that everyone does his best to obey the same obligations, and does so out of mutual respect.

This suggests the nice possibility of turning your unavoidable blunders and meltdowns into a source of moral assistance for your kid. How? By acknowledging them and using that admission to establish a sort of level moral playing field between children and adults, thus encouraging kids to have confidence in their own judgement. In other words, it could actually help not to be an ideal moral model. There's a comforting thought for when you lose it with your kid.

*

ON OUR LAST DAY IN LONDON, WE WENT TO THE Imperial War Museum. Gideon chose it from a *London for Kids* book. It surprised me (unlike the dinosaurs at the Natural History Museum or the zoo).

But he was just shy of three on 9/11. His mother and I tried not to let the pictures upset him — I think we put the sound down but still kept the TV on all day. He must have seen those images the same hundreds of times we all did. Since then it's been lots of war: Afghanistan, Iraq. "There's always fighting in Iraq!" he says in exasperation, as the news drones on. He's a kind of war baby, as I was in 1942, except war is in some ways more pervasive for him, due to the omnipresence of media. So at the museum he scurried about among the tanks, missiles, and hands-on submarine controls. He was disappointed there weren't more swords and daggers, à la Robin Hood. Those must be in another museum. It's not the kind of visit I'd pictured making with a kid of mine. I try my best to interpret war for him, but he has his own view, which I can only partially penetrate. So I have to hope my fairly ham-handed tales of Winston versus the Nazis or our chats about Iraq strike some useful chords. Surely it will have to do with good guys and bad guys, nuanced and filtered through his own conscience and values.

When we emerged from the tube in Paddington Station, where you catch the express for Heathrow, we went to the Paddington kiosk and bought a new bear, large and red with plastic rain boots. The first Paddington liked Canada so well that surely another would also enjoy it; plus, how nice it would be for Paddington One to have company on the return trip. Gideon caringly strapped them both into his seatbelt with him, and when we reached cruising altitude, positioned the computer so they could all watch the DVD, as we settled in for the eight-hour flight home.

*

(POSTSCRIPT ON DEALING WITH MORAL COMPLEXITY: Gideon knew Robin Hood had been an outlaw but seemed unsettled when he learned I'd been in jail myself. It happened when he asked about my friendship with lawyer Clay Ruby. I said Clay and I had known each other forever and, beyond that, he once got me out of jail just in time to avoid a beating that police had promised. I said I was only there briefly and always for noble causes like justice for workers or peace in Vietnam. But he looked puzzled, as if he had unfinished mental business with it. A year later, we bought a Peter, Paul, and Mary CD with a song that he'd learned in school. We played it in the car. Right after that track came a song I'd never heard. It began, "If you've been to jail for justice, I want to shake your hand." He leaned forward in his car seat and said, "You've been to jail for justice." I nodded. He stuck out his little arm. "I want to shake your hand." I think it was the affirmation from an impeccable source that helped it fall into place for him.)

8

WHAT WOULD WE DO
WITHOUT ROMIR?

Two hours out on the road to Agra, Gideon, who was 12 then, said, "What would we do without Romir?" We were on our way from Delhi to see the Taj Mahal. It was our second day in India. "Unfortunately," Romir had explained, "the Taj is everything it's made out to be. You need to go there."

He said it in a plummy, leisurely English. No trace of that familiar parodic Indian accent, which Romir loves to mock. He talks like an Oxford don, though he grew up in India and has spent most of his adult life in the U.S. When Gideon said he wanted to acquire some Hindi before we came, Romir told him to begin by learning to speak English like most Indians. You do that by bobbing your head from side to side as you talk. Damned if it doesn't work.

He sat in the passenger seat, speaking Hindi with

Surinder, the driver, or to us in English, often keeping everyone in the conversation. By then — after just two hours — we'd acclimatized. "If a guy came running straight at us right now with a machete," said Gideon, "I wouldn't blink." There were four lanes of highway, and each direction somehow accommodated about five lanes of traffic: cars, three-wheelers, scooters, bicycles, camels, horses, ox carts, pushcarts, holy men, the odd elephant, pedestrians, squeezing in and by one another. If you thought you could make it, you went for it, honking constantly (buses and trucks had signs on them saying "Please Honk"). The honking was informative and lifesaving, but even if no one was coming through, it seemed wise to keep it up in case a situation arose. It was precautionary and self-preservative. A few forlorn road signs read "Maintain Lane Discipline." Thankfully, no one did: it would have been catastrophic. Occasionally a truck barrelled right at us, in the wrong direction. Its driver had grown bored or was in a rush; who knows? Surinder didn't flinch, nor did anyone else. In our dozens of hours on those highways, we saw no accidents and no road rage. (Though once, in the dark returning from Agra, we heard Romir mutter, "Oh shit," and figured it was over. Then it was gone, whatever it was.)

It was like Mulberry Street, from Dr. Seuss's first book. The kid is walking home from school. It's totally uneventful aside from "a plain horse and driver," which were always there and unremarkable in Springfield, Massachusetts, in 1937, so he invents things to tell his dad that he saw on the way. By the time he gets home, the walk includes marching bands, elephants, maharajas — no wonder we thought of it. The only thing that ever managed to surprise us, we agreed, was the rare stretch of road, never more than a few hundred feet, with nothing and no one on it. That didn't happen often, and it took our breath away.

But we'd have been lost without Romir. When Surinder stopped to get a permit and Romir wandered off for some pipe cleaners or tobacco, we were swamped by beggars and peddlers. A kid about Gideon's age with a snake offered to pose it for a picture. Gideon shot the photo, then another, then the kid adamantly demanded money. "Pay absolutely no attention whatsoever to any of their shit," Romir had instructed us, "and I will come back and abuse them." Then he chuckled and added, "Leave the abuse to me."

And he did it, but with a performative quality. It concealed other emotions. He said he never knew how to respond to the begging and peddling — still, after all the decades. If you gave money to the teenage moms with babies strapped on, it probably went straight to an organized gang. He tried to carry crackers, so they could consume the gift instantly. The desperate peddlers were impossible to deter or humiliate; he'd often finally, when no one could see, stuff a wad of rupees in their shirt pocket and tell them to back off discreetly. If others saw, you'd be surrounded and deluged, all of them equally needy, with further waves waiting to replace them. You could give them everything you had and it would simply be just, fair, and inadequate. A Gandhian self-impoverishment and martyrdom seemed like the rational response, perhaps the only truly ethical one, pointless and unavailing as it would be. Eventually, you'd join the destitute yourself so that you'd no longer be responsible for responding to them.

Romir knows the ins and outs of all this in concrete terms. He was an economics doctoral candidate when we met as grad students in New York long ago. Now he's a retired international development consultant. His Ph.D. thesis was on Indian agriculture, and he had lived among the peasants. His consulting firm focused on alternative energy approaches in less developed countries like India.

We saw ourselves as Maoists back when we met. He and his wife, Ella, an American army brat taking philosophy, as I was, later went to live in the depressed blue-collar city of Trenton, New Jersey ("Trenton Makes. The World Takes" was the city motto. How's that for depressive?) to make contact with the workers there and prepare for the inevitable revolution that we used to speak of unselfconsciously.

We sometimes spoke scornfully about the "neo-Malthusian" claim that overpopulation is an intractable obstacle to decent global living standards.

It's capitalist double-talk, we'd say, sitting in his and Ella's East Village walk-up — it's an apologetic smokescreen to excuse deprivation and inequality. Under an appropriate socialist reorganization of the economy, we assured each other, everyone could be fed, housed, educated, and cared for. "What crap that all was," he says today. We were sitting in the airy dining room of the India International Centre in Delhi when the subject arose, after our visit to the Taj. The place breathed the optimism of the early Nehru years. India's vast population is an overwhelming problem, Romir went on. What could we have been thinking by being so dismissive? It's as though his compassion, commitment, and dismay about India have only augmented as he grew less confident about what the solutions are — or that there are any.

*

HE AND ELLA FOUND ME ON THE INTERNET AGAIN in the late 1990s. We'd been out of touch since shortly after I returned to Canada. They lived in Washington, D.C. She was a lawyer with the department of labour; Romir had the consulting firm. There were two grown kids, Leah and Ravi. When Gideon and I arrived at the D.C. airport, I spotted them from a distance. "My God," I cried, "they haven't changed." They had of course. But they hadn't stopped, the way some people do as they age. You could still see the same people, continuing to grow. It's when you stop changing that you cease being who you were.

As soon as we arrived at their house in Arlington, Virginia, Romir got down on the floor with Gideon and showed him an array of Indian tops. He took us to a nearby schoolyard, bringing along some kites, and taught Gideon to fly them. Kite flying always seemed arcane and highly skilled to me; in India apparently everyone does it. You just jerk them a little on the ground and catch a breeze. Gideon had his up in seconds. When we bored him with our reminiscences over breakfast, Ella produced a DVD trove of Robin Hood episodes from the 1950s for him to watch. She'd discovered he was a Robin buff and that we'd been in Sherwood, the real one, a year before. In coming weeks she shipped us dozens more that she found on eBay.

When we all drove up to our cottage on a lake north of Huntsville that summer, Romir insisted on stopping at Fishing World on Highway 400. It has acres of fishing gear. People have been known to enter and never be seen again. He bought Gideon a fly-casting rod. It's an elegant way to fish and rare in our part of cottage country. He taught Gideon to fly-cast: play out the line, flick it behind, make the essential pause, repeat as often as necessary, then cast it out. No metallic whir of the sort we're used to, just a silent flight over the water and a light settling in.

A year later, when he was in Toronto for a cousin's wedding, we sat in my backyard and planned the trip to India. He and Ella had a condo in Pune and tried to spend a few months there each winter. Ravi was taking a hotel management course at a university in Aurangabad, a mere five or six hours' drive from Pune. It's where you stay when you visit the famed caves at Ajanta and Ellora. I said I only had a small window: two weeks, including reading week in February. He worked it out, day by day, as we sipped coffee in the shade; then he called his brother in Mumbai to have him renew Romir's membership at the Delhi International Centre, so we could stay there.

I asked if the trip might be hard for a 12-year-old. He said India can be handled by kids, but they should be prepared. Ella says she doesn't think India is for everyone. Ravi, who's interned at hotels all over the subcontinent, says, "We don't get many drop-ins." Looking back, I think Romir had in mind some of the challenges that faced his own kids on their early visits. He corresponded with Gideon, suggesting things to read. Gideon said he'd like to learn the language; Romir proposed starting with the sideways head bob.

*

WHAT DO YOU DO WHEN YOUR YOUTHFUL POLITICAL plans for changing the world don't quite work out? I used to be tormented by the thought of the Bolshevik who died storming the Winter Palace in 1917, looking up toward the gates and realizing he'd never know if the revolution had been victorious. Did he think he'd failed after dedicating everything to his quest? Did he die with full confidence or in doubt? And that was all before the birth, not to mention the brief glories, long decline, and sudden evaporation, of the Soviet Union. It didn't get clearer; it got murkier. Even on the orthodox Marxist model, only one generation can truly fulfill its hopes; the rest are too early or too late. What about them?

The answer is you grow up, so that other generations can be young and take their shot at the revolution, whatever their version of the world most people deserve but don't get turns out to be. Everyone has a right to that chance, and everyone else can continue to contribute — or try to — in whatever terms they feel still make sense. Milton Acorn wrote, "It takes a long time, with never a moment without effort / Burning a hole in time for all time." Political engagement is a shifting thing: even when you choose to opt out, you're still having an impact. It's an ongoing learning process, and then you hand on whatever you've gleaned, hoping others will find use or value in it.

*

AMONG THE SIGNIFICANT LEFT-WING CANADIAN figures of my lifetime is Mel Watkins. As a young economist in 1968, he produced the Watkins Report for Liberal Finance Minister Walter Gordon. It had a remarkable public impact and precipitated a debate on Canada's economy by demonstrating and lamenting our dependence on U.S. corporate power. Having made the point theoretically, he entered politics, not content with standing outside and criticizing. At the same time, he moved from the Liberals to the left, into the NDP, and raised the same issues there. He was a founder of what came to be called the Waffle Group. They insisted that you couldn't have independence in Canada without socialism or socialism without genuine independence. It was a challenging, useful way to clarify choices, however it looks at this distance. In response, the NDP expelled him and the Waffle. He went to work with Native peoples in the north, on economic issues. Eventually he returned to Toronto and continued to engage in all the major controversies. He is the only left-wing Canadian of my era who was regularly portrayed in editorial cartoons. Ordinary citizens knew who he was. I worked with him for many years on the editorial board of the left-wing nationalist journal *This Magazine*. In the 1990s, when most of us departed and handed it to another generation, Mel stayed on, the one among us best able to connect with the takeover cohort, learning from them at least as much as he offered.

Mel had three children. The eldest, Ken, had a daughter, Madeleine, Mel's first grandchild, who developed a neuroblastoma at age two and died of it two hard years later. I told Mel that, of all his notable contributions to our era and future generations, it seemed to me his presence and support for his kids and grandchild during that illness were the most impressive and the most enduring. Madeleine's mother, Theresa Burke, some years later became Gideon's mother. Madeleine Watkins would have been his half-sister. Gideon never knew her but refers to her as his sister.

So what happens when your own political project hasn't quite panned out? The advantage of getting older is you acquire a new option: getting out of the way to let later generations take their shot and doing what you can to abet them with whatever you learned that might be helpful. It feels faintly ridiculous to keep on politically *hukking a chinak* (banging a teakettle), as my grandparents would have said, as if there were nothing to do except carry on as you have till the bitter end.

In Gideon's case and that of his friends, their political project will include dealing with the diversity and inequity that are highly visible to them globally and which they also experience up close, daily. When a contemporary of mine who'd visited India said she couldn't bear to look at our photos because they reminded her of the awful poverty she'd seen there, he responded (to me, later), What did she expect to see in India? He was ready for it, partly because we knew Romir. It seems to me what Romir provided — along with keeping us from getting hysterical on the road to Agra, swamped by beggars, or laid low by Delhi belly —

was a subtle contribution to Gideon's ability to deal with his own emerging, unfolding political project. What would we have done without him?

Part IV

THE OWL OF MINERVA TAKES FLIGHT IN THE GATHERING DUSK

9

THE *GLOBE* YEARS: ARTS AND ENTERTAINMENT, 1991–1999

My 20 years as a weekly columnist for Canada's august newspaper, the *Globe and Mail*, began in 1991, roughly coinciding with the end of the Cold War. I'd say they're somewhat related. Till then I'd done everything possible to ensure I'd never occupy such a podium. The media responded in kind.

They generally viewed me as toxic for being a leftist, communist, or possible recipient of "Moscow gold" — though I was occasionally acceptable, perhaps once or twice a year, either to prove their open-mindedness or provide a frisson of dissent, a walk on the wild side.

From time to time I'd ask, like Oliver Twist, for more. In 1981, I wrote a loving takedown of the right-wing epigone Barbara Amiel in the marginal left journal *This Magazine*. Peter Newman, Amiel's editor at mighty *Maclean's* magazine, for which I sporadically wrote, told me he "loved every word" of the assault. He added that he'd deny saying so if I repeated it. I agreed not to quote him but asked for a column like hers. Oh no, he snapped back. It seemed to take no thought at all. We were in a restaurant, and I went over to the bar where I saw City-TV founder Moses Znaimer. I told him I found Newman's attitude perplexing. "The spectrum of what's acceptable in the mainstream media," Znaimer explained gently, "runs from A to B, and it's all right of centre."

That was the reality of the Cold War years, an era almost impossible not so much to describe as to imagine for anyone not there. To those born after 1980 or so, it sounds like the Arthurian age or Harry Potter. It's easier to picture yourself in Homeric Greece. I was born to it; it was the only reality I knew till it ended, so of course I never expected it to end.

(If this text had footnotes, I'd drop one here explaining that I'm not now, nor have I ever been, a member of the Communist Party or any party. In fact, I had antagonistic relations with the CP at best. For instance, they always reviewed my books or plays brutally. That may have had to do with my Canadian nationalism. The party tended to elide all versions of nationalism with Nazism.)

As the '80s droned on, I made limited headway. A column in *Canadian Business* magazine that ran awhile, but they were uneasy enough to always label it Guest Column. A weekly column in *TV Times*, one of those guides that sat on a coffee table in the front of the TV. They had the merit of lying around the house for a whole week and being consulted often. For me it was a breakthrough. I had an attachment to TV because we were the last on our block to acquire one in the 1950s, and it retained a sense of the forbidden; it connected me to secret things that others knew about, like sex. I was eventually fired after criticizing *The Cosby Show*. Then the very *Globe* itself, for their own TV mag, but I was only allowed in every other week.

I was dismissed from that following a right-wing (even for the *Globe*) editorial coup. It happened just after the raucous free trade election of 1988, in which I'd been up to my neck, on the other side from the *Globe*'s new über-Tory editor, William Thorsell. He told staff he'd rather not have "a Rick Salutin" as a columnist. Someone figured out that meant me. During the next two years, I attacked the *Globe* in print, both in *This Magazine* and in the very mainstream *Saturday Night* magazine. (When Conrad Black bought it and made John Fraser his editor, Fraser told me, "You're my key to proving I'm not under Conrad's thumb.") I wrote a piece for him describing the *Globe* and the CBC as Canada's first ministry of propaganda since the Second World War. In response, the CBC blacklisted me and the *Globe* offered me a weekly media column — the two classic strategies. Seven years later that morphed into an op-ed column. This is what I mean by saying I did everything possible to ensure I'd never be there.

But the Soviet Union was gone, as though it had never been. Poof. Whatever I now was, I couldn't be a spy or agent for a nonexistent evil empire. The basis of Soviet demonization hadn't been its mere ideas; it was an actual nation with a formidable military and nuclear arsenal that also functioned as an alternate socio-economic model, especially in its early years. Now that the Soviet Union and its allies had vaporized into history (or History, as Marxists say), you could feel the ruling forces in the West exhale. They'd been holding that in since 1917. A simple left-wing POV in media contexts was no concrete threat; it might even sell papers. This was also contemporaneous with the election of three NDP provincial governments, two of them in the substantial economies of Ontario and British Columbia. As the actual geopolitical threat declined then vanished, some space opened up.

I don't mean my arrival at the *Globe* was a dialectical result of the unfolding of History. Like everything, it was largely happenstance. The *Globe* was looking for a media columnist. A journalist there, the late Val Ross, suggested me to arts editor Katherine Ashenburg. Katherine had a trick of doing bold things as if she didn't realize they might be controversial. Thorsell went along. He'd purged most of the *Globe*'s perceived leftists (everything's relative), like June Callwood and Tom Walkom. He may have overshot. After its readership base in the business world, the *Globe* has always had an important tier of readers in the universities and the arts, who hold more progressive or, as Alexander Cockburn liked to say, pwogwessive, views. They may have been recalibrating by bringing me in. I frequently ran into people of the *vrai* left who scourged me for taking the role of token radical or beard. It also bespoke the paper's sense of grandeur: We are the *Globe*. We contain multitudes. Besides, they hardly embraced me. I was freelance for all 20 years: I submitted a column each week and in effect they decided whether to run it. No security, no benefits, no desk, and — once the heavy security arrived post-9/11 — no pass card. I had to be buzzed in.

I hesitated briefly, to no avail. A friend said, You spend all your time watching that stuff anyway and getting aggravated, you might as well be paid. In fact, for years I'd nursed a fantasy that I'd have a radio show simulcast with the national TV news. I'd tell listeners to turn on their TV but mute the sound. Then, with actors who could mimic voices of public figures, including the lugubrious anchors and journalists, we'd provide a true soundtrack to what was being (mis)represented. That's more or less what I got to do.

*

MY FIRST *GLOBE* COLUMN WAS A DEFENCE OF *FRANK* magazine, the scuzzy satirical journal that everyone in

Ottawa reviled and read. *Frank* had run a "contest" for young Tories, who were invited to "deflower" Caroline Mulroney, the prime minister's 16-year-old daughter. His popularity was at low ebb and still plunging, so he'd started bringing her to Conservative Party events, especially of the young, in order to quite blatantly boost his standing. There had been outrage among the elites over *Frank's lèse-majesté*, particularly at the *Globe*, where Thorsell was a huge Mulroney acolyte. Mulroney, like any good politician, knows how to fan those flames. If Thorsell was in an editorial meeting when Mulroney called, his secretary would come to the door and stroke her chin. Here's the column.

*

THERE IS SOMETHING IRONIC IN THE CONTROVERSY over a mock ad that appeared in *Frank*. The ad announced a Deflower Caroline contest for young Tories, including an entry blank requiring "proof of conquest." The reaction has been intense, to understate wildly. Media Watch said the ad encouraged gang rape. *Maclean's* issued a bad-taste alert. In this paper, Michael Valpy, not a big Mulroney fan, wrote that he stood shoulder to shoulder with the PM on this one, as another father with a teenage daughter. He said *Frank* was put out by dirty little boys and pronounced a journalistic hex on them, wishing them "down the tube." Even longtime *Frank*-ophiles felt similarly.

The anger is understandable. This society has only

started to challenge its routine sexual aggression toward women, and the *Frank* ad was widely read as another disgusting example. That may be *Frank*'s fault — they wrote the thing — but I'm pretty sure it wasn't their intention.

Frank does satire; it didn't mean to advocate the attitude in the ad: it meant to satirize it. Based on what? Brian Mulroney's own behaviour with his daughter this past summer. On the floor of the Tory convention in Toronto, there was Caroline, whom we'd seen little of before, always at Brian's side, where Mila used to be. When the first family 'coptered down to see the Bushes at Kennebunkport, Caroline walked beside George and Brian, with Barbara, Mila, and the boys in the rear.

Political decisions are behind such choices. Did you notice that, midway through summer, male cabinet ministers began wearing V-necks and cardigans? Wasn't that an effort to counter the impression of white men in suits running the country, by putting them in sweaters? Think about how almost all politicians utilize their families and, where applicable, their pets. In the case of Caroline's sudden prominence, had something slipped in the "Mila factor," so valuable till now? Was it those rumours of marital tension? And why replace Mila with Caroline — why not one of the boys? Was there a calculation, to offer the troops something new and distract them? Writing about these ploys is important; it helps expose the scuzzy methods used to try to control us. Sometimes you can't prove them, but they remain proper subjects for comment — and satire. Yet I saw no such discussion in the mainstream media. It fell to *Frank* to deal with the story, in its satirical fashion, by suggesting that Brian was showing his young, attractive daughter around in another desperate attempt to halt his drop in the polls. It may be a disturbing thought, for fathers and other people. But it's hardly out of bounds, especially with what's been learned lately about how children can be used by those close to them — sometimes consciously, sometimes not.

(If the press didn't notice, others did. A friend says she heard teenage boys on her street chattering with the usual male zest about those "amazing" changes in Caroline. They hadn't realized she'd grown so gorgeous, etc. My friend was so unsettled she walked her bike up the street to listen in. This was well before *Frank*'s ad.)

Frank could have made (or tried to make) the point differently without the sexual implication, as it did on its next cover. There Caroline says, "Tory wives tea? No way, Mom. I'm going to the Hard Rock!" And Mila replies, "At 12 per cent in the polls, you'll do as you're told," while dad glowers behind. That's a clearer, gentler kind of satire, the kind we're used to from the *Air Farce*. But there's a place for things that upset us. One reader said the ad was in the Swiftian tradition, because it raised questions no one wants to think about, as Swift did by proposing to solve the population problem by eating the babies of the poor.

Ours is a society that uses female sexuality to sell just about everything, from leather fashions to butter to politics to newspapers and newsmagazines. (Every issue of *Maclean's* does exactly that on its People page.) *Frank* blew it by not making that context clear in this case. (Though the antique term *deflower* — kin to *slut* in William Kempling's lexicon — was probably meant to suggest the kind of lads *Frank* pictures at Tory conventions.) If the context were clear, there might still be objections, but the point would be made. Instead, *Frank* gets attacked for the very thing it meant to attack — and Brian Mulroney and his strategists get off the hook. Sounds like a situation for . . . satire.

*

"Couldn't you have at least waited till your second column to get fired?" said my irreplaceable friend, the late Catherine Keachie, when I told her my brilliant idea for a first burst. "Now no one will even know you were there. It's your self-destructiveness again. It's always your self-destructiveness." But Thorsell let it pass and remained a supporter of the column all the time he was in charge, especially when I wrote about him. After he published a piece saying he didn't understand why journalists would want to "comfort the afflicted and afflict the comfortable" — a hoary cliché — I patiently explained that the rich (a) deserve it, (b) like it, and (c) it's the most satisfaction the rest of us are likely to get, given the distribution of power. When Brian Mulroney fell from grace and left office, then was revealed to have taken bags of money (well, envelopes) from the delightfully dubious German fixer Karlheinz Schreiber, I described Thorsell as Mulroney's "faithful retainer" no matter what befell, in contrast to Peter Newman, his faithless retainer. "This one gets you fired for sure," editors at the *Globe* told me. But Thorsell stayed staunch. "He's into grudging respect," Val Ross said. I think she was right. I think I'm into it myself.

(Besides, that column clearly pulls some of its punches while keeping a wary eye on potential harumphing from *Globe* readers or editors, whose reactions I'm trying to guesstimate as I go — but I digress.)

With this kind of platform and unwavering support from the class enemy personified (Thorsell), I couldn't really sustain the stance I'd grown comfy with: marginal outsider, voice silenced by the media gatekeepers. I'd become a classic case of what Herbert Marcuse called "repressive tolerance." My Marxist friend, John (not Ralston) Saul, said, "That bastard Thorsell will stop at nothing to shut us up — now he's even put you in his paper!"

Things had changed, but they also hadn't. The

range of views allowed in the MSM had expanded, partly due to the demise of the Cold War but also due to the impact of feminism, the assertion of minority voices, and perhaps the arc of history bending — tentatively, as always — toward freedom. Even so, today, more than 20 years later, if you're a young journalist or aspiring pundit, your chances of making a living are reasonable if you're right wing and neo-con; they remain nonexistent if you're seriously left or anarchist. You can slip your work in occasionally — that's the advance. But a steady living is out of the question. Right-wing people working in the media never seem to grasp this. Many of them have been gainfully employed writing editorials or columns since they toddled out of university; they really think it's their brilliance and not their acceptability that's decisive. A left-wing writer and researcher like Yves Engler, who's published fine books on foreign policy and the auto industry, subsidizes his research by working as the night clerk in a small Montreal hotel. It gives him lots of time to read, once the customers go to bed. It never occurs to him to try to support himself by getting a mainstream media day job — he couldn't.

So The System has opened up but also fortified itself. In the years I worked with the agonizingly collective editorial board of *This Magazine*, none of us expected any kind of pass into "the slicks" — *Maclean's*, *Saturday Night*, and their like, back when

Canada had a vigorous magazine industry. Since the Cold War ended, there's been regular movement back and forth between "alternates" like *This*, as it's now known, and the MSM. *This Mag* and others have become, effectively, a farm system. But you park your politics at the gate. Virtually none of the people who did serious time at *This Magazine* and are now employed full time in places like the *Globe and Mail* or the *New York Times* wears a left label. I'm just sayin'. By contrast, right-wingers at those and other places (the *National Post*, Sun Media) make their politics their calling card.

If anything, the politics of the mass media have shifted further right, even while they occasionally open to a wider range of dissenting views and personnel. In 1988, year of the free trade election, every daily paper in Canada but two — the *Toronto Star* and the *Edmonton Journal* — editorially supported Brian Mulroney and his wretched deal. By 2011, only one paper — the *Star* — failed to support Stephen Harper and his incomparably more right-wing agenda.

*

THE EXPERIENCE OF BEING IN THE *Globe* FELT ODD professionally. When I began writing, at the end of 1970, I resisted any professional identification. If people asked what I did, I'd say I write, not I'm a writer. What I identified with instead was left politics — as I'd identified earlier with Judaism. I saw writing chiefly as a means to serve political ends. When I lugged my first serious journalistic assignment, from *Esquire*, up to Montreal during the October Crisis of 1970, I asked left-wing journalists I met there to consider me not a journalist but a comrade. They in turn wanted only to know how to score a gig at *Esquire*.

The ambiguity persisted for years. In the mid-1970s, I lucked into contact with Kent Rowley and Madeleine Parent, Labour leaders originally from Quebec, who'd been fighting the noble fight for the working class (I say non-ironically in their case) since the 1930s. They asked if I'd like to help organize non-unionized immigrant workers at small textile factories in Toronto. It was like being tapped on the shoulder by a guardian angel. I'd returned from my student years in the U.S. as a leftist committed to the workers' cause, but unfortunately I didn't know any workers. This let me fill the gap in my résumé. For years I worked with them as a volunteer. I'd write all day — a play, article, TV script — then at four, when the factories let out, I'd get in my clunker and drive around Toronto urging workers to sign union cards. That led to strikes and arrests. I basically led two full-time work lives. Occasionally — after a horrible review, for instance — I'd ask about going on staff, and they'd say, sure, if I really wanted to, but honestly it was harder to find writers who were on their side than organizers — and I knew they had problems getting organizers. They once hired someone they were sure was a police spy, but, what the hell, he knew how to organize. (When I implied they might be paranoid after their experiences with McCarthyism, Kent said, "The trouble with people like you is you'll never admit anyone you know could be an agent." It had the ring of truth.)

I dove into cultural politics too, as a founder and early president of the national playwrights' union or campaigning against cuts to arts funding — it all seemed part of making the Canadian revolution, a notion that didn't sound (too) weird then. Even in *Harper's*, where the article commissioned by *Esquire* eventually ran, I used that kind of language. The editors on Madison Avenue never winced.

In the late 1980s, I pretty much vanished down the maw of the fight against free trade with the U.S. It combined the varieties of politics I'd been doing in a national coalition of farmers, unions, artists, and more. I wrote a lengthy pamphlet that cartoonist Terry Mosher (Aislin), whom I'd met on that first trip to Montreal, illustrated. The coalition printed millions of copies that ran in dailies across Canada during the 1988 election campaign. It had enough impact to help temporarily turn the tide against Mulroney's deal — along with a virtuoso debate performance by Liberal leader John Turner. It was the kind of electoral politics that I'd always scorned as shallow and diversionary. By then I also had a contract to write a book on that election. That was coincidental, based on a long-standing yen to do an election book in which I'd reveal the deeply undemocratic nature of elections: its title was *Waiting for Democracy*. Now I was part of the beast I was planning to pitilessly expose. When we lost the election and the deal went through, I felt devastated — surely our country would perish and be devoured by the U.S. — yet exhilarated by a kind of engagement in conventional public life that I'd thought could never be mine.

Then, suddenly, I'd become a writer, full stop, for the Canadian establishment's pet newspaper yet. I'd gone from communist to columnist.

A year into the gig, in 1992, the Charlottetown Accord referendum unfurled. Mulroney had moved on from free trade to pressuring Quebec into signing the Canadian Constitution. Pierre Trudeau repatriated it in 1982, but Quebec, under a separatist government, declined to join. Perhaps Mulroney felt it was his way to eclipse Trudeau. But his first effort, the so-called Meech Lake Accord, failed after a national trauma and Trudeau's intervention. Next came "the Canada round." Premiers met obsessively, ignoring all else, to bash out an agreement that everyone, including Quebec and Native peoples, could buy into. Their final session was staged in Charlottetown, cradle of the original Confederation deal. I happened to be there that week and saw them wandering around town, clearly visioning themselves as Fathers of Confederation. Since the Meech fiasco had been criticized for excluding the *vox populi* — like the original version of Confederation, come to think of it — they proclaimed a national referendum, after they'd stitched together the text's final version.

If this isn't ringing a bell, it's because that referendum has vanished so far down the memory hole you can't find the original entry point or any traces. Free trade and Meech Lake still surface occasionally. The disappearance of Charlottetown is a clue that something great and inspirational probably happened there and mustn't ever be allowed to recur. This is the first of many columns I wrote on it. I couldn't stop, week after week. It might seem tenuously related to media, which was my brief at the *Globe*, but by then I'd decided to deal with anything, as long as it had received a mention sometime, somewhere in a media outlet: papers, magazines, TV, pop music, ads.

*

IT MAY SEEM IMPLAUSIBLE, BUT I THINK I'VE uncovered a huge referendum story not reported in the media. There is no No side! At least not outside Quebec and not in the sense that there's a Yes side.

In Quebec you have two sides relatively balanced between the main parties, along with a referendum law that strictly controls both. But the referendum law passed by the federal government for the rest of Canada has no spending limits and almost anything goes.

Now compare the sides. For the Yes side, every government down to territorial level; all three national parties; virtually every newspaper and business group; even labour! Plus the entire throw weight of respectable opinion or, as columnist Dalton Camp says, "almost everybody who is anybody." Camp calls Yes "the side of all the good people." He notes that "presidents of the chartered banks have been summoned to do their duty," while Peter Newman has sent a "dunning letter" to members of the Order of Canada, paid for by our governor general.

Over in the other corner, you have . . . um . . . You see the problem. Rage in the streets? Inchoate popular resistance? Rabble in arms? There are a few identifiable leaders — Preston Manning, Judy Rebick, Deborah Coyne — but they're not really members of the club. Pierre Trudeau is the only certifiable establishment man in the lot.

What is the sound of one side campaigning? Watch some TV. I don't mean the news; I mean TV. Last weekend I could barely spot the baseball and football among the syrupy government ads for national unity: Olympic athletes hugging, Canadian soldiers keeping peace. Those don't even count as Yes propaganda. Nor do the "neutral" referendum spots explaining, "These proposals reflect the needs and aspirations of every one of us. It's for you to judge" — as sun shimmers on a lake and a heavenly choir sings. Tuesday we got the first of more than five million dollars' worth of ads from the official Yes committee, an "independent" body run by a consortium of party hacks. (Of course there isn't a No committee.) Everyone watching TV will see an average of 13 such ads next week. There are also secret daily polls and focus groups done for governments and paid for by us.

There will be no paid national No ads on TV. Zero. The Reform Party will run some ads in the free 90 minutes given each side. As for newspapers, I saw a teeny ad from the National Action Committee on the Status of Women begging people to send a few bucks. Coverage more or less reflects this. Last Saturday's *Globe* had a healthy swatch of stories about the Yesses, and one forlorn item on some No's criticizing those Yes ads. None of this inhibits the Yesses from snivelling about what underdogs they are ("Now it's our turn," said NDPer Gerry Caplan), which the press reports without even raising a brow.

Of course coverage is a problem. The media are geared to deal with elites, with respectable figureheads for parties and organizations, or with experts. When those types are almost all on one side, what do you do? During Meech, CBC News tried to solve the problem, its boss said, by interviewing (skeptical Newfoundland Premier) Clyde Wells 69 times. Now even Clyde is onside, sort of. So there's already a repetitive sense of figures like Manning, Coyne, and, as Jeffrey Simpson wrote, "the ubiquitous Judy Rebick." I don't really think Rebick is in more places than she used to be; it's the media who seek her out. It's not her fault that all the "somebodies" are jostling for space over on the Yes side.

Anyway, trying to find leaders for the No and otherwise equating it to the Yes — even in the holy name of balance — just conceals the real story. The Yes was negotiated by an elite behind closed doors, who then stepped outside and asked everyone else to ratify their deal. The No "side" is a kind of angry resistance from below. A few people give it voice, but it really signals a whole different force in politics. It's hard to report this kind of popular resistance and maybe harder to face. The *Globe*'s Robert Sheppard brooded, "What happens if . . . the considered compromises of elected representatives are tossed aside by a relatively uninformed mob?" I think it was awfully generous of him to say "relatively," but he still conveys a deep sense of threat to the status quo in both journalism and politics.

Back in the days of radio before TV, comics Wayne and Shuster used to broadcast a yearly hockey game between the Toronto Maple Leafs — a mighty puck power then, I swear — and the Mimico Mice. The Leafs always won 99-1. The Mice scored their goal between periods, before the Leafs skated back on. That's how I see the referendum "sides," except that, amazingly, the game is more or less tied better than halfway through. But nobody knows if the No people will hang on through the one-sided media storm yet to come — from a Yes side confident it has the money and techniques to turn anything around — and only the Mimico Mice to beat.

*

WHEN THE REFERENDUM WAS CALLED, MOST OF the punditry — among whom I now dwelled — said it would pass unnoticed since citizens were suffering from "constitution fatigue." Instead, Canadians plunged in, as they had with free trade but without the distraction of an election attached. This was an up/down vote on one fateful proposal. I'd see them reading material on the subway; callers to talk shows were shockingly well informed. They asked in detail about implications for the senate or why a clause about restraining inflation was even in there (hint: the banks did it). By the weekend before the vote, they were phoning each other, asking if anyone knew a constitutional lawyer, and cancelling social events to do last-minute cramming. I saw a cashier check out groceries with one hand while reading a pamphlet in the other. People entered the polling booth still undecided, sometimes sobbing. What was that about? They'd been handed responsibility for an actual decision concerning their country, instead of surrendering it to representatives who ignored them between elections. It weighed on them and they welcomed it.

The outcome was a defeat for everyone who counted. Most provinces voted no, including Quebec and the Native peoples for whom it was tailored. Ontario barely supported it, and the Blue Jays were in the process of winning a World Series there, so yes was on everyone's lips. It had strong support only in Atlantic Canada. It proved you could hold a popular debate on a complex issue and reach a decision that no one except the spurned elites were bitter about. You could bypass the representative system or at least move beyond it after it articulated the issue. Of course it was never mentioned or tried again.

It was my first political action as a mere writer, unaligned with any constituency: no groups, coalitions, comrades. It hadn't much to do with left or right and suggested those categories don't encompass all causes and needn't subtend every debate. Wow — there could be politics after the Cold War. Other factors persist, like the simple human impulse to confront forces that affect our lives and affect them back. Win or lose, human beings want to show up and make their voices heard, to transcend their narrow, particular lives and everyday concerns. Everybody seeks transcendence. It can take the form of mind melding with a hockey team, a TV series, or a band. And even when it's explicitly about politics, you don't need an ideology to guide you through it, though many of us had lived in, and were coming out the other end of, an exhaustingly ideological epoch. Charlottetown was political but not ideological. It felt like living back before that moment in the French

Revolution when left and right took their places to either side of the Speaker in the National Assembly.

You didn't need to be on the left to feel disoriented by the new dispensation. My favourite nemesis on the right was Barbara Amiel. This is from 1992, in the early afterwash of the post–Cold War.

*

MACLEAN'S HUMOUR COLUMNIST BARBARA AMIEL was in rare form last week. She'd just been in Davos, Switzerland, where "groups of distinguished people" gathered "by invitation only" for the World Economic Forum. Mostly, she wrote, leaders of poor countries pleaded with "Western businessmen" to "please come to the disaster areas of the world and make them work." Like they've made New York City or Washington, D.C., work, I guess. Nelson Mandela was there; Amiel thought he was "a bit past things" — which sounds not too bad for someone locked up inside Robben Island and other sinkholes for 26 years. In Davos, people could "lie on their tummies in the sun or wander about the mountains yodelling" while begging for investment. But Amiel seized that bucolic moment to lambaste the only two places in the world where "scientific socialism has still got a gun at the throats of the economy." One is South Africa where, last I heard, capitalism remained discernible; the other, and I'll need a drum roll for this, is Ontario, where [then NDP premier who after being defeated in the 1995 election left the NDP and joined the Liberal Party] Bob Rae "is introducing economic communism."

See, there are these proposed amendments to the provincial labour act. The most drastic — banning scab workers — has been law for 15 years in Quebec, where Premier Robert Bourassa and the new entrepreneurs we hear so much about seem happy enough with it. Another amendment aims to close a loophole so that immigrant women cleaning office buildings or working in cafeterias will acquire exactly the same successor rights that all other workers in all other sectors already have. Amiel says this means "the free market would become an anachronism." She talked to a "prominent Canadian banker" who actually spoke "jovially" about Rae. "He's scared stiff and we're able to tell him what's wrong. We can't let Ontario drown" — a spineless view from which Amiel dissented. She's willing to bet that under Rae, Ontario's laws "will increasingly be replaced by the coercive structures of communism." In no time, the only way Ontario will differ from "the old Soviet Union" — presumably Stalin's — will be in the "degree of cruelty and repression." That degree part isn't very comforting. Are we talking Lubyanka Prison but no gulags? Gulags but no show trials?

The same day my *Maclean's* arrived with Amiel's column, the *Globe* ran a story on the Ontario government headed "NDP Seeks New Image as Tight-Fisted Managers" — even though this refit, the article went on, will likely "anger party supporters." ("With socialists like this," NDP militants already grumble, "who needs capitalists?") Next day came news that the province will exempt dozens of doctors from the "controversial" $400,000 cap on billings. As for Rae himself, this is the left-wing leader who shrank from public auto insurance — something not even [very right-wing Conservative Premiers] Sterling Lyon or Bill Vander Zalm renounced. Rae still hasn't brought in a minimum tax on corporations, as per his election platform. Something must account for the gulf between the Ontario government's dank reality and Amiel's images of it. I have a theory.

She is suffering a severe case of communism withdrawal. Like many journalists and pundits, Amiel was heavily hooked on the red menace. She uncovered it everywhere; her career is largely constructed on a relentless attack against it. The sudden, total collapse of the Soviet empire and its cognates caught these people entirely by surprise. They felt victorious and vindicated, but they had also become serious addicts. When their supply dried up, their habit didn't. They have coped in various ways. Peter Worthington says the collapse of communism left him stunned. Lubor Zink tried to pretend it hadn't happened. George Will acknowledges a gap in his life. But perhaps Amiel's habit was heavier than the rest. Imagine.

She awakens every day and the fix is no longer there. She has delusions and hallucinations. Political delirium tremens. The ideological shakes. She's wired. She stares at the wall, she sees Bob Rae — and thinks it's Bob Che.

Or maybe for her, this is the cure. You can't just go Cold War cold turkey. Bob Rae as methadone. Bring you down. Keep you straight. It could work. Bob Rae: diplomat's son, privately schooled, the socialist who, for his TV speech, looked like [former Ontario Conservative premier] Bill Davis after a facelift and a stint on the fat farm.

Not just anyone will serve. Amiel met British Columbia's NDP leader, Mike Harcourt, in Davos, for instance. He was so cuddly and "business friendly" that she's thinking about buying some provincial bonds. But Harcourt's stance as a socialist is, more or less, "I never promised you anything so don't complain." Rae, on the other hand, says, "I wish I could do something but I can't." That suggests a margin of conscience, a twinge of left-wing guilt. Not much but enough, perhaps, for Barbara Amiel to slake her desperate need.

*

So LEFT AND RIGHT CONTINUED A GHOSTLIKE existence after the Cold War, like phantom limbs, as if their absence was unthinkable, and not just by ideology junkies. Dichotomies satisfy a primal urge. Manichaeism was the ideology of an earlier Cold War. I have no idea whether dualism can eventually be obliterated the way polio was — even it's made a comeback.

But the sides could never look the same. That's because in the "final conflict" anticipated by Marxists between capitalism and socialism, global capitalism simply declared victory. It wasn't so much that it won, as that there was no one left (or no one left, left) to contest the claim. Not on the face of things anyway. Maybe, as Marx said, the old mole continued to burrow away in places like South America. But where we were, economic debate more or less fell off the table, at least until the collapse of 2008.

It was replaced by a vapid non-debate over unsubstantive issues. I first noticed it when I travelled with the leaders' campaigns during the '88 election. Each policy announcement was immediately trumped by questions from reporters on how the programs would be paid for. Deficits and balanced budgets leapt from relative obscurity to front rank status. Journalists themselves didn't seem to know where it came from. They just suddenly acquired the lingo, as if they'd been vaccinated while sleeping. It is now so ingrained that it feels like one of those things that had no beginning and will have no end.

This is from 1993.

*

THE DEFICIT DEBATE HAS ALWAYS HAD A theological quality. Statements are made without evidence or any idea of what would count as evidence.

Blind faith that cutting the deficit will create jobs, for instance. Or that job-training programs will miraculously lead to jobs. Or the unproven credo that government borrowing "squeezes out" business loans. Politicians, economists, and journalists mouth these like a catechism. "Finding the right balance between economic progress and human welfare remains at the heart of Canadian politics," wrote one pundit last week. This has the obscure and paradoxical quality of true dogma. Since when are economic progress and human welfare opposed categories? They write, as Augustine believed, because it is absurd. Heretics like former chief economist of the TD Bank Doug Peters, who says only economic growth will heal the deficit, are disappeared from official view like schismatics in the medieval church. . . .

The religious element lacking till now was a good old-fashioned revival on the deficit, but *Maclean's* and CTV's *W5* jointly produced one last week. They brought a "cross-section" of Canadians to a resort on Lake Simcoe. It included no one who did manual labour and no one from the resource sector or manufacturing. Maybe they were leaving it to a deficit holy roller like Diane Francis at the *Financial Post* to stage a down-market tent meeting. The "imperative" of deficit elimination was assumed as an article of faith. No infidels, like the unemployed welder who told a TV reporter, "To be honest I could care less about it; I gotta put food on the table," need apply.

The group had two days to concoct a plan to eliminate the deficit, with help from professional facilitators and economists. By noon of day two, with just hours to go, a cutting frenzy began. The facilitators pushed hard, calling out areas of expenditure and asking people to take the pledge: who'll cut old age security for those over $40,000? Who'll go to 30? to 20? "Put up your hand if you agree," barked one near the end, just the way Oral Roberts would implore his congregation, impatience and disapproval implied in her voice. Finally they agreed to a nasty package of cuts. Cheery music played as they paraded up to accept Christ — I mean, sign the plan. Even the economists seemed appalled. Carl Beigie from the C.D. Howe Institute, which hit the down beat for the current deficit mania, called the scheme total insanity. International development specialist Leigh Anderson said at best the cuts would make a dent; at worst they'd shatter the economy. A small price with eternal souls at stake.

*

SNIPING AT MEDIA, ESPECIALLY THE *GLOBE* ITSELF, was always part of the column. I'd been given a kind of special dispensation for it. Papers normally discourage journalists from pissing contests with their competitors — and definitely not among their own writers. They tell you readers aren't interested in internal bickering, it's "self-indulgent" — though I think that stuff fascinates everybody. It's like watching family dinners blow up. Maybe the *Globe* thought once I was invited inside, I'd be grateful and polite — which I tried to be. You don't speak the same way in someone's living room as you would yelling at them from across the street, even if you're making a similar point. But they couldn't claim surprise since my attacks on media — and them in particular — was why they hired me. So no one ever told me to stop. The only censorship — more like censoriousness — came when I criticized reviewers and reviewing. I incurred no scowls when I criticized the pope, the prime minister, the *Globe*'s own editorials, or its editor. But I was in the arts section, and they saw themselves as patrons of the arts. They disliked being labelled as cultural sadists. When I impugned the value of book reviews, they suggested I might not want to revisit that. When I wrote part two a week later, they demoted me from the front of the section to an inside page, the only time anything so visceral happened in my time there.

Victories for whatever could now be called the left were scarce in those years. One occurred during the battle of Dooney's Café, from 1996 to 1997. If I'm about to dwell on it lovingly, that's because it sometimes felt like global capitalism's only definitive setback during the decade. Here's the first of many columns on it.

*

I was at Dooney's on Bloor Street West Wednesday morning. John Barber's column in the *Globe and Mail* that day revealed that the bistro had, without warning, been leased out from under its long-time proprietor, Graziano Marchese, to Starbucks. The mood on the patio ran from despair to anger, with anger predominating. A student crew from Ryerson University's journalism school was doing a TV assignment there. They asked for an interview. The first question was, "Would you explain why closing this place is such a tragedy?" I think I grimaced. Maybe as future journalists they expect to cover only global disasters like Bosnia or Hurricane Fran, so they sound a little snide about the loss of a local café. I said something to that effect, and then tried to explain, tragedy or no, what many people feel.

I said we all deserve places in our lives where we can go and be comfortable, other than our homes, and where we can be welcomed by others, other than our family — and I knew I was on the verge of humming, "Where everybody knows your name." For many people today, that's such an alien prospect that, to describe it, you have to mention *Cheers*, the TV bar from the song. Where do you think all the family values mania comes from? I asked. If there's no place in the world that feels like home except, literally, home, then people like (U.S. Republican presidential candidate) Bob Dole will become hysterical about protecting it. People deserve to feel at home in more places than their mailing address. That's what a local like Dooney's provides. Good luck finding that in a Starbucks. I thought they'd snicker, but the interviewer said, "It really does sound kind of tragic."

I had this *Cheers* discussion with kids once before, at a high school deep in suburbia. I thought when they moved downtown, they too could have neighbourhood institutions. But now they're at university, and with chains like Starbucks everywhere, their sense of community is still based on *Cheers*. Even then it was vicarious: thinking you had a place where everybody knows your name, because you saw it on TV. Now *Cheers* comes only in reruns: the hair and clothing already look dated, so it's not only a vicarious and mildly psychotic experience; it's retro too.

I admit a small personal bias. A close friend, describing how I reacted to the Dooney's news, said it's "as if somebody was going to tear off his living room." But it's amazing, given the disintegration of community in our time, how communal the reaction has been. There are posters up and down Bloor. Local kids were chalking the corner with a star and a dollar sign and a "no-go" slash across them. An articling student offered to work free with the legal team. A massage therapist said she felt like blowing some of those Starbucks up. A teacher said they do not make a better cup of coffee than Dooney's, John Barber's judgement notwithstanding.

It isn't Starbucks' fault that it represents everything contrived and commercial that a real community isn't, that it's about being inside an image, rather than a real place. The very name comes from the coffee-drinking first mate in *Moby-Dick* — like something made up by people who took American lit in the 1970s and had a cat called Melville. CEO Howard Schultz told the *New York Times* that Starbucks is "aiming to introduce a European concept of coffee culture." Well, you don't need to introduce coffee culture to Borden and Bloor. You go into Dooney's, order an espresso, and sit there. It's not Disney World; you don't take a little train and get off at Eurocoffeeland. Do we ever get to have anything real, instead of a corporatized version of what used to actually exist somewhere in the world? And where it still exists, like Dooney's, does it have to be destroyed in order to "introduce" an imitation?

At Starbucks, they have coffee "cuppings," like wine tastings. More image. For what? A cup of coffee? (And by the way, I adore coffee. I had a defining moment on an Air Canada flight descending into Milan where they wake you for breakfast two hours after supper to pour some sludge in your cup, and I raised my hand and said, "No! In 30 minutes I will be in coffee heaven!") Starbucks' Toronto man, Roly Morris, says, "We're offering a lifestyle product." Poor Graz. All he put into Dooney's was a life.

When his lawyer, Brian Shiller, asked if he could

come down to Dooney's wearing jeans to discuss the case, Graz said, "You can wear anything you want, but I'd like you to bring a little compassion." You aren't going to get that out of the 24 hours of training Starbucks gives its "baristas." Hospitality isn't a course he took; it's what he decided he wanted to contribute to the part of the world he has a chance to make a difference in. Think about the "hospitality industry" and all the kids who "take" it in college. What a weird phrase: *the hospitality industry.*

Barbara Crooks, a British Columbia journalist visiting Toronto, says she goes to her Starbucks in Vancouver each day, and they know her, say hi, get her regular order ready. Hey, if that's what you've got to add a little grace to your day, it's better than a kick in the teeth and a cup of brown water. But do we all have to make do with a have-a-nice-day from whoever's stationed by the door on that shift — from people called baristas? At Dooney's the help are called Petra, Dominic, and Suzanne.

The man who sold to Starbucks is landlord John Hix, who had a free lunch at Dooney's almost every day for nine years and, says Starbucks, approached them — without giving Graz a true chance to negotiate a new lease or match the offer. Hix is an architect with a big reputation for concern about community and environment. Go figure. He's not returning calls, but his wife, Neeva Gayle Hix, says, "We love Graziano. . . . I believe totally in love and support him in this. . . . We have a heart and you'd be surprised at what a heart Starbucks has too." This is the dregs of the 1960s love-and-peace vocabulary, a sad dénouement to that era, where only the words survive and nailing a big tenant is what counts.

And what about others, from the 1960s and elsewhere? Are we reduced to protesting about coffee? Was that part of the snide reaction of the student film crew? On the other hand, there once was minor local protest against distant power called — the Boston Tea Party. A Toronto Coffee Party? Dare to dream.

*

It was the only time Starbucks backed down anywhere on the planet. Their normal m.o. when entering a new market like Toronto was to cruise neighbourhoods and pinpoint the best locations, buy the leases up from under the tenants, and start making money. They didn't know what hit them. The Friday after the news broke, all three Toronto dailies (Toronto now has four that are reasonably distinct: the *Globe*, *Star*, *Sun*, and *Post*; it gives us a false sense of diversity compared to every other city in North America) ran columns denouncing the takeover, each written by a Dooney's regular.

They picked on the wrong bistro. That weekend other Starbucks locations were picketed by the newly constituted Friends of Dooney's. A number of patrons had been union organizers or political staff for mayors and premiers. They knew how to rattle the cages. Starbucks mobilized their PR firms in turn and ran a full-page ad saying they were shocked to discover they'd accidentally torpedoed a "beloved community institution." Shocked! They would work tirelessly to undo the utterly unintended harm.

The manoeuvring and positioning began. It lasted nine months. It was insufficient for Starbucks to back out of their lease; they had to make sure the landlord, a malevolent force on his own though lacking global clout, wouldn't still boot Dooney's, which was at the end of its lease. So Starbucks had to maintain the lease and sublet back to Dooney's, in order to salvage a benign image during their move into Toronto. The landlord, for whatever buried reasons, sued Starbucks to prevent that. Starbucks brought their legal staff from Seattle and hired the highest-end Toronto real estate lawyers available to win the right to let Dooney's keep serving lattes to what they'd viewed as potential Starbucks customers. Eventually, after a 4-day trial, the judge upheld their right to sublet in a 49-page decision. The day it came out, the café looked like a law library. Every table had its copy, with people poring through it and highlighting phrases.

I had liaised with the president of Starbucks Canada and said if he followed through on his noble promises, I'd buy him a drink when it was over. I had Churchill's "In victory: magnanimity" in mind. When we met, at the rooftop bar of the Park Plaza, he said what everyone at coffee HQ wanted to know was, "Is it safe to go back to Bloor Street?" The Friends of Dooney's had terrorized them. His team felt if they hadn't managed to restore Dooney's, they'd have been pursued to the ends of the earth and beyond the grave. Graz, the *patron*, subsequently became godfather of my first and only kid in 1998; they go fishing at our cottage every summer. I'm not allowed in the boat because I don't take it seriously enough. Graz kept Dooney's going for ten years; then when rents on Bloor went even further through the roof, he opened another place in the hood for a while. As we speak, he's preparing to start up a new bistro, farther west on Bloor. He wants to know if it's okay to call it Dooney's. Of course it is. There are former regulars still careening through the streets up there, hollow-eyed and zombielike, looking for the only real home they had.

What replaced the red meat of left/right politics, aside from shitty little shootouts like Starbucks versus Dooney's? Personal stuff basically.

Writers who might have engaged in the past with political parties or movements, signed on instead for PEN International, the writers' free speech organization; Amnesty International; or Doctors Without Borders. They joined general human rights campaigns in the name of anti-racism, feminism, or gender equity. These aren't class conflicts in the old sense, but they aren't merely individual pursuits; they mobilize collectivities and act as pressure groups or constituencies that are part of civil society — another term that emerged suddenly one day, full blown. There was nothing wrong with any of those causes, but it feels as if something got abandoned. I think it was the engagement with the raw economic and social forces that mangle lives everywhere. It's comparable to the Clinton-Lewinsky scandal in the U.S. in those years: an affair involving some kissy-face in the White House plus an unconsummated blow job. It led to Clinton's impeachment by Congress and then his acquittal. I thought it was the only real accomplishment of Clinton's presidency: he took on four hundred years of American sexual puritanism and prevailed. He survived in office and his reputation survived. That was historic. Puritanical attitudes impede human progress and ravage lives over many generations. Battling them matters. In retrospect, Clinton's persistence through the Lewinsky scandal paved the way for important changes in gender attitudes a decade later — acceptance of gay marriage even in the U.S., a lesbian premier of *Ontario* — and yet . . . yet what? Something had gone missing in politics: that raw part, the confrontation based on who holds economic power. The Marxist formulation of it had been class struggle, RIP. You couldn't go back, and you didn't know how to move forward.

Something else slipped away while I wasn't looking — Canadian nationalism. It was so fresh and invigorating when I returned from my years in the U.S. It gave me someone to be. I had a conversion experience that I wrote about for Canadians, on CBC Radio, and Americans, in *Harper's*. It jogged everything into a perspective that was adaptable to almost any issue. It located me, and others like me, in a happy confrontation with tired old "continentalists."

It was multifarious. You could be a cultural nationalist as I was — demanding respect for our own work rather than subservience to foreign authors and to institutions like the Stratford Festival. Or you could be an economic nationalist calling for Canadian ownership rather than American corporate exploiters. If there weren't Canadian capitalists ready to do the job, then public ownership was the inevitable default position. You could even be a labour nationalist: we were the only country in the world with branch plant unions! I ploughed all these fields both as participant and writer. Its high point and greatest defeat was that tumultuous free trade election in 1988.

The point about a phenomenon like the Canadian nationalism of the late 20th century isn't whether it was right or wrong; it may have been both. But it was also of a time, and in politics that matters. To implement your beliefs, you need to find others with whom you can act. If they aren't there, you can try to recruit them, but then you may have to become a proselytizer. Some of us aren't comfortable doing that, and anyway, it doesn't make for healthy political movements. To act politically, it's best to find a way of being in tune with your times, even while those times keep changing as new generations arrive.

This is from 1996.

*

THEATRE DIRECTOR CLARKE ROGERS DIED SUDDENLY, as they say in the obits, last week. He killed himself at his home in Flesherton, Ontario. A memorial service was held at Theatre Passe Muraille in Toronto, where Rogers was artistic director from 1982 to 1988. The theatre, an amiable space with a gallery and bar incorporated in the audience area, overflowed. Writers, actors, and others who'd worked with Rogers talked about him and played scenes from shows he'd worked on. A striking thing about the event, it seems to me, was that it was not like *The Big Chill.*

No one flew in for the occasion, back from a big career in New York, London, or Hollywood. The people onstage were accomplished and skilled, but, like Clarke Rogers, they were still here. Many were as good as artists you'd find anywhere in the world and some were better, but they lacked the surface signs of success in our culture: celebrity, wealth, global fame. In this way, Rogers's frustration about his own career in middle age probably mirrored that of many contemporaries — though I don't mean to say that's what "caused" his death; speculating on reasons for suicide is, from what I've seen, pointless.

This is a generation of theatre people, now mostly

in their 40s and 50s, who have been widely accused of cultural nationalism. They liked to do plays written by Canadians, often set in Canada, on Canadian subjects, and acted in Canadian (as opposed to British, American, or indeterminate) voices. Looking back, in the light cast by last Sunday's memorial, it seems to me there's a more personal way to describe what they were out to do.

They were artists who insisted on the right to define the experience they were going to express rather than having it defined for them by others. This may seem self-evident, but it's not. All dramatic art attempts to express human experience. But in the Canada of the 1950s and early 1960s, the experience being expressed was often that of Shakespearean or Shavian England. Modern scripts might be by Americans such as Eugene O'Neill, Arthur Miller, or Sam Shepard. The Rogers generation said, "We'd like to express our own experience, please." It was less about nationalism than self-respect, modest pride, maybe self-interestedness. If that seems outdated, think of whose vision many Canadian theatre artists are now expected to express: Andrew Lloyd Webber's, whatever the hell his reality consists of.

What happened to this generation and its vision? Under what you might consider normal development, they'd have moved up from the alternative or experimental theatres to established institutions like Stratford and the big regional companies. They'd staff, run, and program those places. They would, in other words, become the new establishment. Along the way, they'd modify and soften their demands, incorporate pieces of the loathed past, and in general compromise. Meanwhile, a new generation of artists would emerge, disdainful of this nationalist/conservative establishment, whom they'd challenge and eventually replace. Everyone would be able to remain in theatre and pursue their vision — or sell it out — in their own good time. This matters because as people in theatre get older, they inevitably find themselves tired, as one actor I knew said in the 1970s, "of not having real furniture."

None of this came to pass. The directors at the little theatres weren't allowed to take over the big ones. The actors and writers didn't become a new establishment. They drifted out of theatre and into radio, TV, film, or teaching. The actors worked at Stratford and Shaw, on regional stages or in the U.S., and in TV and film. Many continued to do "Canadian" work when they could find and afford it, usually at the same small stages where they'd begun. Actors such as Saul Rubinek and Maury Chaykin, for instance, built careers doing secondary parts in American films but kept homes here as well and are always planning drama projects based on their roots. What's remarkable about the whole group, I think, is how undisillusioned they are with that past and how they'd still love to be carrying on its tradition.

Probably everyone is required to compromise as they live their lives, but there are different kinds of compromise. It's one thing to be asked to water down your original vision; it's another to be pressed to abandon it. For Rogers's generation, compromise was especially difficult. If your notion of your art has to do with a kind of local control over its content, giving up that element won't be easy on you. Rogers may have been specially unsuited to that compromise. Among those who insisted on defining their reality themselves and not taking it from elsewhere, he was even more so.

There's now another generation of youthful theatre artists in their 20s and 30s, often working in spaces even smaller and more alternative than those of 25 years ago. Some already feel the call of real furniture and wonder how long they can afford to continue. Though they share the aim of defining the reality they're going to depict, they sometimes express an apt contempt for the old nationalists of Canadian theatre. I think it's too bad for everyone that the old nationalists can be hard to find and don't provide the kind of complacent, successful targets that artists on the rise deserve to have in their sights.

It's true the Canadian cultural nationalism of that era expressed itself in other realms in which it seems to have won more lasting success: fiction, poetry, music, film. I think that's because, as novelist Graeme Gibson once theorized, theatre needs a very high level of social or national maturity to sustain it. Those other forms can survive privately; the product lingers on a shelf even as its society wanes or dies. But theatre exists only in the living presence of an audience, which will be provided only by a confident or searching society or, at any rate, by a society with some collective sense of its unity and its need. Without that, theatre gasps for breath, at best.

*

THE LUMINOUS ACTOR AND PLAYWRIGHT LINDA Griffiths, who'd been tempted by a U.S. film career that was offered to her on a platter, told me that she recalled making that decision consciously: to stay here and pursue a waning vision. The strangest part, she said, was she knew her choice would lead to a diminished career, yet she made it anyway. It was a case of embracing her fate. The same thing was happening with Quebec nationalism, which slightly predated ours and slightly outlasted it. Its high point was probably the 1995 referendum on Quebec independence, lost by an infinitesimal margin. Of course it lingered on, like the English-Canadian version, and both may at some point revive. The deaths of causes are often declared prematurely. But the sign of a political passing in the short run is this: what had been pulsing and urgent in your own experience has become an object of historical study and curiosity to others. You know it's over when they ask if they can interview you about it.

10

THE *GLOBE* YEARS: OP-ED, 1999–2010

IN 1999 I MOVED FROM THE *Globe*'s ARTS SECTION TO the op-ed page. The newspaper war was on: Conrad Black had started up the *National Post*, in direct competition to the *Globe*. Some long-time *Globe* people, like Thorsell and Margaret Wente, who was in a management position then, talked as if they'd be delighted were Black to buy the *Globe* or bring it to heel. The *Globe* imported a new publisher, Phillip Crawley, who came from the no-hostages environment of the British dailies. He replaced a former Green Beret from the U.S., Roger Parkinson, who'd clearly been too mild-mannered. Crawley struck a Churchillian note, saying any *Globe* employees caught consorting with the enemy would be exiled or executed — something grim. He had the unbelieving mien of Rocket Richard when he learned hockey players of a later generation actually socialized with members of opposing teams. As John Cruickshank, who became publisher at the *Star* but back then was still chafing under the Conrad yoke, says, Phillip was a great wartime publisher.

I'd become a first-time dad a year earlier. I was also awaiting a cardiac bypass after some tense nights alone at the cottage that summer with angina. It was complicated. This is the first column I wrote in the new space.

*

SO HERE I AM. OP-ED AT LAST.

For eight years I've written a weekly column on media for the *Globe and Mail*'s arts and entertainment section — the pansy patch, as it was sometimes known at the paper. It was an interesting time to do so since it coincided with the latest phase in what I think of as the Great Reversal of the last half of the 20th century: between politics and culture.

Fifty years ago, a hearty band of artists went before the Massey Commission on the arts. They bewailed Canada as a wasteland of hockey-besotted, beer-swilling Philistines — a word you don't hear today. Arts eminence Mavor Moore, now 80 and writing an opera, was part of that group. He says that, into his 50s, his family still asked when he planned to get a real job. But last week in Victoria, I ran into Tony Penikett, who used to write stage and television scripts but went into politics and became premier of the Yukon from 1985 to 1992. He says that throughout the time he headed a government, his mother asked when he planned to get a real job. If he'd been a best-selling author or news anchor, she'd have been fine with it. In fact, if you want to date the Great Reversal, you might place it in 1968, when U.S. President Lyndon Johnson announced he was quitting because newscaster Walter Cronkite said he should.

TV major-domo Moses Znaimer recalls that in grade school in Montreal in the 1950s, poet Irving Layton came to his class and wrote on the board "99.9999 . . . per cent of people are Philistines." And Irving Layton was a successful writer. This fall, his son, David, got almost as much attention for his first book — about being the son of Irving Layton, the poet — as his father got in his whole career. It's a world we never made, Irving. Newsmagazines, which used to place culture on the cover once in a dog's age, now routinely put the latest mediocre movie there. Local TV newscasts spend more time on bar bands than politics.

Last week on the University of Victoria campus, a grad student stopped me and asked what I'd be saying in a lecture that had been advertised. I laboured to explain my ponderous thesis about the Great Reversal between politics and culture. "Oh yeah," he cut in, "the postmodernism thing." To me, it's a mystery; to his generation, it's already a cliché. I mean, who in their early 30s wouldn't rather be Evan

Solomon (the TV host) than Bernard Lord (the New Brunswick premier)?

I don't mean to do a reverse whine on the new prevalence of culture and the decline of politics, though I suppose it comes in the cursed category of getting what you wish for. Those artists who went before the Massey Commission actually believed a mountain of culture would save and civilize our society. I'm just pointing out that the switch happened and was in its way as unexpected as the demise of the Soviet Union or the end of apartheid.

So TV's Adrienne Clarkson is now Canada's governor general. Vincent Massey, of the Massey Commission, was also a governor general, but he came from a political family that patronized culture. Adrienne Clarkson is culture itself. Maybe that's why it looks so muddled and peculiar to see her interviewed on TV. You can't interview her: she's interviewed too many million people herself. You keep expecting her to tell the camera to widen the shot or move closer. You have to do something else with her on TV. I don't know what, but something.

Or take the appointment of a new CBC president this week. Why does anyone care? CBC is a small player today in a mondo-channel universe, most of it private. But we live in a time when politics has abdicated its role of providing a sense of national reality. Our leaders say there's little they can do; we're adrift in the fickle currents of global commerce and capital flows. So people seek a sense of public things elsewhere, in a cultural institution such as the CBC, which can stand in as evidence that Canada still exists. I'd even say this helps explain the wide resistance to Onex's attempted takeover of Air Canada, and it must drive Gerry Schwartz nuts. Canadians seem to see Air Canada as one of those few national institutions we still possess. As if they're saying, Well, we lost the railway, but there's still time to save this one. They may even think of Air Canada as public (in the old sense), though they "know" it was privatized years ago. It is, in other words, a symbol, like hockey or butter tarts. It's a matter of culture.

Anyway, here I am, bidding farewell to the pansy patch, yet not really escaping the reach of media and culture. It's a welcome move for me, especially with culture having acquired that new prestige. Life is generally more interesting in the lower-rent areas. I'm happy to be downgraded, as they say at check-in, to the editorial pages.

*

A WEEK LATER I HAD THE BYPASS, A QUAD. (I WAS scheduled for a triple, but once he got in, the surgeon said, he decided to give me a freebie.) A few days after I got home, I read a column in the *Globe* by Marcus Gee, celebrating the fall of the Berlin Wall a decade earlier. I found it so smug that I called and said I was going to file. I'd missed exactly one column. My new copy editor, Larry Orenstein, a fellow cardiac case, said it was the briefest time off ever for that level of malady. He told Marcus that he should file his own claim with the Ontario health plan for providing me such speedy rehab.

It was a good time to leave the media beat. When I started the column, in 1991, the term, *media* was equivalent to mass media: it meant newspapers, TV, radio, books, films, recorded music. Those are now described as one-to-many media and unidirectional in nature. Eight years later, mass media had begun acquiring a sepia tone, like Canadian nationalism. They were challenged by new media, which were many-to-many and reciprocal in direction. New media felt in some deep way like a return to Harold Innis's beloved oral tradition. The realm of print, into which I was born, as I was born into the Cold War, had also seemed destined to last forever. Now people had begun referring to a four-hundred-year Gutenberg parenthesis. Just another phase in history. I didn't have the feel for new media, which more or less means the internet, that I'd had for mass media. Noam Chomsky was my go-to guy on media criticism, and he dealt entirely with mass media. In fact, he wasn't even really interested in media so much as in propaganda. His insights were as applicable to the Spanish Inquisition as to the *New York Times*.

I lucked out doubly on the timing of the transition since I'd been teaching a half course in the Canadian Studies program at University College of the University of Toronto. (I know that seems like one "university" too many, but the academic world has its traditions.) I'd done it since 1979. It got me out of the house once a week in the worst months of winter and kept me in touch with students. Around the time I started at the *Globe*, the course was rejigged as Media and Culture in Canada. I used the shift to indulge a long-time curiosity about the cryptic media writings of Innis. The students were patient while I stumbled through his texts for the first few years and, I sincerely hope, slowly learned to make some sense of them. That's the teaching process in essence: everyone's learning, when it works. It was also another fortuitous case where the odd variety of things I found myself doing seemed to cohere.

*

TEN YEARS AFTER THE FALL OF THE BERLIN WALL, with instinctive deference to the custom of dividing history into decades, the first major post–Cold War uprising against global corporate dominion occurred, in Seattle. A meeting of the World Trade Organization, called to ratify a humungous universalization of everything that had been odious in the little Canada-U.S. trade deal that kicked it all off, collapsed due to street protests and a dawning awareness of the Trojan Horse nature of the agreement. Resistance mounts with agonizing slowness; on the other hand, it's amazing that it happens at all. Similar demonstrations occurred in Washington, Genoa, and Quebec City. I attended the Quebec Summit of the Americas. The tear gas made me nostalgic, and the water cannon was an interesting new wrinkle. Almost the whole old city, where I went in 1969 to rent a garret and become a writer, was sealed off. Since there were no more communists — if you don't count China or Cuba, which you don't — the necessary Manichaean other label fell on "anarchists." Some protesters really were; others were the usual grab bag of citizens unwilling to defer to authorities in the face of their own experience and common sense. It felt like an anarchist scare might succeed the communist scare. This is from 2001.

*

THIS COLUMN HAS, AS THEY SAY, NO HOOK, OTHER than a fear the news media will begin to discuss anarchism rather than just referencing it. So far, they've been content to simply substitute the term for *communism*, *terrorism*, *Islamic fundamentalism*, and similar frights: "Anarchy reigns in Genoa 'war zone.'" "Men in black behind chaos; anarchists, hardliners plan 'actions.'" "Chrétien: Canada will punish anarchists at next G8 summit." Its meaning is more or less assumed. Anarchists are violent; they believe in chaos. There are wry asides ("anarchists, by definition, are not supposed to be organized") on how contradictory it is to belong to an anarchist group or go to an anarchist convention!

There hasn't been much by way of analysis or

in-depth attention with sidebars and headshots of Mikhail Bakunin, Peter Kropotkin, and Emma Goldman. That's the vacuum I'm rushing to fill.

What about all that chaos and anarchy? It sounds like a big pillow fight. How can they oppose organization and order? Actually, anarchists don't. They oppose order imposed from above; in other words, they oppose authority and power. Anarchism isn't about disorder but about the absence of authority. You could say it's taking the notion that power corrupts really seriously. It assumes people are naturally social and don't require laws to force them to get along. In fact, the natural human state is anarchy, which comprises the only true order. The coercive order of governments and laws distorts that condition. "If there is a devil in human history," said one anarchist, "it is the principle of command." You can disagree with this, but it's arguable and interesting.

The anarchist rejection of governments is based on this faith in the human impulse to self-regulate; every government by its nature imposes an order on society. But the principle of anarchism is not primarily antigovernment: it's anti-hierarchy. In our time, many people on both the left and right think the power of government has declined, while that of the private sector has grown. But the fight of anarchists has always been against all forms of domination, so you can see why they take a big role in protests against both corporate and state power.

Yeah, but what about the bomb throwing and guys in black smashing up cars? Isn't that what they mean by direct action? Well, what's the alternative to direct action? It's indirect action, which is exactly the electoral systems we have. By voting, you transfer your power to act to representatives who, inevitably it seems, end up lording it over you. *Direct action* is the general term for people exercising political power themselves. That might mean the American Revolution, going on strike, creating co-ops, or refusing to fight in a war. The violent impulse is one strand of direct action, but so is the nonviolence of Gandhi or Leo Tolstoy — figures in the anarchist tradition. It was an anarchist who said, "It is impossible to seize power in order to abolish it."

It couldn't possibly work; it's never even been tried. Actually, it has, for brief periods. During the English Revolution of the 17th century, the "masterless men" in groups such as the Diggers and Ranters applied anarchist principles. The Paris Commune of 1870 ran the same way. The most extensive experiments came in the Spanish Civil War of the 1930s, when whole cities operated, successfully it seems, on anarchist models. All these were brought to an end by the armed forces of wealth and power, not by internal failure. The jury is still out. You could say the same of democracy or Christianity.

Let me finish by saying something personal about the new appeal of anarchism. For me, that appeal lies in an ability to reconcile individualism with a commitment to society. I detest being forced into the anti-individual position. Voices on the right tend to claim individualism as theirs — even if most of them are locked happily inside big institutions such as the Fraser Institute, the *National Post*, or the Departments of Foreign Affairs and International Trade. Those of us who incline, even if grumpily, to the left are expected to defend the collective against the individual.

Yet think about it. Which individuals flourish under the dominant economic and political culture today? Mainly the rich. Only they can afford the best health care, education, leisure, culture, plus music lessons and theatre trips for their kids. And even for them, there's a strong downside, especially if they have a social conscience. This system preaches individualism but actually grinds most individuals into poverty or preoccupation with survival, destroying the chance for their individuality to thrive. Anarchism declines the choice. It teaches, in Emma Goldman's words, "how to be one's self and yet in oneness with others"; or, in Mikhail Bakunin's, "Man is not only the most individual being on earth, he is also the most social." That is, you can only truly be individual(ist) by being truly social(ist). I love wiggling out of those dichotomies.

*

I RECEIVED MASSIVE MAIL ON THIS, MOST OF IT STILL snail, often from anarchists. They wrote in surprise and gratitude; they were used to being stereotyped in the MSM. I was amazed at how many anarchists read the *Globe and Mail* (speaking of stereotypes). Shortly after, during a widespread power outage, I was riding with Gideon on my bike. We stopped at the complex intersection of Harbord and Spadina; it bundles cars, streetcars, bikes, pedestrians, and buses, all with special signals of their own that were now entirely extinguished. But the traffic kept flowing with no one in charge. People glanced to either side, nodded at each other, and somehow synchronized on timing; it was clear proof for the viability of societal self-regulation. Anarchism, given a chance, could make its case. But whatever was germinating got cut off on September 11, 2001. This column appeared four days later.

*

As I BEGAN TO WAKEN ON WEDNESDAY, THE EVENTS of Tuesday started to seem more dream than reality, the kind you stir slowly from and with vast relief as you realize what you thought had been real was not. If only.

What marked Tuesday's attacks was not "sophistication," a word I've heard enough of since then. Certainly not in the sense of technological sophistication: they used plastic knives! Nor logistics, cost, or coordination. It was all relatively simple and stripped down. That's what's scariest. Once it's been shown to be doable, it becomes redoable, with relative ease. Except for one item, harder to duplicate and on which it all depends: the willingness of those involved to kill themselves. This is what marks these attacks as 21st century rather than 20th.

The great motivator of political action in the 20th century was ideology: socialism, fascism, national liberation. In its name, people were ready to murder massively and, in a better version, to die for their cause, their fellow humans, and the future. But willingness to die for a cause is not the same as a deliberate choice to kill oneself for it. Political ideologies are secular and this-worldly. Their horizon of hope lies in this world, where their followers want to build something better, all of which will be lost to them if they die, though not to others who may benefit.

The worldview that motivated Tuesday's events is different. Its horizon is otherworldly. It sees this world in the frame of another world, the supernatural, and an afterlife. It is, in other words, religious; not just religious but fundamentalist and simplistic. Robert Fisk, the British journalist, says it pits theology against technology, the only force that has shown an ability to equalize. This is religious, as opposed to political, terrorism; and the difference is the choice not just to die if necessary but to willfully commit suicide. It sees its cause not in social change but in a cosmic "titanic struggle between good and evil," according to experts quoted by the *Globe*'s Marcus Gee. In an eerie parallel, President George W. Bush said this week that America was in a fight between good and evil. There are days when it seems that George Bush and Osama bin Laden deserve each other.

Bizarrely, the rise of fundamentalist religion as a political factor in many parts of the world owes something to American policy. The U.S. chose to nurture Islamic fundamentalism in Afghanistan in the 1980s to undermine Soviet control there, in the course of which it worked with, armed, and trained — Osama bin Laden. In a similar way, Israel chose to encourage fundamentalism among Palestinians to undermine secular left-wing forces. I point this out for two reasons. As a wise reader wrote to me recently, "There is a fundamental principle of Vedic philosophy (Hinduism) that asks one to examine, when confronted with adversity, what one 'owns' in it." And if the West had some role in creating this force, perhaps it can do something to uncreate it.

It won't be easy. It truly feels — pardon this cultural reference — like a genie you can't stuff back in the bottle. You can't hunt it down because no country is its home; its home is despair, delusion, and faith in values such as cosmic war and an afterlife. You can't "make them pay"; they're already dead. You can't threaten their families and communities; that's what started the cycle. But if you can't destroy it, you can try to defuse it.

By that, I mean deprive it of the soil it lives in. Take a precursor: Japan's kamikaze pilots during the Second World War. They were dependent on the emperor's blessing, their nation's applause, its mythology, etc. Remove that and it would have been hard to find candidates. Today's soil is the despair and sense of injustice in places such as the Mideast. Communities have been created that laud these gestures, as one sees at Palestinian funerals. "Terrorism experts say the approval of the community is an important reason why terrorists do what they do," wrote Marcus Gee. You defuse this by eliminating the worst cases of wretchedness that sustain it. An obvious example, since Palestine has been a tinderbox of religious terror and the Israeli occupation has been the tinderbox of the tinderbox, would be to end the occupation and hand those lands back to Palestinians. It would be hard, because of the settlers, but it would eliminate the tinderbox. A similar case would involve ending sanctions against Iraq that have led, the UN says, to the deaths of a million children.

The fanatics themselves wouldn't vanish. And fanaticism itself may be a human perennial. But there would be massive relief among huge numbers who yearn mainly to live decent, unharassed lives. The despair, mania, and hate that sustain the fanatics would largely be withdrawn.

Would this mean "giving in to terrorism"? No, it would be a strategy to cut off its oxygen. It would also be the right thing to do, but think of that as merely collateral damage.

*

ISRAEL AND JEWS WERE THE SOLE TOPICS I WAS cautioned about ("You might want to consider not writing on that") by tetchy editors after moving to op-ed. Ed Greenspon, the only Jewish editor in chief the *Globe* has had, told me his life would be a lot easier if I avoided them. I don't know if he was getting heat from his mom and her friends in Montreal, from higher up in the building, or from people he ran into socially. There was no point asking: they tell you what they want you to know. Ed was a straightforward guy who usually meant what he said. He'd have preferred to have an easier life, but I didn't stop (I always thought about it and then persisted), and he didn't do anything about it except, I guess, have a harder life. I'm sure that wasn't due to angry letters from readers. Those run off the back of someone with Ed's experience. The pressures he felt came from people who didn't need to write letters. They'd corner him at dinner parties and galas or call his cell. (The only newspaper editor I know of who took calls from ordinary readers was Peter Worthington at the *Toronto Sun*. He was a populist.)

In 2005, I was offered an award for "media excellence" by the Canadian Islamic Congress, a legit group with a wacky leadership at the time. Mohamed Elmasry had called any Israeli over 18 a valid target for Palestinian militants since everyone there served in the army. But they had as much right as anyone to advocate and be heard. They were no wackier, in my view, than B'nai Brith or the Friends of Simon Wiesenthal Center, and they should all be free to give out gratuitous awards. Like many Arabs and Muslims in Canada, they felt cruelly and unjustly treated by "the media" and were embarrassingly grateful when someone was simply fair-minded. It wasn't support that thrilled them, just not being kneecapped.

I knew the award wouldn't sit well at the *Globe* and tried to avoid it by delaying a response till I'd written an unflattering column on them to provide an excuse for them to withdraw their offer, but they didn't. So I responded and said I couldn't come to Ottawa for their convention and award; I'd been told they were strapped and didn't like to spend. Undeterred, they agreed to expenses. Out of tricks, I said I'd be there and say a few words, as they'd asked. Then I did something bizarre: I wrote a preemptive column, explaining why I was going and that I planned to engage them critically while there since I believe in respectful disagreement. (I do, but it's the only time I wrote a strategic column based on it.) The dinner was in a parliamentary dining room with many MPs present. They were taken more seriously by politicians than by the media. After my peculiar acceptance speech, only Mohamed Elmasry seemed puzzled; he sensed there was more to it than simple contrarianism. I don't think he suspected that I feared losing my job, though. For them anyone who had a column in the *Globe and Mail* looked impregnable.

Aharon Appelfeld, who taught me Hebrew during my year in Israel, said any choice to be Jewish in the modern world is a complex one. I find it growing more so, less in relation to my own choices, which I agonized over plenty in the past, and more to do with choices made by my fellow Canadian Jews, including lifelong friends. One, who's never belonged to a synagogue or any Jewish institution I know of, asked, when his kids were little, if I'd give them Jewish lessons. He said that, when they were grown, he wanted them to know why people hated them. He is the epitome of unimpeded success and prestige here. If he has encountered anti-Semitism, it didn't slow him down a step — and I doubt he has. It makes me realize that I lack any solid understanding of what group identifications are about, any of them — Canada, Israel, Leafs nation, Ford nation — even as I acknowledge they are elementally embedded in all our behaviour. They are at the core of how most people see themselves. But what are they? What are they based on? Often on nothing, or close to nothing; sometimes, on a great deal. I feel truly humbled by my lack of understanding on these matters at the same time that I recognize their power. (I know that sounds quasi-religious, but one of the classical sociological theories of divinity says that the deity *is* the social entity.) In the case of Canadian Jews today, the group identification has two main components: anti-Semitism and Israel. It's been stripped down to those, from a far longer, richer catalogue. They seem conjoined and inextricable. Here's a modest attempt to decouple them. It was written in 2008.

*

MEDIA COVERAGE OF ISRAEL'S 60TH BIRTHDAY HAS gone on for more than a week. Almost all of it was celebratory, though there were sympathetic references to the Palestinian *nakba*, or "catastrophe," that weren't often included in coverage of Israel's 50th or 40th. Even the *National Post*, among dozens of articles, had one by Jeet Heer on the "ethnic cleansing" of Palestinians, which a *Post* editorial rebuked the same day.

Something that struck me was the fairly narrow notion of the Jewish experience outside Israel, in the Diaspora, that was implied. A Toronto prof, quoted in the *Post*, said, "Everything they do to us . . . strengthens our deep-seated perception that fuels our identity of being a persecuted people." This rings true to me not as how things are but as how many Canadian Jews see them. I have friends and relations, often wealthy and accomplished people, who feel anti-Semitism is always imminent, though they've rarely or never experienced it. It shapes their attitude toward Israel as the only refuge for Jews and makes them less willing to hear criticisms of it than most Israelis are. It seems to me irrational, and I wish I understood it better.

When we were kids in the 1950s, we studied a book called *Sufferance Is the Badge*, based on Shylock's line, "Sufferance is the badge of all our tribe." It interpreted Jewish history as a tale of torment. But that was in the shadow of the Holocaust. When I was married in my 20s, my mother-in-law did a painting in her art class that showed religious Jews clutching Torah scrolls as they fled. Their beards and prayer shawls streamed behind. My father-in-law, a manufacturer, called it caustically, *The Jews Running*. I think he meant it was sentimentalized and overstated, and he wasn't buying that version of the Jewish past, at least not outright.

All this resonated in the aftermath of Hitler and was helpful in raising support for the fragile state of Israel. But, at bottom and for understandable reasons, it distorted two millennia of Jewish history that were rich and complex. Almost all Jewish literary and intellectual accomplishment occurred in the Diaspora. There were golden ages of relative integration, along with expulsions and pogroms. That's a big chunk of time. Crisis comes and goes in all collective and individual lives. Jews prayed for a return to Zion, but only in the messianic future that God alone would bring about. Anyone who tried to "force the end" was considered a heretic. They didn't just make do in the Diaspora; they settled in and often thrived.

It seems to me that a more nuanced, positive view of the Diaspora might open many Jews to a different relationship to Israel, in which they feel freer to offer criticism. It would also correspond better to their real lives. And it would fit the increasingly diasporic nature of a globalized world.

There are now many diasporas. The stats show Canada is becoming a diasporic country, and so do your eyes as you walk around our cities. The young know they're more likely to be wanderers than their parents were. These shifts are accompanied by tensions and sometimes disaster.

But they have many upsides. You even see it in the Obama campaign. Who could be more diasporic, with his Kenyan father and Kansan mother?

There's a debate in Israel now over the meaning of the Jewish Diaspora. A historian has written a book claiming there was no expulsion and exile during the Roman era. Most Jews stayed put and converted to Islam. Those Jews outside Israel increased by converting others: Arabs in North Africa and Khazars in Eastern Europe. It won't change basic attitudes, but it enriches and complexifies the nature of Diaspora.

In a world of nations, you celebrate national birthdays. But in a world of diasporas? That may call for something completely different.

*

Palestinians and Israelis have been locked in each other's deathly embrace for a century. Yet theirs is probably the most resolvable international conflict in the world, in the sense that the terms of a settlement are clear to everyone. That hardly matters, given the other elements at play. Yasser Arafat was the Palestinian leader whom Israel reviled most, both before and after accepting him as their "partner for peace." It was a superb example of demonization, which is just another word for dehumanization, and is the signature stumbling block in all politics, as far as I can tell. If that's so, rehumanization is a worthy project. Here's a piece from 2004, after Arafat's death. The Israeli army had besieged and held him prisoner in his West Bank office for months.

*

It was Yasser Arafat's task to represent the Palestinian cause at a time when it seemed almost hopeless, especially in the West. What chance would you give a cause that could be readily portrayed as denying the right of Jewish people to a national existence in the aftermath of the Holocaust? That could therefore be depicted (falsely, I'd say) as an extension of Nazism.

His achievement was that, under his leadership, that cause finally made its mark. It became seen as legitimate and urgent. He achieved this although his own presence, in the West, was a PR nightmare. He was unkempt (nearly drooling), both ingratiating and menacing, inept in English, a manoeuvrer rather than a straight talker. (A great example? His declaration that the official Palestinian position on destroying Israel was *caduc*, an obscure French term implying "inoperative, so don't worry about it.") But he rallied support to his cause, as much despite his own traits as due to them.

Yet he failed, in his lifetime, and his cause may fail too, as Edward Said, the elegant Palestinian advocate who also died this year, apparently felt at the end. Arafat's moment of triumph, the peace agreement signed at the White House in 1993, was probably his great failure. He agreed to police his own people but got no guarantees back on issues such as Jewish settlements, borders, Jerusalem, or right of return. Without those levers, his power declined.

In 2000, he felt he had to turn down what Israel managed to position in the media as "the most generous offer" ever made to Palestinians. In truth, it was far less and added little to the earlier deal. When I asked Mustafa Barghouti, of the nonviolent grassroots Palestinian movement Mubadara, why the Arafat side failed to counter Israeli exaggerations, he gave me an answer I didn't expect: "Sheer incompetence."

Yasser Arafat's death reverberates because it also seems to represent the failure, so far, of his cause. That failure, in turn, symbolizes the collective human capacity for failure in a just cause. I know there are other just causes. But Palestinians have, in this era, become emblematic of them, as South Africans were under apartheid. South Africa came to eventually embody the capacity of the human community, acting through international institutions, to win victory in a just cause. Palestine so far is its grim opposite.

Funerals are important, even if they evoke ambivalence, as this one does among Palestinians. But this funeral is important for how Israelis respond too. Israel's justice minister said the burial would not happen in Jerusalem because it is "the city of Jewish kings, not Arab terrorists." That is the voice of Jewish arrogance, not Jewish righteousness. Jerusalem is also a city of Jewish prophets, who denounced their own kings, even King David, when those kings abused people under their rule, including non-Jews.

Israeli officials are reported to have called Yasser Arafat "the founder of modern terrorism," a ridiculous claim. Terrorism has a far longer history and includes two of Israel's prime ministers. Nelson Mandela was once a terrorist. Then, suddenly, he became South Africa's national saviour for blacks and whites. The term *terror* wasn't withdrawn or redefined. It just went away; it became *caduc*. Other national and moral priorities took over. The whole thing never was about terror, not really.

For decades, the Israel-Palestine imbroglio has been a litmus test for whether people of goodwill can sort through a horribly tangled issue of right and wrong. It has been confused and obscured by the Holocaust, the price of oil, Hollywood's notion of terrorists — don't get me started. Were it elsewhere in the world, with other players involved, most people would have sorted it out by now with ease. But put it this way. The Holocaust has for so long been the reference point for questions about crimes against humanity that it is in danger of losing its ability to instruct. The world needs other reference points. The cause of the Palestinians stands in that role, as one real test of whether humanity, to the extent one can meaningfully use the term, measures up.

*

I WAS REALLY A ONE-TRICK PONY AT THE GLOBE. The trick was being there at all, since I disagreed with a great deal of what else was in the paper. Of course, I tried to improvise and perform beyond my basic trick, and I hoped not to be predictable (*trying* not to be predictable is hopeless). But I felt a certain obligation to represent the "left" position, whatever else I was up to.

When the newspaper war settled into its serious phase, the *Globe* brought in an editor from the U.K., Richard Addis. There, papers are in an endless state of war. They fight each other and fight internal civil wars. Nastiness and hostility course through them. Editors sometimes assign two reporters to the same story, then let them fight for the space, and perhaps their jobs. Addis seemed amiable, but I saw him do it, as if his blood had risen inside him. At a lunch he threw for freelance columnists, he suddenly turned to one clearly insecure writer and announced, "Oh, and your column will be moving to Mondays." Changing the day of your column always seems ominous. It's like being evicted from your house. There was no reason to say it in front of everyone, and I don't think Addis even followed up on it. It was more as if he hadn't fed on any raw meat in a while and reflexively took a bite from the arm that looked juiciest.

He laid on the lunch because there was a small panic when Robert Fulford, my old antagonist from *This Magazine* days, decamped for the *National Post*, after feeling insulted by the way some subeditor treated his copy. Addis wanted to shore up the rest of us, not that he knew who anyone was. He wasn't from here. He and the other Brits in upper positions at the *Globe* hoovered up a lot of time from the local *Globe* editors, getting them to translate what the hell was going on here. Literally, translations. What's a riding? What's Meech Lake?

He told me he'd asked his editors to position all the *Globe* columnists on the ideological spectrum, working inward from the poles. Well, they said, Margaret Wente was way out to the right, about as far as the *National Post*. On the other end was me. They told him I was at least as far to the left as she was to the — well, no, actually I was a lot further in that direction than she was in hers, in fact — and it was as if he couldn't get his left hand far enough out there without some kind of clown extension. "So you see," he shrugged, "the schema didn't really work."

Conrad Black was at the centre of the war and intrigue. The *National Post* was the only paper he created in all his years of buying and selling. I wrote about him often. I especially liked his way of playing a character called "Conrad Black." When he married Barbara Amiel, it felt like the union between a person with maximum motive to wish me harm and one with maximum ability to deliver it. After he took over the Liberal-leaning Southam chain of papers, I wrote, based on one of his pronouncements, that if I were working for him, I'd feel a mix of shame and fear. He wrote to the *Globe*: "Mr. Salutin concluded that if he were an employee of mine, he would contemplate that fact with a mixture of fear and shame. The fear might be understandable, but the shame would only be justified by reasons proper to him and unrelated to the identity of his employer." He wasn't one to avoid confrontation; he liked to mix it up. During a 2000 strike at one of his papers, the *Calgary Herald*, he stepped out of a directors' meeting and, instead of ducking into his limo like the other nobs, crossed the street to shriek in the face of a striker. I wrote about it. When I got home late one night soon after, there was a message from the secretary in his Toronto office. (He was still based at Canary Wharf in London.)

She said there was a personal and confidential letter for me. Please call in the morning and she'd fax it over.

I slept badly. Things had been rough at home, and I felt I may have slipped on the piece about the Calgary strike. You weren't allowed to do that with Black. He knew the libel law and loved to brandish it. At that moment he was on a tear, suing NDP members of parliament and union leaders in what looked like a strategy to destroy the Canadian left, such as it was, by bankrupting it with court costs. I'd never been sued, or even threatened, because I knew how to offend legally, I thought. But under emotional stress, who knows what you might miss. Next morning I made the call and got the fax. "Comradely greetings from the other side of the barricades," it began. It was basically fan mail.

Black said he understood why I misrepresented his attitude toward journalists as bitter, envious, and resentful. He said he knew that's how the game is played. But he insisted he couldn't possibly feel that way about journalists since he employed so many. Eric Peterson, my dear pal and theatre colleague, had come over to hold my hand as I got the awful news. He said he could picture Black gazing out from Canary Wharf, basking in how his empire was thriving and, absent anything pressing or worrisome, thinking to himself, *Perhaps I'll write Salutin in Toronto. See what that stirs up.* I responded immediately that, au contraire, employing journalists is a precondition for exploiting them. But I said I appreciated his genial tone and would be glad to buy him an espresso at some grotty Marxist bistro on my side of the barricades next time he was in town. (When I told the regulars at Dooney's, they said they'd pelt him with biscotti if he showed his smug face. I said that was unacceptable if he came as my guest.) His secretary called back almost instantly to say, more or less, He doesn't go out. But he'd be glad to have me to tea at Canadian HQ, so we set a date. It went well. We paid no attention to the tea and cakes because we were so deep in conversation.

Before he went on trial for fraud in 2007 in Chicago, I asked if he'd come as a guest to my media class at the University of Toronto. I've had lots of people there from the other side of the barricades: Preston Manning of the Reform Party, Jonathan Kay and Terence Corcoran from the *National Post*, Lorrie Goldstein from the *Toronto Sun*. Black asked what he would talk about, and I said, Bias in media, of course. He said he'd do it dependent on his court dates and came two weeks before the trial began.

*

CONRAD BLACK, THE ONE AND ONLY, WAS A GUEST in my undergrad half course on media and culture at the University of Toronto last month. The topic was bias in the media. When I said he was coming, you could hear a hundred student jaws hit the floor.

When he actually appeared, unaccompanied, a few weeks later, there was a sharp collective gasp. As if the simulacrum had entered the room. I don't know if anyone else would have had that effect. We aren't used to the images that pervade our lives, and often overshadow them, taking corporeal form. Or if they do, they're framed as images: on a stage, with a spotlight, handlers, etc. There were no news media in the room, just him and us (well, one student writes for the *Varsity*, a campus paper).

He stood at the front, looking a bit more subdued than "Conrad Black," almost seeming nervous, a hand stuffed in a jacket pocket. Still, he did a good-enough version of the familiar character, like most people playing themselves. I felt there was more to the odd sense in the room than just a famous person, in person. It was as if it somehow proved to the students that they live in a society that really exists because he, who's been at the pinnacle of its wealth and power, was in the same physical space at the same time as they were. So society is not a fiction, in contradiction to the claim by a Black heroine, Margaret Thatcher, that there is no such thing as society.

A story did appear in the *Varsity*, and a number of students posted replies including, "Put the fucker in jail and throw away the keys." Conrad (he said we could call him anything) replied to each post. For example, he wrote, "The Red Queen said it better: the sentence, followed by the verdict, followed by the charge, followed by the evidence (if any). I am relieved that he thinks life imprisonment would be adequate. . . . I want to thank . . . all who attended for receiving me very hospitably. Best wishes to all, even the lugubrious ——, whatever the source of his disturbance. Sincerely, CONRAD BLACK."

Frank magazine recently ran a hilarious prank based on a fake Support Conrad Black website, including an On-to-Chicago Caravan. Michael Bate, *Frank*'s editor (or proprietor, in Conradese, which is weirdly hard not to slip into when you write about the guy), sounded muted, even impressed, by how "gracious" Black, who smelled a rat at the last minute, was about the hoax. I said he seemed to make a better victim than a bully — and he'd been a damn good bully. "He missed his calling," said the savage satirist from *Frank*.

In an *ave atque vale* in Saturday's *National Post*, Black voiced some unexpected views. He seemed pleased that global economic forces have "enabled Canada to keep its generous social benefits." In the past, he called those programs a "hammock," "institutionalized compassion," a "dragnet for the aggrieved," and "endowed martyrdom" that "will require repeal of universality and retrenchment." He also said, in the *Post*, "I have never been happier to be Canadian." No mention of the "plain vanilla place" this once was (he has high praise for Toronto's new opera house) or "the pandemic Canadian spirit of envy," he described back then through clenched jaw.

I am absolutely not against anyone changing his mind. I see flip-flopping as a sign of adulthood. If you don't flip-flop, you're either perfect or you've stopped growing (statistically more likely). A dose of misfortune sometimes, but not always, gives people a different focus along with more compassion for others, including those who must go into court without a lot of money for legal support. It would be nice to hear people acknowledge it when they shift even partially, but few do; that seems even rarer than change itself.

I talked to my 94-year-old friend Jack Seeley, in Los Angeles, just after Conrad came to class. Jack is the wisest, most principled person I know. He still practises psychoanalysis, mostly with kids. I said I always felt Conrad Black was one person who could have been on either side, politically. Jack said he thought that was true of most of us, a notion I think I'd shied away from, because it's disconcerting, but as soon as he spoke it, it sounded utterly true.

*

WE WENT UP TO BLOOR FOR A CUP OF COFFEE AFTER class, though not to Dooney's, and talked about being on trial. When his limo pulled up at the curb outside, Black tried to grab the cheque, but I beat him to it. Then we stood and I said, *Hazak v'ematz*. It's Hebrew. It means "be strong and of good courage." Moses says it as Joshua is about to take over and lead the people of Israel into the Promised Land while Moses stays behind to die. It wasn't all that appropriate, but the general sentiment felt right. He asked me to repeat it, so he could, then headed off as his chauffeur held the door open.

I think it's possible that Black should be in jail, as I've told him, but not for any of the things he was convicted for. Jail does no one any real good (including those of us ostensibly being protected by putting people there), and his crimes as I see them, like polluting the public discussion and using wealth as a weapon to bludgeon democracy, aren't illegal.

I feel the same about, say, the late Peter Worthington, founder of the *Toronto Sun* and the many other *Sun*s. Worthington had blood on his hands, almost literally, for collaborating with the apartheid regime in South Africa. He was, on the other hand, a delight personally. We'd also done print combat before we met on a TV show — he in his mighty tab and me in *This Magazine* with our little clutch of readers — and I was unprepared for his puckishness. I gave him a ride afterward and asked if he'd ever had second thoughts ideologically. The sun was setting and he said, in a mellow way, there'd been a moment back in the 1960s when he felt alone and all the juice seemed on the other side. But he stood fast and the pendulum swung again. Whenever we saw each other after that, there was an immediate surge of pleasure. The CBC's Michael Enright once told us to stop acting like long-lost brothers: that didn't work on radio or TV.

I ran into him on a TV panel just before Gideon was born. There had been some medical bumps that morning — as is normal but who knew with a first and surely only child — and I rudely talked over the other guests due to nerves. The host was irritated and the others were miffed too. At the end, Peter leaned in, patted me on the back, and said, "I'd like to thank Rick for having us on his show." It's the only time I can recall anyone physically touching someone else on one of those sententious programs. So even if, in theory, I thought he should be in jail, if I needed someone beside me at a tough moment, I'd have been happy if it was Worthington. In my student protest years, when the cops were about to charge, you always looked around to see who you could count on to stay and who was likely to run or already had. There was nothing commensurate between the most militant talkers and the people you could count on. Maybe when we're a more evolved species, the two pieces — words and deeds — will match up better.

*

WHAT I KNOW I HAVEN'T SAID CLEARLY UNTIL THIS point, is what a pleasure it was to have my little say, week after week — doubtless amplified by having been shut out (or carefully contained) by the MSM during my first 20 years as a writer. It was like the moment you stop banging your head against the wall. This, for example, was a rare, inspiring moment during the American occupation of Iraq. It happened in 2008, when Dubya slipped into Baghdad for a visit.

*

Journalist Muntader al-Zaidi, the shoe thrower of Baghdad, has given us all a Christmas present — like the gift of the Magi — in the form of a new way to react to rage and conflict, one that's symbolic and nonviolent. It evokes respect, even from its target, rather than further rage and violence.

I don't think his act was unprofessional, as claimed by Haroon Siddiqui in the *Toronto Star* or a *Globe and Mail* editorial — since I don't see journalism as a profession, not the way medicine or shoemaking is. It lacks a unique body of knowledge and depends on a skill everyone has — language — plus the exercise of normal virtues such as common sense, skepticism, observation, and integrity.

The humour, restraint, and nonviolence — or, at most, symbolic violence — Muntader al-Zaidi showed are a welcome antidote to the common stereotypes about some inherent Muslim impulse to violence. Violence is a human trait. It's certainly just as Christian — wars of religion, the Crusades, world wars, the Holocaust — and Jewish, if you consider the historical books of the Old Testament or the 41-year occupation of Palestinian land.

Our own violent, martial era of disastrous

invasions and occupations is a good time to be reminded of the merits of nonviolent action. It had its triumphs, in India under Gandhi and in the civil rights battles of America. Nonviolence as a political tactic usually goes with symbols such as sit-ins or Gandhi's march to the sea. There are places today, including the Mideast, where it should be tried. There is, for instance, a nonviolent current in Palestinian politics that might be effective, if it got a (pardon) foothold.

Symbolic acts are therapeutic for people who feel, like many Iraqis and Palestinians, humiliated. You not only lose your homes and lives, you lose your sense of dignity. A restrained, controlled act helps restore that sense. You could see it in the creativity of people raising shoes on poles in recent demos demanding U.S. withdrawal from Iraq or pelting military convoys with shoes — rather than blowing them up with IEDs, which assault terrified young soldiers instead of the decision makers. The latter are rarely exposed, except at press conferences, where the indignity can descend on them if they have to dodge around like targets in a dunk tank.

Such acts can even be helpful for the targets. "This is a gift from the Iraqis . . . you dog!" yelled the shoe thrower. But he gave George Bush a chance to look quick on his feet and more astute than he ever did after 9/11. Remember his doltish "analysis": It's because they hate us for our freedoms. Here he called it an "interesting way for a person to express himself" — as if it gave him something to reflect on, for once. So it was a gift.

As for journalists, the brave Irish reporter Patrick Cockburn said the toss would "gladden the heart of any journalist forced to attend these tedious, useless, and almost invariably obsequious" sessions with visiting Western leaders. Journalists are citizens too, with civic obligations. Meeting leaders isn't their "privilege," as a *Globe* editorial claimed; it's their duty and right. But if you merely ask tough questions, you won't get called on again, likely won't be invited next time, and may lose your job.

The shoe thrower hasn't been seen since his arrest, although he was heard from: screaming while being beaten by security afterward, then apologizing yesterday for his "big ugly act," according to a government official. He used to sign off his reports from "occupied Iraq," which sounds more sincere, as well as both objective and impassioned. And his tosses seem a model of self-restraint and goodwill when compared to two bombings during a visit on Wednesday by British Prime Minister Gordon Brown: at least nine dead in Baghdad and a 13-year-old north of there. Peace on earth, good shoes toward men.

*

THIS IS FROM THE WINTER OLYMPICS OF 2008. IT was headed "First, We Kill All the Sports Shrinks."

WE HAVE A RECORD CONTINGENT IN TURIN. I'M talking about the sports psychologists. Twelve of them. Only seven were in Salt Lake City. Their job is to help win the 25 medals promised by the Canadian Olympic Committee.

I have two problems with sports shrinks. Like other results-based exercises, such as dating services and negative campaign ads, they work except when they don't. And, like much in the social sciences, there is no actual body of expertise, just a shifting discourse. Sports shrinks used to teach athletes to visualize. Then they stressed relaxing. Now their focus is on focusing. Do you really think some expert badgering you to focus isn't going to distract you? Yet, like most experts, they rarely suffer criticism; it's the clients who get the blame.

Let them speak for themselves. Kimberley Amirault, who works with speed skaters, says Canadians may be too nice to win. "Our athletes sometimes get too caught up in not wanting to offend anybody." Now what effect is seeing that in the paper going to have on an athlete? Will they get mean in order to win? Can you make yourself do that? I mean, mean is mean; it's not a, er, means to an end. A psychologist should know that.

Terry Orlick, who has written 20 books, sounds like a motivational speaker whose main model is himself: "I never dread going into a meeting with an athlete. . . . I am always focused. Right there — in the moment — absorbing, listening, learning. . . . I find it rewarding and I am very good at it." If you're an athlete who reads that and misses your gold, then you feel like an even bigger loser, since you know Terry is great at what he does, so it must be your fault. This is therapy? Maybe he's the guy Olympic kayaker Caroline Brunet meant when she said, "If I met a good one, perhaps I would have used one. But the ones I met I think need to see a psychologist themselves."

Here's sports shrink Cal Botterill, whose daughter is on the hockey team. He's worried the pressure of the coc's prediction of 25 medals "could really cost us" since "Canadian athletes are much better at the underdog role than when they're considered the favourites." So is his job to counter the stance taken by his employers? Maybe he should just treat the bureaucrats.

What message is sent to athletes by having all these sports shrinks around: that you guys are screwed up and being a Canadian jock is a losing proposition? Yet there's no evidence that sprinkling therapists or grief counsellors in tense settings like school shootings and natural disasters does any real good. A study in the *Lancet* says disaster counselling "could even delay recovery" among those who might have "recovered normally by talking with friends and family or by blocking out any recall of the incident until they felt they were ready." A psychologist on that study said, "We have an ideology that it's 'good to talk.' But sometimes that's not so." Maybe the athletes would do better without the shrinks. What about the geniuses from "13 major sports groups" in Canada who put out a study saying Canadian Olympians "have a history of choking on their big days." What's their problem and what effect will that have in Turin?

Now consider the athletes, who I find far more aware. Here's Jeremy Wotherspoon, a speed skater who fell at the last Olympics and "disappointed" this week with a ninth-place finish: "It's mostly a mental thing where, as soon as I get close to the first turn, I start to think, 'I don't know what this is going to feel like.' Because of that I back off." He sounds highly articulate and self-conscious. He seems to lead an interesting, examined life. It might be better to lead an examined life and win a gold, but if you had to choose . . . The *Toronto Star*'s Rosie DiManno said the skater had been "thinking himself into a muddle," whereas sports is about "just doing, muscle memory and instinct taking the lead." Rosie, sounding like she was channelling the sports shrinks, said Jeremy should have concentrated not on a gold lost but a still-possible bronze. But he spoke on another more resonant level: "I was too mad at myself for too long." I'm with him; he sounds like a mensch.

*

IT WOULD BE FOLLY TO DENY THE COLUMN WAS therapeutic. Someone asked how I seemed relatively calm and hopeful given the awful events I wrote on, and me a congenital catastrophist, as Harvey the shrink had observed. But I had a cottage on an island where I sat on the dock and a column in a paper where I vented. And that was before I had a kid, putting me much further ahead of the game (whatever it is) than I ever imagined possible. "When did you become a glass-half-full kind of guy?" my editor at the *Star* asked recently.

Take Brian Mulroney, fount of my generation's aggravation. He was the burden we bore, with our dreams of a Canada truly independent of U.S. dominance, possibly even socialist. We got Mulroney who, as a kid, sang for coins before an American magnate, then alongside Ronald Reagan. During the '88 free trade election, when I rode the Tory campaign plane, they seated me in the front row between two RCMP guards, to protect the other journalists from me. Through a partition I could see the back of Mulroney's head. I fantasized having a gun — just a little toy one that shoots plastic darts with suction cups. We all fantasize: it's what keeps us civil the rest of the time. When Mulroney was PM, he said on TV that he'd like to get a gun and go down to *Frank* after they ran that piece about deflowering his daughter. He added that he'd also like to choke whoever did it.

Then came the columns — from the opener

defending *Frank*'s Deflower Caroline contest. It's inestimable how much stress they drained out of me, the way Toe Blake once told me he could see the pressure drain from the Rocket each time a puck he shot entered the net. It was invaluable, since Mulroney never went away. If I could make a national bequest, it would be a column for every Canadian to deal with whatever is nettling them. This is from 2007. It's on Karlheinz Schreiber, a European bagman and dealmaker, who poured money into Mulroney's campaign pockets when he first ran; then, after he left office, into his actual pockets. He accompanied Mulroney, like Tinker Bell, whispering in his ear and handing him envelopes of money. It all eventually emerged, or most of it, only because, under minority governments, things skid out of control. Schreiber was summoned to a parliamentary hearing to explain the payoffs.

*

UNPLUGGED. AS HE IS. NOT JUMPED BY LINDEN MacIntyre in a street, then edited for the *Fifth Estate*. And boy is he different from the views of the pundits of the haute media, sniffing and wincing at any mention of his name, as if they never before encountered pungent odours in the barnyard of politics. "One of the slipperiest characters alive" who'd sell his own mom, wrote Margaret Wente. "Shady," said Lysiane Gagnon, citing a European reporter who stopped talking to the creep because he "systematically led him down blind alleys." Awful thing for a journalist, having to figure out which alleys are blind and which aren't. Former Liberal Party president Stephen LeDrew, in a term worthy of rich airhead Margaret Dumont in a Marx Brothers movie, called him unsavoury. Wait, that's unfair. Margaret always had a surprising weakness for Groucho's sly appeal (Ooh, Mr. Firefly . . . Ooh, Mr. Schreiber).

That's it: he's the Rufus T. Firefly of the Mulroney era, and who can resist? He's the model of an enduring type in life, or I may mean literature, the rogue or scoundrel or scamp — subtype: the con man or flim-flam man — who can be annoying but (if you're not directly involved) awfully appealing.

Here's what I mean. He starts off yesterday telling a parliamentary committee he won't answer questions till his extradition appeal is done and he gets access to his papers and maybe a decent night at home. They schlepped him to Ottawa, shackled, in the back of a police van — nobody's idea of how to prep for TV. It looked like it was going nowhere; I almost turned it off. Then one MP sort of belittles him for not answering even simple questions, and KH seems to reconsider — this doesn't look good for him; he can make something better of it. He starts answering a few questions, then more; it's going okay. You spend your life handing envelopes stuffed with *schmiergeld* to the noble leaders of the free world, you won't be intimidated by some backbenchers getting their seven minutes of glory on cable TV. A Bloc MP asks why he gave $300,000 (in cash, in bags) to Brian Mulroney. He says the guy had money problems; he and Mila even sold off some of the furniture at 24 Sussex; they had to be bailed out. The Bloc member asks, "If I was having trouble making ends meet, would you give me $300,000?" He looks around, the situation he's in, the rest of his life on the line, these people could help salvage it, and says, "Under the circumstances, yes." It's true, it's wry, it's sheer BS; it's the flim-flam man and Rufus T. Firefly at the top of their game.

He can pull this off — the thing that puts the confidence in the con man — because he knows what they don't or would rather not: that they're all part of the same system. They ask disjointed questions about who got money and why, and he lectures back, in his rumpled, accented way, This thing is so complex, I've got thousands of files; it took my genius lawyer Eddie Greenspan five-and-a-half months to understand. He gets it in a way they don't — how money greases everything in our economy and politics. He and they need each other the way cops and crooks often need each other, till it can be hard to tell the difference, or like armies at war. Those on the other side are always "scumbags," just as we are for them, or no one would get a chance to kill and be soldiers. I don't mean the world could never be different, but, in the world as it is, it's often the flim-flam man who sees it more truly and, once in a while, shadily half-reveals that truth to us. That's why he's hard to resist.

*

IT WAS ALSO A PRIVILEGE TO WRITE ON OBAMA. His election was a historic moment, not in the sense of 9/11: one disaster among many that happen to happen. Just people screwing up again. Obama was historic in the meaningful sense of a hint at what our species might be capable of, a hopeful new direction. The wisest thing anyone wrote on him during his first campaign (IMHO) came from Alexander Cockburn, who said Obama himself probably didn't know what he'd do if he won. *If we're lucky*, I thought, *we might find out what post–Cold War politics could be about*. Fat chance. We're still waiting. This is from January 2010, a year after his inauguration.

*

IS IT ALREADY OVER FOR OBAMA?

The saddest event in politics is the death of the hope that things can basically change. This genre of loss involves a setback not just to an individual but to a population, or a large part of it, which placed its hope in a candidate or party. We last saw it here in the early 1990s, when Jean Chrétien's Liberals forsook the hope and change of their red book, on which they were elected, and chose instead the insipid task of balancing the budget by further shredding social programs. Now it's happening in the U.S.

It involves Barack Obama's presidency. It appears at this point that its main achievement will turn out to have been his election itself. That, I rush to add, was a big feat. But it is entirely different from governing in a new way. He promised "change," which is pure rhetorical boilerplate for presidential candidates, and he brought it. But the change he brought was the election of a black man as president, full stop.

Some of the blame is his. He may have succumbed to a near-inevitable hubris or, as someone said of Kim Campbell's abrupt fall from grace as Canada's first woman prime minister, "believing your own bullshit." But the real problems are structural: there's not much any president can do outside the frame of what all others do. The list includes giving big money what it wants, while occasionally badmouthing it, and making war on small countries. You get some choice about which countries.

I mean it. If Howard Zinn, the splendid left-wing U.S. historian who died Wednesday, had been elected president, there isn't much he could have done that differs from a Bush or Clinton. He could have said he had other goals, like cancelling foreign adventures or huge military expenses. That's called "using the bully pulpit," which Mr. Obama has done. But it has zero to do with making even minor systemic changes to, say, health care. For that, you need 60 votes in the U.S. Senate, which means, *inter alia*, overcoming the financial clout that drug and insurance industries have with senators, which you won't be able to do, no matter how much you bully them from your pulpit. The problem isn't the intentions; it's the mechanics.

When politics can't do real things, it becomes by default a realm of entertainment and titillation, requiring ever-new thrills and Susan Boyle–like surprises. If last year's American political idol was the neat black guy, what's better this season than repudiating him in favour of a right-wing former centrefold from Massachusetts who drives a truck?

Does this mean basic change in the U.S. is impossible? No. It means the road to it does not run directly through the White House. The last major social legislation — the civil rights laws of the 1960s — followed a decade of freedom rides, lunch-counter sit-ins, nonviolent clashes with police, etc., giving a president the impetus behind him to pass the laws. Prior to that, the big changes of the 1930s occurred in the context of union drives, radical parties, marches of the unemployed — you get the changes your society is mobilized to demand. Then you wander over to the White House.

One of the silliest conceits (or scams) of the Obama machine has been the idea that a campaign organization that elected a president can somehow be converted into a social movement on issues like health care. It doesn't equate. Elections are too broad, superficial, brief, and personality based.

But there is a movement for the Canadian-style,

"single-payer" health care in the U.S. that about two-thirds of Americans consistently say they want. It includes seventeen thousand MDs and has run campaigns in many states. If they continue to gain momentum, they could one day drop by the White House.

Who knows how long that might take? Maybe the current prez should request a rain check for the position, till the rest comes to pass.

*

OBAMA DID EVENTUALLY PASS A HEALTH CARE BILL. It was good for many people and far better for pharmaceutical companies and private health insurers. But it was a real accomplishment, and one that many of his predecessors failed at. He did other laudable things, like not invading any more small Muslim countries, along with ugly ones, like unleashing drone attacks that killed many innocent civilians and created resentments that will eventually blow back, as they say, in the form of new strikes at the U.S. If he'd been truly serious about change, he'd have probably stayed a community organizer on the South Side of Chicago.

Another privilege of writing weekly is the chance to rethink what you thought you thought. It's easier to be intellectually flexible (or louche) in a column. Nothing feels as solid on newsprint as it does between book covers. Walter Ong said books turn ideas into objects because printed words look like things in a box. Opening a book is like going into the vault and seeing what's there. That isn't true of columns. They're evanescent, so it's easier to be undogmatic — even if columnists tend to be opinionated and simple minded. They are — but the form, the page, and the here-today/gone-tomorrow quality make it hard to take their own rigidities seriously. I had a streak of dogmatism; it took me into religion and from there into the left. So column writing has been salubrious. Here's something on rigidity from 2005. You can't get much more dogmatic than the pope.

*

Cardinal Joseph Ratzinger nailed the papacy, it appears, with a rant against relativism just before the conclave doors were locked. "We are moving toward a dictatorship of relativism," he preached, "which does not recognize anything as for certain." The ploy is not isolated. George W. Bush won his presidency by assuring the Christian right that he was no moral relativist and stood for absolute values such as "life." Up here, the *National Post* often attacks relativism, cultural and moral — sometimes in the form of identity politics or multiculturalism — because these things undermine Western values, Western civilization, or just "our side." This week, the *Post* ran a long defence of the new pope's anti-relativism.

But really, what's so scary about relativism? After all, it isn't even all that relative. As Bertrand Russell once explained in his posh British way, "If everything were relative, there would be nothing for it to be relative to." The point of "relativists" is not that everything thought by anybody is true, but that any view might hold some truth and no one vision can contain it all.

There now, that wasn't so upsetting, was it? . . .

This harks back to ancient Greece and what scholars call, in the pope's native tongue, the *homomensurasatz*, which, I hasten to add, has nothing to do with gay rights or same-sex marriage. It is the claim that man — that is, human individuals — is the measure of all things, since there is no platform for thought above or outside us.

It's clear the new pope finds this kind of thing upsetting; he used the term *agitated*, as he described the mood of questioning in the late 1960s. He sees it, citing St. Paul, as "letting oneself be tossed and swept along by every wind of teaching." He wants people to be "true adults" who don't follow "waves of fashion" — though some might say it's childish to see the world in stark alternatives: rock-solid absolutes versus windblown relativities. In this way too the pope's tone is typical. Much of today's world is "agitated" by challenges to authority, as it was in the 1960s. The last U.S. election was a virtual rerun of those conflicts. For some reason I don't grasp, the species seems to divide between those who need to know with certainty and those who don't or even prefer challenge and uncertainty. . . .

At Brandeis University, where I did my undergrad, there was a sort of plaza of chapels — Protestant, Catholic, Jewish — where, it was said, "three faiths go their separate ways . . . together." At the time, I thought it was pathetically corny. Now I think it was just hopelessly parochial. What about Islam? What about the East? Aboriginal religion? But this pope has declared even other Christian churches "deficient" and anyone who objects as "absurd." I don't think it's easy for Catholics or anyone else to retool their thought processes away from a focus on absolute truth. It means radically rethinking thought itself, from a quest to know, into a process less about truth than about exploring the world and the human condition thoughtfully and, to some extent, for its own sake. You can decide for yourself which you think is the more adult approach.

*

THE MAIN PRIVILEGE THOUGH, BY MILES, WAS access to readers in a continuous, direct way. You write for them, not your editors or ownership. That's why it was irrelevant when people asked if I was bolstering the *Globe*'s credibility and shilling for its heartfelt conservatism. By direct I mean it's not like writing plays or books because there's no reviewing process. No critic passes your column through a filter and tells readers whether or not to spend their precious time on it. That's exhilarating, if you've had reviews dropped like a Berlin Wall between you and your audience. Even when reviewers praise your work and recommend it, they tend to distort and undermine the relationship to the audience. In a play that's badly reviewed, people sometimes say afterward, I didn't think it was so bad. They were watching through the screen of a review they'd read. Even if the reviews are positive, there's distortion: the laughs come a bit too fast, before the lines have a chance to penetrate, because people know they're supposed to be having a good time. Column readers, on the other hand, tend not to be fans. They don't come worshipfully to public readings, where you, the author/priest, conduct the service and they gratefully pose a few respectful questions. Readings always made me edgy. I never quite understood why people came, and as a result, I sometimes insulted those there by asking. You can say almost anything to people at a reading, they're so in your corner. Column readers are a tougher sell; they're not there to buy in, more to peruse and move on.

Print is inherently cruel, said Innis, because no matter how moved a reader is by a book, no book ever responds back. It seems to me we imagine books as having a capacity to survive whether they're read or not. They sit alone and aloof on the shelf, self-sufficient (or shelf-sufficient), patiently waiting to be found and read — but not urgently needing it or at least not letting that need show. If not in this generation, then somewhere down the road. A column, on the other hand, is short and short lived. It has no shelf life; you can't conceive of one existing without readers. Books are chaste; columns need to be known. They're more like plays in that respect. Once a play has rehearsed and opened, no actor considers performing it without an audience. If there's no one in the seats on a given night, the show is cancelled. There would be no point.

The reader response I'm most gratified by is, I don't agree with everything you say — or any of it — but I appreciate how you lay it out. I'm less at ease with readers who read in order to feel reinforced in what they already think — though I know many people do that. I sort of get it: columns that resonate tend to articulate something a reader might've thought, maybe subliminally; the writer confirms that you aren't crazy or off base, your opinion makes sense, and you can trust your gut. But that's not my bent. Here's an unusual case of reader response from 2010, after the death of a bicycle courier on a downtown Toronto street in a clash with a former Ontario cabinet minister.

*

LAST FALL, AFTER THE CATASTROPHIC TORONTO encounter between Michael Bryant and bicycle courier Darcy Allan Sheppard, I wrote a column lamenting the swift intervention by the PR firm Navigator on Mr. Bryant's behalf. I also said we'd started to learn about Mr. Sheppard, and that he was the product of a "failed adoption," plus much foster care.

Soon afterward, I got a letter from an Edmonton man describing himself as "an enthusiastic reader" and the adoptive father of Darcy Allan Sheppard. His name was Allan Sheppard. He said he found my piece "insightful" but "there is one reference you might want to reconsider." It was "failed adoption." More than 25 years ago, he and his wife, who had children by an earlier marriage, adopted Darcy and his younger brother, David. They were four and two and had already been in many foster homes. The stresses led to the breakup of his marriage, although he remained close to his stepchildren. After the boys, who stayed with him, became troubled teenagers, he felt he couldn't handle single parenting them and gave them up to Alberta social services but, by "a unique arrangement," held joint custody and partook in all decisions about them. When they "came of age," they returned to live with him, then went off on their own but always stayed in touch. He saw Darcy a week before his death and urged him (again) to deal with his addictions. He spoke at memorial services in Toronto and Edmonton. He said Darcy told him and others that without his dad, he'd have been dead by 14.

What I found remarkable was the mix of a calm, pensive, fair-minded tone with a deep love and commitment to his son, mere days after his death. I wrote and apologized for getting it wrong. We began corresponding. He asked me to respect his privacy. Last Christmas Eve, we had dim sum at a Toronto restaurant where he and Darcy often went. He got a call on his cellphone, from his other son, David, in prison in Manitoba. His voice had that same, calm, paternal, accepting tone as the letter he sent me.

On Victoria Day, he was here again. He'd just learned that all charges against Michael Bryant would be dropped. He said he understood the special prosecutor's reasons. That doesn't mean he felt "the system worked," as many people have since said. Issues are still in doubt (Why did the Bryant car lurch forward, throwing Darcy onto the hood? Then, later, why didn't Mr. Bryant stop, even after Darcy fell off?), which might have been best dealt with in testimony and cross-examination. Sitting in court Tuesday, it was clear this was far more Michael Bryant turf than Darcy Sheppard turf.

Defence lawyer Marie Henein said, "Darcy Sheppard lived a tragic life that was years in the making." But this is wrong if it implies the life was only tragic. It also included his brother, his kids, his cycling comrades (or my godchild, Molly, who took a bad fall on her bike last summer but was rescued by a guy whose photo she later recognized), and his dad. If there are redemptive elements in this, they exist far outside that courtroom.

Allan says some in his family can't understand

why he gave up so much for his boys. But his sister told him she gets it: "It was your one chance to give unconditional love." Unconditional love is an astounding blessing, and it doesn't seem to matter whether you receive it or provide it. But to give it, you need to be offered an opportunity, then seize it hard. Nor, as he seems to know, does unconditional love mean unconditional approval. The real human skill comes in the gentle blend of contraries, as in that first letter.

I asked this week if he'd mind my writing about him now. He said no, he wouldn't mind. But he quickly added a condition: that I include his other son, David, and the unconditional love he feels for him.

*

IN 2010 THE G20 MET IN TORONTO. I TOOK GIDEON, who was 11, over to Queen's Park to see the start of the big protest. He was reluctant, which I attributed to anxiety based on TV reports about violence. But once we arrived, he was happy to be there. He simply hadn't understood the purpose of gathering to protest. It sounded to him like people just go somewhere and stand. Then he saw it was an event, with people we knew and funny signs like "Undercover cops for peace." Later, after we went home, things got scary downtown: the black bloc breaking windows (of banks and other enemies of the people, so not arbitrarily, at least in theory), hundreds arrested and kettled, a police-car burning. A day later I went on Bill O'Reilly's Fox News show in the U.S. They shot it from a studio in the SkyDome. I'd been on before and always found O'Reilly amiable. He had a vulnerable quality — like Conrad Black. He probably should be in jail too. I always learned something from going on with him. Once he introduced me as a writer for a left-wing Canadian daily. I said I hated to squander the few minutes I got between his lengthy diatribes just to defend the *Globe*, but I had to tell his viewers it's a right-wing business paper. No, it isn't, he snorted. It's a *secular* paper. That's what I mean about learning something. Only in the U.S. and Iran is left wing equivalent to non-Christian.

So, Salutin, O'Reilly began, what do you say about all those criminals up there in Toronto? I take it you mean the leaders of the G20, I replied. Not my greatest riposte but viable. Next day my section editor told me the new editor in chief at the *Globe*, John Stackhouse, was upset by what I'd said. She was delivering his message. It was disrespectful to the West's august leaders and, worse, brought the *Globe*'s seriousness into doubt. He was especially irked that I'd been identified as a *Globe* columnist, which I was, but only on sufferance. Unlike a staffer with union protection, I could be dismissed at any moment, for any breach, though it hadn't happened yet. I always told the shows to bill me as "freelance writer and *Globe and Mail* columnist," but sometimes they didn't, and even if they did, the fragility of my foothold mightn't come through. Perhaps Stackhouse had been contacted by board members or ownership people, who tuned in to Fox News. (I've never seen it myself; it's not on my cable plan, and one of O'Reilly's kvetches when I was on with him was that his show didn't get on any of the basic cable plans in Canada — a clear sign of the unholy bias of public policy here.) I'd met Stackhouse, both before and after his ascension. When it was announced — the same day Ed Greenspon was frogmarched out of the newsroom — I thought it was probably a good sign for my job security. He had been the *Globe*'s first and only "development reporter" in the Third World, based in India, before returning and beginning his long climb up the ladder. This usually involved a stint as head of the Report on Business. He'd clearly been infected by a severe strain of *Globe*-itis; its main sign is an irresistible impulse to twist yourself into any shape in order to reach the pinnacle.

I hope I'm not sounding hostile. In retrospect, I think I was hostile throughout my time there. I don't believe I said or wrote anything that indicated great respect for the paper as an institution. I never thought of it as highly distinguished and was puzzled by the esteem in which it was held, especially by its own employees. There were some fine writers, mostly in foreign bureaus — Stephanie Nolen, Graeme Smith, Doug Saunders — but the writing at the *National*

Post, for instance, was far more readable; and the *Star* did a better job on reporting and investigating. The reason behind their assumption that they were a superior breed was mainly that they were at the *Globe*, which was circular. That and the font perhaps. It's true my lack of respect was part of my shtick as opposition in residence, but it didn't require any faking, and I was genuinely grateful to be there with the chance to participate in the public discussion.

*

I WAS AT GIDEON'S KARATE CLASS SHORTLY AFTER that when I got a voicemail message that I assumed meant the gig was over. For 20 years I'd written every column, starting with my defence of *Frank* magazine, as if it were the last, which may have provided a certain ongoing edge; now it had finally happened. Gideon came off the floor and said, "What?" He doesn't miss a lot. I told him and said it might turn out to be a good thing. "Like the fire at the cottage," he said immediately.

Next morning I talked to the section editor (I never heard from Stackhouse), who confirmed that they were indeed cancelling the column. She didn't say why, and I didn't ask. I wasn't interested in any verbiage she might have prepared, and even if she'd been willing to tell the truth, what would it matter? I wasn't that curious. I could think of lots of reasons they would drop me, all of which would have applied since the first column. The real puzzle was why I'd ever been hired and lasted so long.

I told few people, and there was about a month in which I continued to write columns. Then came the launch of the *Globe*'s big "redesign" — these things happen so often you can't keep track, but it was the official cutoff. Word gradually got out; I began fielding calls from people interested in media issues. I never complained or asked anyone else to, but a sort of campaign to reinstate me took modest shape on the internet, especially by people of the Canadian left. If I'd left the *Globe* on my own steam, they'd have never forgiven me for abandoning such a stentorian perch. There was some stirring of the entrails: a columnist in British Columbia decided I was fired because I'd recently called Stephen Harper "the last Straussian," referring to conservative political philosopher Leo Strauss, who recommended secretive dishonesty when attempting to manipulate the ignorant masses for their own good. Ever since then I run into people who ask confidentially if the reference to Strauss did me in. I seriously doubt it, but who the hell knows. Some of the responses showed how frequently people see the *Globe* as a semipublic institution that must be held to account, like the banks, though neither of them remotely is. Gideon looked at some of the mail and said, "It's almost worth being fired to get letters like this." It was probably the nearest I'll come to hearing the eulogies at my funeral. The *National Post* called to say Bob Fulford had written a column on my disgorgement from the *Globe* and could they have a photo. I declined since I didn't know what he'd write, but it turned out to be a gracious piece in which he said he'd miss me because I was unpredictable. That was good to hear since predictable was something he'd called me in one of our earlier in-print spats, and it's among the terms that really wound me, possibly the only one. (Whoops, shouldn't have revealed that.) Anyway, before long and after I'd resurfaced with a column in the *Star*, he was back to calling me a "doyen of the smug left," which I take to mean predictable. We were back on script.

The final column was on an ordinary subject, but I appended a couple of lines saying I'd miss my relationship with the readers since this was my final shot. I knew the *Globe* had a policy against farewell columns, though I have no idea why, but after all, it had been a score of years, over a thousand pieces, and I said nothing that was remotely bitter or hostile. Larry Orenstein, my beloved copy editor, phoned and said, No way, we don't do that here at the *Globe*. We'd had a great relationship. The only time he rebuked me was for giving away the ending of a movie he was planning to see. He was Jewish in a cultural, secular way and didn't approve of my forays into Mideast policy. But once, speaking about an Israel column, he said, "I don't know what you're doing to me. I'm sitting here reading, and I realize I'm nodding my head." It was as good a reader response as I ever had. I reacted to his rejection of my final column's coda with fury and we had a royal tiff. Gideon happened to overhear. He knew Larry. When we'd each slammed our phones down (or the equivalent since there are no more cradles in which to satisfyingly smash receivers), he said, "It's obvious you're both upset because you like each other so much." He sounded like Joanne Dru at the end of *Red River* when John Wayne and Montgomery Clift are wailing on each other and she furiously orders them to stop it: "Any fool can see you two love each other."

I contacted John Honderich at the *Star* right after being fired. I'd been approached by the *Star* several times while at the *Globe*, but you never know how serious people are. John had been a reporter, editor in chief, and publisher there. He was from one of the five families who hold unique roles at the *Star*; they are charged with maintaining the "Atkinson principles," reflecting the flinty-eyed social justice ethics of the paper's founder, Holy Joe Atkinson. If they act together, they can control the paper via special voting rights. John had been ousted in some scuzzy corporate manoeuvring and patiently, strategically, over many years, worked his way back to finally become chairman of the board, as his dad, Beland, had been. It was a comeback worthy of MacArthur or de Gaulle.

I definitely fit better there than at the *Globe*. We

were a *Star* family when I was a kid. My brother delivered it and I stood in if he was ill. I don't think I even knew there was a paper called the *Globe and Mail*, just as I didn't know there was a part of Toronto on the other side of the Don River called the Danforth. The only other paper I was aware of was the Tory *Telegram*. My Platonic notion of a newspaper columnist was Pierre Berton, who wrote daily, at heroic length, in the *Star* when I was in high school. I even recall his first three columns: a contract with readers, in which he promised to write his best and they agreed to indulge the occasional dud; a walk along St. Clair Avenue near where we lived; and a searing exposé of shady TV repairmen, using special Berton "operatives." Once three of us went down to urge him to write a column about a city-wide high school campaign we were organizing for World Refugee Year. As we were entering his office — he had one, like Clark Kent at the *Daily Planet*, which was modelled on the *Star* — my little brother came out. He was a Berton operative!

Pierre wrote a column after that called "A Visit from Three Typical Teenagers"; it was a twist on the perennial panic over wayward adolescents. Decades later I mentioned it to him, though I said I was sure he wouldn't recall it. "You were one of those guys!" he cried. "What happened to the others?" In his last years, which included many testimonial dinners at which he recited Robert Service poems, I made sure to attend. I also wrote a *Globe* column acknowledging his influence — alongside the Vancouver *Province* columns of Eric Nicol, who broke the news to me that you can be funny in print. Pierre wrote saying thanks, noting that he'd been the one who discovered Eric Nicol.

At the *Star* I'm no longer the loyal opposition, and I don't have to cover all left-wing positions. Others do that. It's nice to go my own way and not feel like a slacker. Nor is there that unease I often felt at the *Globe* or the one-trick pony thing. I still don't have a job. I'm freelance, week to week: no security, no desk. But I feel more like a part of the institution. I've done weekly videos, for instance, for which I go there and sit on a stool with the *Star*'s epic newsroom as background. It's strange: ever since I began freelance writing, I've had a fantasy in which I rent a desk in a huge office. I go in each day to work on my plays, novels, and articles. I say hi to all the folks at other desks, wander over to the water cooler, and catch up on the office gossip. It's the kind of thing you moon about when you live alone and work at home, so you have to leave the house just to see another human being. The offices I fantasized having a desk in were only two: the huge insurance company in the 1960 film *The Apartment*, with Jack Lemmon and Shirley MacLaine, and the vast *Toronto Star* newsroom. Now there I am, for as long as it lasts.

In the end, the *Globe* did me a favour by hiring

me, and then they did me another one by firing me. It was the only honourable way to get out of there and on to whatever comes next.

*

At the *Star*, I've done long series, in addition to columns and videos. One was about religion and politics. For it, I decided to check in with Gene Borowitz again. He was the rabbi and theologian who eased my way into psychotherapy the first time round, in Manhattan. ("You will question all the pillars of your life, but in the end, they'll all still be there.") I'd known him in my teens, when he visited Toronto to teach and preach. He'd been dynamic, funny, and oh-so dead serious about religion. He said "God" as if it was a normal part of conversation. Being overtly religious had seemed to me embarrassing till then. It went with over-the-top evangelists like Billy Graham. But when Borowitz said *Gawd*, in his U.S. Midwest voice, it sounded normal. So did he, unlike other Jewish thinkers I revered, who came with European accents. He hailed from the U.S. heartland: Columbus, Ohio. I could picture him riding the range.

I'd occasionally visit New York to consult him on my theological dilemmas in those years. When I moved there in the 1960s, he helped preside over the end of my absurdly early marriage; he insisted we both treat each other decently. And nudged me into therapy. Since then we'd been out of touch, except once, briefly. But I knew he still, at 91, taught, wrote, and lived in a retirement home in Connecticut. After some calls and emails, I flew down and rented a car. I phoned from outside the Edgehill residence and said it was me. "Rick Salutin!" he intoned, still in that sermon voice, with surprise but also delight. So maybe there was a little short-term memory loss. He told me to never mind. We'd have lunch; he'd meet me in the foyer. "You'll recognize me as an elderly man," he said. Then added, "Oh, wait, almost everyone here is an elderly man."

"I'd know you anywhere," I blurted when I saw him, though age had taken a small toll. We had a long, lovely lunch. He told me about a conflict with his publisher — writer to writer, as it were — over whether they'd call him a philosopher or a theologian in his next book. "I am a theologian," he said. "For reasons that are not clear to me but that matter, this God thing is important to me." It was still there: he sat in the dining room as if God were on his shoulder like Jiminy Cricket. There are people who walk and talk with God (or whatever word) and he's one. They're in touch with this entity in a personal way — which can also seem impersonal depending on culture, but it's relational, to use one of his terms. They are spiritual adepts. He's a highly American one. "You're a God guy," I said. He nodded, "I'm a God guy." I told him, though I was pretty sure he knew, that I wasn't part of that world any more. He wasn't fazed. "But you still understand the language," he said, "and there aren't many of us who do." When we parted in the expansive driveway of the large, comfortable complex ("This is how it looks when you reach my age, if you're lucky"), he gave me a big hug and a kiss. We were never like that in the past. I was too much in awe.

But here's what I wanted to say. In spite of losing my faith, as I'd lost my marriage, my academic vocation, my subsequent Marxism, not to mention much else, I still did understand the language. It enriched me and allowed me to pick up the conversation with people like him and others whose languages I spoke, if they were open to it. The thinking continued, even as the thoughts and conclusions slipped away or were covered over by the tide. All you really need is the language. The content comes and goes. Trust the thinking, not the thought.

ACKNOWLEDGEMENTS

MUCH GRATITUDE TO BRUCE WESTWOOD FOR HIS patience through the many incarnations of this effort. Thanks to Joyce Wayne for her assist and to Jack David for his immediate and sympathetic response, as well as the team at ECW, including Susan Renouf and Nadiya Osmani. A special thanks to Gideon Salutin, whose influence is scattered throughout, though his own formulations and conclusions are routinely more eloquent and persuasive than mine.

Chapters one, five, and seven appeared in their original versions in the *Walrus* during the years that Ken Alexander, to whom I'm grateful, ran it. Three and four were originally in *Queen's Quarterly*. The rest appear here for the first time.

Published by ECW Press
665 Gerrard Street East, Toronto, Ontario, Canada M4M 1Y2
416-694-3348 / info@ecwpress.com

Library and Archives Canada Cataloguing in Publication

Salutin, Rick, 1942–, author
What was I thinking? : the autobiography of an idea and other essays / Rick Salutin.

Issued in print and electronic formats.
ISBN 978-1-77041-260-6 (pbk)
ISBN 978-1-77090-733-1 (PDF) ISBN 978-1-77090-734-8 (epub)

1. Salutin, Rick, 1942–. 2. Authors, Canadian (English)—
20th century—Biography. 3. Journalists—Canada—Biography. I. Title.

PS8587.A355Z53 2015   C813'.54   C2014-907596-0
C2014-907597-9

Editor for the press: Susan Renouf
Cover and text design: Rachel Ironstone
Cover images: bulb © tr3gin/Shutterstock;
grenade pin © TRINACRIA PHOTO/Shutterstock
Printed by Friesens 5 4 3 2 1

MIX
Paper from responsible sources
FSC® C016245
www.fsc.org

The publication of *What Was I Thinking?* has been generously supported by the Canada Council for the Arts, which last year invested $157 million to bring the arts to Canadians throughout the country. We acknowledge the support of the Ontario Arts Council (OAC), an agency of the Government of Ontario, which last year funded 1,793 individual artists and 1,076 organizations in 232 communities across Ontario, for a total of $52.1 million. We also acknowledge the financial support of the Government of Canada through the Canada Book Fund for our publishing activities, and the contribution of the Government of Ontario through the Ontario Book Publishing Tax Credit and the Ontario Media Development Corporation.

Canada

Ontario
Ontario Media Development Corporation

ONTARIO ARTS COUNCIL
CONSEIL DES ARTS DE L'ONTARIO
an Ontario government agency
un organisme du gouvernement de l'Ontario

Canada Council
for the Arts

Conseil des Arts
du Canada

Printed and bound in Canada

*GET THE EBOOK FREE!